SHANGHAIED AND SHACKLED
FROM CALTON TO CANTON
FROM TONGS TO TRIADS

LAUCHLAN CAMPBELL

Copyright © Lauchlan Campbell 2016

Contents

Prologue - Back Then 1

1990 7

July 1991 10

Addiction 21

Border Crossing 24

One Way 32

1st August 1991 36

Shanghai PSB 43

The Barracks 48

Daybreak 54

Day Two 59

Routine 66

Living It 70

The Triad 76

News 80

Winter 1991 83

Merry Xmas 1991 90

1992 94

Appeal 100

A Dangerous Man 107

May 1992 115

Wake Up Call 121

June 1992 127

Lao Da	136
The Shit Patrol	142
September 1992	146
Psychic Pain	153
Xmas 1992	158
1993	161
1994	166
1995	172
1996	175
1997	187
July 1997	207
December 1997	216
1998	219
July 1998	223
1999	230
2000	241
2001	249
2002	255
2003	263
Goodbye	269

Introduction

Here is a true-life story of a father who has taken his two sons out into the world to teach them to look beyond their own backyard. It had been all very innocent to begin with but his sons were streetwise Glasgow boys and no wool was being pulled over their eyes. Scott was 18 and Lochy 16 both had travelled with their father in the past. This story of selfish errors in life and the results of a father behaving irresponsibly, Shanghaied and Shackled tell a tale of life behind bars in communist China an education not advisable to be experienced. A story of squandered opportunity and the desperate consequences of lessons learned the hard way.

Prologue - Back Then

There is nothing that could be called normal about an upbringing in the rat-infested slums of the 1950s Glasgow. Though 'the usual' turmoil and madness seemed perfectly normal at the time. My mother, of the Irish Catholic tradition, enjoying her wee dram, would often announce her favourite cheer to the household, "Here's to the bird with the green wing, a free country, and a Feinian king." All very well of course, while Dad was still in jail for some bank robbery or other.

Dad, a Campbell of course, of the Scots Protestant tradition, would not exactly be chuffed to hear such open rebellious cheer in the presence of his children. My Dad was called Bobbie - he boxed for the army and loved that sport thus supplying his three sons with daily lessons in that particular skill. He was also a known gangster.

I was born on 23rd May 1950, the sixth child of eight survivors – having four elder sisters, Helen, Sarah, Agnes, Patsy and an older brother George (who we didn't know about at the time).

My mother was a broken woman who used to comment, "I'm living on my wits with you lot.'

I also had two younger siblings, Robert, and Tommy – the baby of the family who, surprisingly, would grow to become the tallest and also the most notorious of us all.

My mother fell under my father Bobbie's charms and after the war, they married. She had it tough when my dad was in jail, bringing up children without a husband to help and support her. In retrospect can see how she must have struggled. It was not all bad, she clothed and fed us and if not a good upbringing, we did have her love.

Whilst Dad was in jail there seemed to be no halt to Ma's moonlight flits with debtors hard on her heels. Most of the houses we lived some had one room with a recess with just enough space to fit a bed mattress other house was just a single-end apartment with a kitchen. My sisters slept in one bed whereas the three boys slept beside my mother. We didn't have bedsheets or pillows we often used army coats and blankets to keep us warm in winter.

There was no electricity the house it was lit by a gas mantle. My mother cooked on an open fire. We often went hungry. I can recall being put into temporary childcare and foster homes on more than one occasion during these periods. It was truly amazing for the likes of us little Glasgow 'toe rags' fresh from the gutters of our streets of shame to have Fresh air, sea, and sunshine, and, unusually for us, the food was regular too. I remember Tommy crying, saying that his hands and face were swollen; in fact, he was all swollen, his arms, shoulders, legs, everything. He thought that he must have contracted some terrible disease, so we hurriedly sought help.

"No! It is called 'nourishment' son," explained the matron and apparently, we were all getting it. The carers were very strict and disciplinary often resulting in being slapped around the head.

Tommy just kept on growing and went on to become a tall strapping lad who grew way beyond us all. Robert was neither ginger nor orange-haired, it was simply Blood Red and had the fiery spirit to match it. My oldest brother George and I had what was called fair-haired light brown and my youngest brother Tommy had dark brown hair.

Where Tommy was big and beefy with a gentle heart, Robert would remain wee, wiry even, throughout his teens. We lived in various places, mostly throughout the north of the city of Glasgow. Firhill, Cowcaddens, and Possilpark then onto George Street in the city end. All these places were just the standard post-war red or grey sandstone tenement slums of the late 1800s. We had no idea that there was such a thing as a bathroom until we moved into our new house in Carntyne in 1960. It was there, for the very first time we had more than one room and the wonder of it all, an inside toilet with a wash hand basin and a bath.

The streets were tarmac with broad pavements and gardens rather than the granite cobblestone with tramlines that I had come to know. Being the sporty type, I played football for the new school team at Parkhead Primary every day passing the ground of the famous Glasgow Celtic. By then Dad was home from jail and things were rapidly changing.

It was clear that money was coming into the household. I had seen with my own eyes bundles of money from some criminal enterprise or other. We were also more prone to police raids where the house was torn apart in search of something that was never found while we were all stuck in the bedroom out of sight on those occasions.

The hassle escalated as Dad and his pals pulled off more robberies. Dad was careful, we were never supposed to know, see, nor hear anything about his activities but we could always gather the general gist of it from Agnes or Patsy or often Ma. I would say that we were financially well off then. The house was redecorated and refurnished from top to bottom while we were polished, suited, and booted like toffs; half-boiled toffs my father would remind us. It was after years of living in squalor with no carpet on the floors or curtains on the windows - often no bedsheets either - our lives seemed rosy. We boys got a bicycle, and football boots, along with new clothes.

There was a lot of talk in the house one evening, I heard the words: explosives, Tam Padden, and fingers being blown off. The good life came to a sudden halt. Dad was arrested again and fitted up on false evidence for the hijacking of a whisky truck and an armed robbery committed by his pal Andy Steele.

Everybody knew who had committed the crime even the police would freely admit it- out of court- but Dad, in accordance with the code of underworld ethics, would never testify who the real guilty parties were. The code of silence was expected and respected in those days, but there is also an unwritten code that if someone is doing your time then financial support occasionally should be dropped off to help feed that family. Dad was sentenced to ten years imprisonment, and we were once again sentenced to abject poverty and deprivation.

No sooner had Dad gone back to jail again when Mother hit the bottle. She had seven children to look after, which she brought up herself most time. Then unexpectedly my long-lost brother George knocked on our door, a young man of eighteen who had been sent to the Isle of Tiree to live with a farmer's family. It brought temporary happiness back to my mother; her little lost boy had returned finding his way home and he was my mother's double.

By the start of my teens, I was already anti-authoritarian, in that the authority of the times was the police and they, by my experience, were not to be trusted. Not that I was particularly impressed by the criminal element either.

Ma died at the age of 42 just a few years into another of Dad's sentences, which had broken her dear heart for the final time.

My eldest sister Helen was married with a family of her own as was my other sister Sadie. This then left it down to Agnes - who was 16 years of age with a baby of her own to look after - and another younger sister Patsy aged 15, me 14, Robert 13, and Tommy 12. My sister Sarah took Robert and Tommy, and at 15 years old, I moved in with my sister Helen. Just as I began my sojourn into the wild side of adolescent exploration.

By that time, I was at secondary school in Shettleston and it seemed I had acquired a 'bad attitude' as they say, yet when those opinions are that of authority figures such as school teachers, then those disrespectful attitudes soon come under the heading of 'misconduct reports.' I was there less than two years when such reports led to my expulsion from Wellshot Road Secondary School.

I was transferred to Dennistoun School where the famous Glasgow superstar Lulu was born and raised. It was also close to the famous Dennistoun Palace dance hall where she danced the hucklebuck before going on to sing her anthem, Shout. Living in Carnytne was my new free life beyond the sewers. While sport and football remained a passion, they took second place to music dance, and girls. I would soon meet and team up with many more young and angry young boys of my age and ilk. We were to become notorious as the infamous 'Tiny Calton Tongs'.

No more than confident youth, yet more able than most when it came down to aggression and the defence of our territorial boundaries. This by then included the Barrowland Ballroom on the Gallowgate. I along with Davie Cochrane, Rab McIntee, Gerry McNamara, Cabe, Kinny, Jimmy Johnston and many more would dance the afternoon away with the girls. I held the reputation as one of the best dancers and took my gift seriously stepping the mob and usually holding the floor a bit of a show-off to impress the girls.

Those days were dominated by sectarian gangs such as the Bridgeton boys, Garangad Shamrock, The Cumberland Street mob, Maryhill, Ruchill,

Possilpark, every area of Glasgow had a gang. Confrontations were never far away. It was considered a good night outing if it ended in a brawl a party or both. It was akin to living in a war zone with no brothers in arms.

There is nothing odd in the way that we three brothers Campbell all ended up in religiously nonaligned teenage street gangs. Tommy quickly emerged as the undisputed leader of the notorious Carntyne Goucho boys of mixed religion. The Goucho held an alliance with the Calton Tongs with me and my other brother Rab running with them. Those were wild but good days even if it was only good luck and nimble feet, that kept me alive. Dad had taught us well, boxing our ears until we learned the arts of self-defense. The attitude it sometimes seems, is ingrained in the psyche of the native Glaswegian. The motto on the Mercat cross for example reads *Nemo me impune nassasit*. Which, in English reads *No one may assail me with impunity* and in old Scots, *Wa nae meddle wae me*. Simply translated in Glasgow to say *No messing* with me but these were not my ways.

I wanted out of that weary old town.

I went to London in 1973 with a friend Ralph McLaren. He was a tall handsome easy-going person and his girlfriend Mary was pregnant. When visiting they had decided their child would be born in Scotland whilst Ralph was returning to work in London – so he had a spare ticket going back.

I decided to utilize the ticket saying, I would join him to find a job. I told my wife that as soon as work and a flat was found she would join me with our infant son Scott.

All plans do not always come to ruination as this one did. It was not long before Ralph and I ended up in Holland taking LSD and hitch-hiking across parts of Europe, ending in Spain. We then returned home eight months later with a globetrotter badge, a ponytail, an earring and an attitude directed at legalising drugs.

My mother-in-law, old Mary slapped me around the head, telling me "Away ye go and get a haircut and a job, you lazy so-an-so ye are"

My wife was pregnant when I left for London, we had two sons and I would see very little of them as they grew up. The irresponsible father still had big ideas driving me on towards new horizons.

My marriage finally dissolved in 1975 and I then returned to London and discovered the Velvet Underground punk New York bands, and heroin. I met up with artists, poets, musicians, and dope dealers alike. London was the most exciting city I had ever lived in besides Amsterdam. Squatting in Finsbury Park and my pals were Pappy, Frank and Vinnie Docherty, Peter Slowey, Andy Mac McCarthy - all southside of the city boys.

My brother Robert had a council house in Whitechapel east of the city and had married his first love Vonny McLaren and his pals were also mine - Marsy, Robert Faulds, Robin Murphy, John Kilmartin nicknamed Cool - all good dependable men from all over Glasgow. Our flats were always a mad house, with all night music, all sorts of drugs, and plans on how to get even more.

Frankie Miller's the great Glaswegian singer had a band called 'Full House' he was our local hero we saw him on many occasions around London and he became a friend to my brother Rab, the McLaren family, and other Scots living in London.

By 1976 I was off again to Holland selling student cards with a friend called Boatman from Glasgow. We ended up in Morocco with a stash of LSD. Then in 1978, off again, this time to Saudi Arabia to work as a painter and decorator and had the job as interior designer for a company called Armco. With the money hard earned from that trip went back on the road again and this time there would be no going back.

1990

It will always be a long hard journey following the Silk Road from Iran, through Afghanistan and Pakistan on into China. Even if you do sometimes, have the luxury of motorised transport. Marco Polo traversed this route by donkey, camel and on foot, and I hold a deep respect for the endurance of that intrepid traveller. Still to this day, many traders continue to tread these ancient routes were there remains a booming trade in all manner of goods. Yet alongside the usual honest backpack travellers and group tours you meet up with international nomads crossing the borders in Asia on the regular smuggler's trails. I would run into some of them repeatedly, at arrivals or departure areas in airports or border towns in Malaysia (doing a visa run so as to stay longer at their watering grounds).

I have met gold and gem smugglers, technology and data smugglers alongside drug and arms smugglers. Smuggling is more than a fulltime occupation for these people, it is a way of life, which I came to know and learn over many years of almost perpetual travel around these trade routes.

You tend to meet, and travel with some interesting acquaintances whilst going over centuries of old mountain trails shortcuts into bizarre new worlds in pursuit of the rainbow's gold or in other people's case to get a photo of mount Trish Mir at sunrise or collect a healing stone or touch a prayer flag. It is certainly interesting when you discover why some folk travel as for me having no direction in life other than just smuggling through.

Then also my life went to the other extreme flying more air hours than pilots, getting free airline booze, sleeping in cheap hotels or brothels. After three months of constant traveling, buying and selling gold and technology would then rest a few months relaxing on a beach. This was a pastime well suited for me, preferring beach life to jetting over concrete cities to only earn money. There were many places to meet up with people in this international trade. Hong Kong was the central meeting point and I was having dealings in 1980 with a syndicate there.

On several occasions during that period, I was smuggling gold to South Korea, Bangladesh, and to Tibet Nepal and India. For example, my return trip prior to this one had been from Hong Kong to mainland China, Chengdu city then to Lhasa capital of Tibet, then overland stopping at towns on the way down to the border at Tatra Panni, then onto Katmandu in the Kingdom of Nepal. On my return then travelled overland back through Tibet, a barren dry land but with a charm to be experienced. Then eventually took a bus and train across China to Shanghai before finally boarding a ship to Kobe a port in Japan.

I had also been smuggling cannabis resin, but I drew the line at dealing in heroin, it was not my trade (although more profitable and easier to conceal). I considered any form of THC acceptable and thought it should be decriminalized if not outright legalized and I smoked cannabis myself, every day.

I was also inclined to smoke some heroin putting myself down the road to oblivion, then coming around on a cycle of despair and self-loathing, before pulling myself back up and out of that insane state of self-abuse. I had not yet worked out why I did this. Heroin is aptly named *Nasty* bringing delusion of tranquillity to those lured to the dream, only to be awoken with a serious drug addiction an extremely short time down the road.

.oOo.

By 1990 I had my brother-in-law, Billy Haddifon, and my son, Lochy, traveling with me - cycling from Katmandu to India. We were en route to visit the Dali Lama at his retreat in Dharamsala with his growing Tibetan community exiled there. It wasn't typical of me to go to a place just to say I had been there but I never bought a tee shirt. However, after our visit in Nepal to the lake in Pokhara, where we both ate and talked with the displaced Tibetans, we did find it a sorrowful state of affairs. They were affluent enough and intriguing to say the least. The respect they held for their spiritual leader was humbling and all they wanted was to return to their homeland without communist interference.

I sold the three bikes in New Delhi and got most of my initial investment back. It was hard work cycling and Lochy and I were going to head to Dharamsala by train. Billy wanted to take a break, staying at the guest house in the Pahar Ganj area, until our return.

I did not try to get an audience with the wise man himself knowing he would have other matters to attend and didn't need to be bothered by two curious Scots.

We ate well and enjoyed the scenery looking at the multiple Tibetan crafts that had a well set-up little industry going on. The tourist trade was booming by what I could see around me, with travellers wearing *Free Tibet T-shirts*.

On our return to Delhi, we discussed a future trip as both Billy and Lochy were leaving for London two days later. We spent that couple of days hanging around the swimming pool at the Imperial Hotel. Billy and Lochy drinking Kingfisher beer and myself smoking cannabis.

I waved goodbye as they walked through immigration to board the flight from New Delhi to London with promises to do another trip together in the not-so-distant future.

I, on the other hand, had already purchased my cannabis upon arrival from Nepal, from an Old Italian hippy I met when first coming to India. He had married a local lady from Manali up in the hills and her family-owned land and produced good quality hand rubbed cannabis resin. Whilst I waved Billy and Lochy onto the flight, the resin was being moulded into a suitcase ready for Japan.

My onward trip to Japan was a successful one. I had money to spend, thus contacted my other son Scott via my brother in London. I had phoned and asked if Scott would like to join me. A few days later I called again and it was all arranged. Scott would join me eight days later. I was delighted.

July 1991

It was so humid in the Summer of 1991, that the sweat dripped from my eyelids, it was to be a special occasion for me, meeting up with my eldest son again. Scott had travelled with me before in the past when he was sixteen, going to the Philippines, Thailand, Bangladesh, onto Burma and Malaysia. Now nineteen years old, it was great that the two of us were getting back together. Whilst waiting on his arrival inside Islamabad airport, I could feel my heart rate triple at the thought of having him together with me on this adventure to traverse over some of the world's most awesome scenery.

When he finally, stumbled through into the arrival area, I called his name. Scott turned opened eyed and smiling. We embraced and shook hands before heading for the car and the driver who had been hired for me by an old friend.

It was a relief to escape the usual airport hustle having the driver with me. During the ride to our destination, I was telling my son our first stop was Peshawar at the North-West Frontier. It would be good for him to see and experience dealing with people from another culture having visited the Philippines with me, a Christian country by majority.

I had contacted my old friend Attollah from Afghanistan he still had a carpet shop in downtown Peshawar. Attollah had secured places at a hotel for us to lay back and relax. I recalled having many a contented dream filled night at his carpet shop just laying back on the spread rugs and cushions puffing on a hash-filled hookah that would bring joy to any a weary wondering soul. My son would have no complaints this fine night. The drive back to Peshawar was a good laugh as I produced a few hashish joints in ready for my son's arrival and after a few puffs felt the ice breaking.

At the entrance to the carpet shop in Peshawar, Attollah's sons were among the group of raggedly attired children leaping and waving at us then leading the way into the building. We walked along a creaky corridor then upstairs into a huge welcoming carpet shop. Upon seeing us, Attollah and his brother Hammed immediately embraced us with greeting from Allah for our safe arrival. Both these men had well lined and sun scarred faces. Although younger than me, they looked older.

Planting our bags onto the floor, it felt like I was arriving all over again. The North-West Frontier of Pakistan was bandit territory. Peshawar was abundant with not only figs and fruits; it was also the most open display of weaponry and drugs in any town ever visited by me. It was a mystic place of exotic sights, minority groups with deeply lined faces, some with clear bright eyes peering over veils. It was also full of bearded Jihadists, with bandoliers strapped over shoulders, and Kalashnikovs guns in plain view.

I felt the sheer bustling, crowding, cramming of such grand phenomena can be overwhelming. Talk about 'culture shock'? This is a culture 'quake' shaking you to the realization of what other people's lives are about in comparison with your own. Scott was beaming in the sheer joy of our welcoming. After Attollah showed gratitude Once more to Allah in prayer for our safe arrival. We then settled down spreading our limbs and sighing in a contented anticipation.

Atollah's two sons Khalid age fourteen and Aktar 9 got on with the chores around the shop. Knowing these two boys well, I loved to watch their antics, and their exited enthusiasm. They knew my arrival always had a surprise in-store for them but they were too well-mannered and polite to inquire.

The children were very sharp and I watched, as Scott was enticed out of his goodies - giving away cassette tapes, a tee shirt, etc. - as Attalla's lads tested the veracity of their trading prowess. Feeling well settled my son and I smoked our first hashish hookah. We looked at each other and laughed till our heads done a spin equalling that of the mystic Persian 'Dance of the whirling Dervishes'. We snacked on some dates and nuts and then were smoking our second Hookah. We were both totally awe-stricken by the sheer beauty awaiting us over the Karakorum Highway from Pakistan to China feeling literally on top of the world. The next part of our journey through and beyond China would entail catching a ship from Shanghai to Japan.

Gaping at the magnitude of the road ahead sighing in self-contentment, "Aye there's still a way to go yet my son," I said.

Peshawar houses about one million Afghan refugees in shantytowns, many, including Attollah and his kin, still bore cruel scars from the Russian wars. Learning to assemble load and fire, the standard Kalashnikov is child's play around there and Attalla's sons were already busy teaching Scott - till he could load and reload another clip.

I was keen to show Scott a different world from Glasgow - hanging around street corners, swallowing cheap wine and beer, and smoking low-grade cannabis. Suddenly I wanted Scott to see other possibilities and to open up his horizons. I wanted to help him escape to freedom from the prison he and his brother were born into, even if he did not even see. Alternatively, was it I who was deeply deluded.

Atollah had a spread of food fit for a prophet and laid it out for us sitting on the floor with a nice colourful carpet The spread was full of sweets from almond nuts, cashew, walnuts, and a few others unknown to me some sugar-coated others not, but all exquisitely aromatic. There was a range of dried and fresh fruits, dates, figs, and apricots from the Hunza valley. Then there was goat and chicken kebabs, fresh barbecued, lamb, and stews, hot nan bread with fresh tomato, onion and yoghurts.

My son and I ate well and were more than contented with our host. As we sat in bliss, Atollahs visitors came and went about their usual custom. I nodded off in a happy food overdose. Scott on the other hand was having an adventure of his own, deeply embarrassed and pursued by a highly esteemed homosexual Afghan agent. I could barely hide the smile as he sought refuge behind my coat telling me to tell him to, "Fuck off".

It ended up a good night ablaze in Afghan hashish pollen. We smoked, we laughed and had fun. Just in the wonder of those stars outside above those mystic mountains, praise is to Allah.

.oOo.

I had not told my son about filling my cigarettes with the devil's dust and I was still lost in delusions counting the Kali dosh, instead of the probable consequences. The reality was this me taking my son along on a drug smuggling trip. Taking him through dangerous terrain and where one wrong step could well turn to disaster. I had deluded myself with visions of living in my houseboat up the Mekong River - going from Thailand, to Cambodia, and Vietnam - and was already drifting in paradise.

I got up most mornings with the sun; and immediately reached for some powder to fill a cigarette. I did this while awaiting boiling water for my instant coffee. Then once in my heroin daze, I usually took a shower. I dressed in the local garb, Shalwar Kamiz, paying attention to the detail of stashes in the folds of my garb. Satisfied by the vaguely shabby, but clean impression that reflected back at me I set out to rouse my son.

Going next door, I knocked a few times before it opened. They're stood Scott wrapped in a bed sheet looking the part as a Bedouin Nomad. That is always a good thing in those parts, to fit in like the locals and learn to quote some words from the Koran.

Darra and Barra were tribal areas of the North-West Frontier in Pakistan were large quantities of firearms and drugs were freely and openly on display and for purchase. While if you were prepared to buy the ammunition, you can discharge it freely all day at your leisure. This after all was tribal land and territory. This was something Scott wanted to try out.

I on the other hand was more fascinated by the weave of the colourful wall hangings. They just seemed to hang their abandoned to the weather like old billboards that no one noticed anymore. Who had made these colourful weaves of art, and where are those people now?

Scott took me from my muse by asking me, "When are we going to Darra, Dad?"

I had to concede, "Tomorrow." I also had been fascinated by the lawless areas and to return to have some gun firing practice again.

"Ali Baba here we come," Scott whooped delightedly sparking up a hashish joint and confirming with me with a nod of his head, "Tomorrow then Dad."

.oOo.

It had been arranged that the long-bearded Jihad with bandolier gun and a Jeep, whom we met at Atollahs shop on Scott's arrival, would escort us. We were leaving at around 9 o'clock that morning and I nodded off while smoking on the bed – I was lucky not to get burned. I showered and went to awaken Scott, holding a cannabis joint in my hand. I walked through his door and handed it to him saying, "Get ready its AK47 day."

Scott was up in a split second, his boxer's shorts in a twist and headed to wash up.

We arrived at the rendezvous just after nine. Atollah was standing by the sidewalk deep in animated conversation with two turbaned gun-carrying characters. The sun was well up a hot haze had already begun highlighting the pollution in the air. A blue diesel cloud wafted by and the air hung oily. I approached Atollah and greeted him, *As-salamu alykum,* embracing and shaking hands.

I was introduced to our guides.

Scott nodded hellos and we all jumped into the jeep.

It was about an hour's drive to Darra, and the day was young. We were eager and keen to get about some shooting practice. The checkpoint was a simple wooden barber's pole across the road and guarded by tribal police officers of the Pathan clan.

After an exchange of a few words with the driver, we were through.

The first firearms shop was little more than two hundred meters from the barrier. We stopped and watched the men and boys at work huddled over untidy workbenches, filing, tapping, screwing the parts they had just made and assembling them into deadly weaponry. Our escort friends directed us around the back of the shops. Scott was out in front eager and ready. I stood at the back and watched as the two people fixed up their guns ready to fire. Scott braced himself and took aim - one single shot. He was impressed by the lethal power at his fingertips, blowing and puffing at the rush.

After he had discharged a few rounds, his gun was moved up to rapid fire. Scott jumped as if he had just been shot himself. The gun gave a novice the feeling of healthy respect for weaponry. Something that was necessary and required for survival in the region.

The entire scene was being recorded from various angles on our camcorder. It was a gift to Scott from my brother Robert, in London, before his departure.

Looking every inch the part of the freedom fighter, Scott donned two of the bandoliers and casually hung them around his shoulders with a Kalashnikov slung low on a strap crossing over the bandolier at the chest. Then with seeming casual ease, he would stutter off a half clip of rapid-fire shouting, "Free the Glasgow two."

I walked onto a small hill to take another photo angle, all the while thinking I was a BBC presenter. Scott disregarded the targets set out for him and blasted a hole in the sky on rapid fire.

Just across the path were dope shops in all shapes and forms, pollen and hashish piled up to the rafters by the ton. In another shop raw opium and morphine in no lesser abundance. No wonder there were so many guns on hand and so many wretched souls lying around in doorways, out of their long-bearded sculls - deluded, dysfunctional, dirty and dishevelled. The contrast slapped you in the face with a cold shiver.

There, on the one hand was millions even billions of dollars' worth of dope. On the other foot - literally at your feet - were the results of all that profit.

I wanted Scott to see this was not in the tourist brochures. This was the downside and it had to be seen to understand that this was part of the harvest reaped from the trade. I was not just trekking merrily over poppy fields in a happy hippy trip. I was checking out the harvest where it was a means of living to farmers. There were very little other crops or government substance to earn them money, in order to eat. I had known some of the people, they were once brothers in arms, now returned to their valleys and their farms destitute.

Death did not scare me but how to die did. I did not like these sights around me but knew Scott had the picture. We decided we should make tracks back to the hotel. It had not been a bad day. Scott was excitedly babbling on about the balances of Karma. I was just glad we were on our way as far away as we could get from the shadow of death that had been cast over those wretched lost souls (who once were warriors). Shivering in the thought that, for the grace of Allah, I might end up like them, addicted for life.

It was late afternoon and we had only eaten watermelon during our stay in Darra, so we were hungry. Atollah suggested that we do a detour to his home to rest and eat. Before departure I stood for a moment to take in the surrounding scenery but only seeing shadows in the fading light looking up at the strangest sky a mixture of purple blues deepening reds darkening yellows as the sun had started dipping. Its vastness made me feel small and somewhat insecure in my insignificance. It was a quiet trip to Atollahs place lost in dark thoughts of stretched skin stooped shoulders and heroin addiction.

Arriving after a twenty-minute drive we stood at the entrance of a refugee camp, Atollahs house was there somewhere in that maze of walls built from mud. Some were better built with partial brick but most were mud adobe with corrugated tin roofs. It looked like a row of camels snaking across the horizon.

A bunch of raggedy children immediately surrounded Scott. Some pale skinned with blond streaked hair a feature that made them stand out. Atollahs brother greeted us, and we were led through a hand dugout alleyway. It led to a small doorway into a well-kept back yard and beyond to the house living area. It was very basic in fixtures - no television, no telephone and next to no furniture - but it was warm and inviting. It was colourful with an abundance of scattered cushions, beautiful floor carpets and rugs. The kitchen was in one corner of the back yard where we had entered.

The women of the house toiled busily beside a clay-baking oven, their heads covered and their hands nimble. We all sat down and were immediately served tea with sugar-coated almonds. Atollah was smiling a picture of well-being as he sat cross-legged on the floor packing small pieces of cannabis into empty cigarettes.

Scott was escorted and kept busy with Aktar displaying rugs in the other room; there was no closing time with these traders. It wasn't long before it was time to eat and we were served another excellent meal with mutton and a tasty sauce. The evening hazed by just chatting and smoking hashish.

Attollah was telling us about his new wife to be. I knew money would come into this conversation, and before long the trading began. I ended up buying $3,500 worth of rugs to be sent onto Japan. I was to send the money once shipment was received. I liked that sort of trade when you didn't need to lay out first, so we shook on it.

It was pitch dark when we stumbled, stoned, from Atollahs house. Only a slithered moon lighted the sky. Scott having done some trading with young Aktar now had a rug wrapped under his arm, but he was minus one Sony Walkman, another fair trade. Our guides drove us back to the hotel. It was a good day out but stoned and tired, I just wanted to get to bed.

We spent a couple of more days around Peshawar and changed some traveller's cheques at the local smuggler's bazaar. We visited the Peshawar Museum admiring some wonderful old carvings and learning a little more about the Buddhist influences here. I bought a postcard of the fasting Buddha. Gandhara period Buddhist statues along with other such artifacts are readily on offer in Pakistan. On a previous trip I bought two small stone Buddha's in the market probably hacked from Temple walls looted by thieves in Afghanistan during those warring years that never seem to end in this part of the world. I sent them to Scotland via Japan for safety.

It was also nice to stop in at the Dean Hotel for a cool beer - a rare treat and watering hole in an Islamic country. You needed to have a permit before the purchase of alcohol - which was attained at the local tourist office in Islamabad. I had acquired them for us before my son's arrival.

Scott certainly enjoyed a few beers after long hot treks through dusty streets. It was a pleasure just to sit down somewhere cool in the shade with a beer, it gave your soul some cheer in Peshawar's hot dusty town in mid-July. More so since Scott was quite badly sunburned during those first few days and in danger of mild heat stroke. His neck was lobster red, and it looked like he was about ripe to fry.

I kept up the jokes and even Scott managed an occasional ventriloquist dummies smile. After a few more days around Peshawar, we returned to Islamabad gazing at the sublime sky by the outskirts around the Maury Hills. The colouring suggested such an inviting cool that you just wanted to swallow it up with your breath.

I had hired a taxi for the day so that we could do a bit of sightseeing knowing enough from experience not to waste precious hours, or sometimes days, waiting for local buses – which were likely to stop to pick up the goat etcetera. On our return to Peshawar, we stopped at the old Fort built by the British and looked around that area, which seemed to have gone from grandeur to ghetto.

By the evening, I was in a state. It felt like I had just gotten to the end of a long day's trek uphill, when in fact it had just been a taxi ride. It was a clear sign of desperation due to my being without having heroin by my side. I'd been reducing my use, since the arrival of my son from the UK, and was down to three smokes per day. Whilst fumbling for my room key, I walked to the hotel, Scott behind me. Getting to my door, I just couldn't get things right, dropping the key then turning it the wrong way till it nearly broke. When I eventually got inside the room, I immediately packed a cigarette with powder and let out a sigh, not having taken any with me when we had left this morning thinking to cut down. I realized that I would soon have to do without that poison and whilst still in Pakistan as well. I had to clear my head of the drug delusions before reaching China. I still hadn't told Scott about my addiction, kidding myself I was in control.

.oOo.

The subject of smuggling cannabis to Japan had been broached upon one afternoon as we sat talking during a beer at the Dean hotel. I had finally explained to Scott that my life in Asia was not all just traveling - outlining a brief history of my occupation. Starting in 1979 in Hong Kong, I was mostly trading in technology buying a $300 seventeen-day round trip ticket to South Korea then onto Japan. I would sell the products on in black markets in downtown Seoul and was paid in Korean Won. I then would exchange this money back to US dollars. Having to scurry up some narrow-darkened side road to a faceless moneychanger located near the American military base at E Tae Won. I had visited a few American military bases in Asia it is where you find fast food, the red-light seedy massage parlours, and all the good old treatment for the troops on tour of duty.

Then I went onto Japan and purchased high tech goods at Akihabara electric city, some items being cheaper there than at 'Tax free shops. I would complete a ten-day return with a stop-over in Taiwan on the way back. This stop-over created a loophole for people who wanted to visit the People's Republic of China. The reason being you were not allowed entry into mainland China if you had a Taiwan stamp on your passport. The British High commission in Hong Kong issued me with a one-year passport to use for this purpose. I used it to go back and from Hong Kong to Japan alternating from one passport to the other to look like fewer entries had been made.

Most smugglers would only stop off there to sell Korean Ginseng, most would often opt to go direct to Hong Kong. Many syndicates would provide air travel and hotel expenses for backpackers plus $600 to $2000 dollars per trip for travellers prepared to carry gold. Not bad back in 1979/80. They were known as the 'milk runs' and it kept the wheels rolling for the ever-growing population of semi nomads around the world. It also closed a heavy steel gate on others.

I didn't need to work for someone anymore, had independent finances of my own, and could make a profitable return of about $1500 in ten days at my level, just by trading in technology.

It was great fun flying all over the place, but it could also become tiresome trudging around bars, brothels hotels and airports. I would mostly be meeting up with people in the same or similar trade as my own and that ranged from travellers on the milk run to more serious shady characters - and I had met and knew a few.

I secured 20kg of cannabis not fancy gold seal, just the fresh aromatic battered pollen; I knew the route through to China to take and, most importantly I knew the cannabis suppliers well. They were old friends of mine - Afghan refugees whom I first met in 1980 when I had sent £5000 worth of their carpets, given to me on credit, onto my brother Robert in Bethnal Green, London. He had sent me the cash, thus indirectly assisting in the feeding of a network of Afghan families in dire need, all along the North-West Frontier of Pakistan. They were dependable proud Afghan people whom I had grown to love and trust.

I put my cards on the table with Scott, outlining my full plan. I told him that I wanted to build houseboats on rivers from Thailand into Cambodia and Vietnam. It was my dream to live away from noisy cities and the rat race in general. I reminded him of the time when we visited Myanmar and sailed along Inlay Lake and how serene that experience was. Then went on to say that he needn't worry or get involved, but just to tag along as an adventure holiday.

"How can I help you carry the cannabis and not be involved?" Scott inquired.

He had a good point.

As we discussed it further, with me trying to reassure his anxieties and relieve any fears. Making it clear that if, in the remotest of possibilities, anything went wrong, never to acknowledge any involvement with these drugs. It was out in the open and the way ahead seemed clear. It was agreed that the venture would be like the two as one. Scott was part of this smuggling enterprise and regardless of whether that had been part of the plan or not. Thus, the following day was spent buying travel supplies adding mostly dried fruits, oatmeal, nuts and plenty of well-wrapped dates. Enamel cups, spoons, bowls, and two tin openers (in case one malfunctioned).

My first priority was to pack the cannabis so that it did not need to be disturbed until we reached a hotel in Shanghai. I had a nylon duffle bag with seven kilograms stitched inside the bottom I had had a suitcase made with the five-kilogram cannabis completely concealed inside the lid and bottom. Then finally having another eight-kilogram wrapped up in towels and other clothing jammed at the bottom of a backpack. This was the most dangerous, least concealed, of the illicit cargo and the one for me to carry. I had little fear of being stopped and searched going through such remote borders and relied on dirty laundry and sharp implements placed at the top of my bag as a health hazard for other people to search and look through. As a result, they had never yet reached the bottom of my baggage.

Addiction

Atollah laid snoring, his head against a well-padded carpet cushion. He had a lopsided grin on his face, which brought a smile to mine. Both his sons had camped down hours before, and Scott lay asleep on the floor stretched out, his head resting on folded rug. I lay there curled up, preoccupied in tangled thoughts, psyching myself up for the oncoming of the inevitable heroin withdrawals before I drifted off into a heroin nod.

It was Atollah who woke me by calling out something to his sons and I roused immediately. Stretched a little, yoga being something I had practiced in the past, I was deluding myself thinking I might be able to break the vicious cycle of heroin addiction with a few stretches, and controlled breathing.

Once Scott had risen and rubbed the sleep from his eyes, we made a quick exit from the shop. We all embraced each other one more time, with promises to return. We went back to the hotel to freshen up, collect our bags and go. I had already sorted out our money and had given Scott cash to keep aside for any misfortune that might befall us (or just in case we were split up or robbed or some other unplanned disaster not uncommon in these parts of the world). I had Japanese Yen, US Dollars, Chinese Renminbi, and British Sterling a mixture of currencies amounting to roughly two thousand British pounds each. We said farewell to the hotel staff then we hit the street awaiting the arrival of our transport. Patan our driver would take care of our every need – including accommodation and food. He was another big strong character and a friend for many years to me. He was almost 60 years old at the time and kept himself very fit and well groomed. He had a big bushy beard - with a mixture of brown, henna red, and grey streaks - which really set him apart.

We took our final glimpse of the passing bustle of daily life in Peshawar. Looking at the people, the broken buildings on that parched and dusty landscape, the weather-beaten faces and the cold harsh reality of the drugs industry with its weaponry and warlords. Welcome to the North-West Frontier of Pakistan.

It was only a few hours' drive from Peshawar to our first stop at Besham. I was smoking around one gram of heroin per day and had about eight grams of heroin to sustain me to the last border town. I would then stop check into a guesthouse for a week to wrestle with the demon of withdrawals. Having brought this on myself and would just have to suffer the consequences - this I knew well. For every action, there remains an equally balanced reaction for every cause, an effect. That is Karma and there is no escape. You deal with the demon you will pay the price in pain. I planned to leave Scott to his own devices, exploring the breath-takingly spectacular scenery. Whilst I would lie lost in the costs of my weaknesses, crashing in stinking sweaty withdrawals on the dark side in some room, out of sight of the glorious and magnificent mountains.

Besham is a small village where the air was clearer and cooler, the landscape was greener and more welcoming to the eye after the hot dry drive. I decided to cut the sightseeing short, and just stay the one night in Besham before our next stopover in Gilgit. We had arrived safely and after a nice meal at a roadside hut had a look around the small town. We checked into a small motel and then spent a quiet evening out on the veranda before heading off to an early bed. I needed to have my nightcap smoke and was dreading the comedown.

The following day on the way to Gilgit, we stopped off at Taxila to visit the museum there. Taxila is still a centre for Buddhist research, adorned with Gandhara art and other sculpture. It also has many archaeological sites dating back to 1000 years BC. We visited Dharamarijika, dating back to 300 years BC and a well-known Stupa and temple there. We spent that night in the cool and calm, beautiful green, landscape at a lodge in Gilgit.

The following morning, we set off, we sat back and relaxed as we headed up the Hunza Valley. We would stay about ten days around Karimabad and I could spend that time recuperating from my self-abuse. Thankfully, Scott would get some sightseeing before our next move. I had told Scott about my addiction and he was deeply concerned saying he would keep a close eye on me whilst wrestling with the heroin withdrawals.

.oOo.

I finally arose from my stinking pit on the sixth day, having no more bile left in me to puke, looking haggard, thin, and smelling of bad odours. I could smell my demons in the discarded items strewn around me and took baby steps to the toilet in an attempt to overcome my fear of water. I had been down this path before, taking a towel and turning on the water tap. My whole body turned to goose pimples the fear of purity when wetting my skin. Then gently rubbing my flesh and overcame the shock of accepting water. It took at least 20 minutes to wipe myself over having to squat down still feeling weak.

Washing gave me the illusion that I had washed away my poisons and was clean on the outside, but I knew by past weaknesses it would take some time yet to feel clean on the inside. I was feeling better this day and walked a short distance around the room. The following day I ventured from the lodge once more out alone but not having the energy to deal with traders often trying to sell precious stones apparently worth many fortunes. It was the old 'too good to be true' story so walked on listlessly out of earshot. This was indeed a beautiful land of calm serenity. Its people 'laid back' unhurried and easy going in their ways. Perhaps this then was the secret of inner peace and longevity or the results of it. Who knows? People seem to live long lives there going into the hundred years of age and more was common and was wondering why that was it reminded me of that book I had read "One hundred years of solitude." It was something to do with finding peace wherever it is your heart lies. This was sure a lovely place even with my blurred and deluded vision.

Border Crossing

It was ten days on the Hunza valley then we packed our bags for the final part of the journey to the border. I was eating again and feeling my spirits lifting. The road was narrow, high and at times perilous, the jeep swung and swayed on the sharp bends and any attempt at bypassing a car coming the other way could be fatal. It was therefore a sudden surprise for us when we were stopped high into the hills by armed Pakistan police on foot, waving our driver down. The jeep came to a halt.

"Now where the fuck did, they come from and where did that travel-hash-piece go?" I spoke to nobody in particular. This is just the kind of unexpected event we should have been ready for but were not. The tossing of the jeep had shaken my travel cannabis loose so that it had rolled onto the floor. I picked it up put it down the back of my trousers waistband. Our windows were open during the drive and just hoped there was no lingering cannabis aroma. The pleasantly smiling officer in navy blue uniform popped his head in the driver's window.

Scott opened his door and stepped outside onto the narrow road with me at his back; Scott smiling away merrily. The paranoia was oozing from me just as the stink of heroin sweat had done in the days before.

Patan chatted away and the police became friendlier. It turned out that one even allowed Scott to examine his gun once the magazine was removed. Finally, they waved us on in good speed and we were back along the high and winding way.

We finally reached the Pakistan Chinese border at Sust where we joined the general bedlam of people and traffic. The area around immigration was mobbed mostly with Pakistanis. Scott and I had said good-bye to Patan, before departure paying him two hundred dollars for his services and company and all was well as we embraced before he returned home. Having secured our immigration entry forms we sat by the wayside; I helped fill out some people's visa applications for them; we proceeded to fill in our own forms while those thrusting pen invaders impatiently awaited our help. It took two hours before we got through immigration and customs. I was nervous just in case something did go wrong but watched as my bag went through x-ray, sort of knowing cannabis didn't register. I still had that moment of uncertainty that it might go wrong, and that definite moment of relief when it didn't.

We made our way over to a tea hut at the other side of the checkpoint, in China, I let out a sigh of relief audible enough for Scott to comment. "Dad what's all the panic about? Don't worry."

Hearing this did not make me feel any better at all. In fact, it set off alarm bells in my head. What was I doing? I wasn't used to having responsibility for other people and that this particular risk was to my own son. I pushed those thoughts aside and was tired and feeling weak. The stress nerves were jabbing my neck, the adrenaline charge diminishing and a sense of security on Chinese soil.

We had the choice to catch a bus then and there or leave the following day. I put the options to Scott, who replied, "If you're tired Dad let's just spend the night here."

It was late afternoon and we were hungry so with the use of sign language soon ascertained that there were no guesthouses around there, but a friendly family offered us the comforts of their floor. It was agreed we would spend the night at the border in this tea hut so we sat with a smile of gratitude on our faces and we ate in silence. The food was bland and tasteless, but a few fried eggs helped the taste buds, nevertheless. I was thankful to have something in my stomach and my son by my side. Feeling the tension sweep over me as tightness in my neck stung like a dart. My nervous system goes haywire when I am stressed. I slowly kneaded the muscles around the shoulder helping me relax a little.

The shifting shadows from the dull glow of the kerosene lamp seemed to dance reluctantly with the flicker from the fire in the stove -as if grudgingly combining their light, or was I just stoned? I thought to myself. What, in god's name, was I doing?

That night as I lay on a matted rug, my son sleeping by my side, I could see the outline of his face. He looked just like his mother, and I slept with that in mind and not with the stupidity of sending my son through those hazards with so much dope

The following morning early, we ate two eggs each and some hot baked Nan bread, we thanked the family, gave them some money then got onto a bus lugging the twenty kilograms of cannabis resin along with us. The bus was full of border traders heading to shop in China. It never ceased to amaze me watching them barter and exchange money before even departing, it is a great place to meet up as you can be sure someone will know where to find what you desire.

Scott tried to keep a conversation going as we bumped along a desert road pointing out mountain ranges on the landscape, he had read up on it, telling me that the Chinese claim Mount Everest is in China. Then pointing out that the Kunlan mountain range has moving glaziers. I must have been unconsciously nodding at his comments, but my mind was wondering down dark passages during that trip. We finally arrived and disembarked with the last few passengers at a place called Tashgurgan - a dry and dusty oasis town. This was to be our second stopover in China, a desert oasis at best but at least we could have a room with beds and a shower. That was something to look forward to after any long dry dusty trip.

At the hotel reception, we had to show our passport open at the visa page and fill in a registration form. Scott and I sailed through leaving the mob of Pakistani people pushing more pens in our faces. Getting into the room and dropping our bags, I immediately started to undress, feeling the poison still being expelled from my pores leaving an overbearing stink on me. The water was cold but plenty of it and just what was needed. Rubbing plenty of soap over my skin I washed those demons off me and then had a shave.

When I came out the washroom Scott put a cannabis joint into my hand, "Cheer up Dad," he joked, "you've got a face on like you like you didn't get any Valentine cards this year."

I did not respond; my mind was preoccupied with what lay ahead. Scott showered and dressed. Then we took a stroll outside and bought delicious lamb kebabs with hot bread, from a street vendor just minutes outside the hotel. It was a pleasant surprise that the vender also had cold beer in a cooler under his stall. Scott purchased two cold beers and said, "Cheers Dad," raising our spirits with a great lip-smacking sigh.

As we stood on a tree-lined dirt road smoking a joint and finishing off our beer a contented feeling came over us before returning to the hotel to get our heads down.

I awoke feeling refreshed after a good night's sleep leaving my son in blissful slumber. I stepped outside and inhaled the cool morning air. Several Pakistani people were standing around the entrance smoking cigarettes. I went to look for a breakfast to start of the day but returned shortly with no result. Enquiring at the hotel desk for a menu and was informed that western style breakfast was available by room service. I ordered two western breakfasts with extra toast then returned to the room and awoke Scott.

It was a warm bright morning with the sun well up. Our bags were still packed from arrival so it would be a quick brush our teeth, zip up and go. The breakfast was somewhat artificial in its content except for the eggs they were duck and tasted fine for me, the toast tasted like sun baked sponge cake, and the tea was green, but it was all consumed.

Scott had paid our bill and we boarded bus outside the hotel and got seated. It was not long before the driver checked with the hotel reception assured everyone was on board before driving off into the desert oasis of Kashgar. It is known as one of the silk roads most famed and exotic stopovers.

I had been there on many accessions in my imagination, now I was going to the market there for real. I had a flutter of excitement charge through me, a feeling that I was going to meet someone I knew.

The bus drive was uninteresting except for someone pointing out a herd of horsemen and a gathering of yurts. I elbowed Scott to draw his attention to it, and he mumbled he had seen them away back, and returned to his dozing (knees up to this chest). I gazed out of the window until we arrived. It felt like that half the trip was already done when I stepped of that bus into that famous desert oasis.

.oOo.

The journey into Kashgar was disappointingly sparse and uninviting, the architecture was mostly standard institutional communist block style. There were scatterings of local styled housing which almost looked out of place among the regimented rows of flats. We checked in at the old British Consulate building converted into the 'Chinibagh Hotel.' Nobody could miss nor mistake this building; it stood out like an architectural gem amid the mundane regimented blocks around it. I had secured a twin bedroom with toilet, shower and a balcony overlooking the beautiful gardens of the consul's old quarters. At the entrance of the hotel a guard stood with an oversize uniform. We smiled at him and entered the reception. We checked in and headed to the room dropping our bags with sighs of relief, we cleaned up, each having a shower and changing clothes. Then we headed out to the open-air café just opposite for a cool beer. It was a busy little venue the tables were mostly occupied by other travellers. It is always an opportunity at these places to acquire interesting tips and advice such as moneychangers, best rates, and places to see, etc.

Scott managed to get a vacant table situated in the shade under a grape vine creeper, which arched and spiralled across a makeshift roof. Having ordered our beer, I was looking around me for any old acquaintances but seeing nobody recognizable. I did notice one person with his back to the restaurant wall preoccupied with rolling a joint, seemingly oblivious to digression. I returned back to the room and a few minutes later had a piece of hashish. The guy rolling before I left had gone. Scott rolled up a few joints and passed one over to the three people at the next table, you meet people and you share, sometimes it is knowledge and experience. Other times it could be food or water now it was cannabis and conversation. We chatted for hours smoking hashish and snacking on hot bread and kebab washed down with a local fine wine. Evening turned into night with each of us telling tales of daring deeds, incredible happenings and close encounters. We all got so drunk I could not recall getting to my bed.

The following morning, I slept later than usual rising around 7am with a hangover. My mouth tasted like I had spent the night kissing camels. I took a long shower, brushed my teeth and mouth-washed a few times. It did not remove the fuzz from my brain but it did enough to clear my thoughts enough to head across the road for breakfast. Leaving Scott sprawled on his bed somewhere deep in noddy land. The sun was well up and the easy dry heat lifted my spirits sitting relaxed in the shade, drinking coffee.

It was no surprise when a local person of Turkic origin asked me, "You need a guide sir?" He introduced himself as Sabir.

There are many minority groups of China's autonomous Xingjian region, earning a living by trading in local products. That part of China still had a semi open black market ie money exchange and selling hashish to travellers was a common sight. I bought a piece to try out the quality even though I had 20kg in my room. This was a different type of hashish however and had a lovely aroma similar to Lebanese hashish in colour that I had smoked in the 1970s. It was good quality and cheap. Sabir sat down at my invitation and offered me to a free tour of the market place the following day. Kashgar market was something still to be seen for me. I first read it in a book tracing the footsteps of the intrepid Marco Polo along the Silk Road and had read about saffron and silks among other exotic spices, worth their weight in gold that had exchanged hands there, from as far afield as Europe and all the way to Beijing. I agreed to meet Sabir the following morning.

The following morning around 9am I got up and went across the street and sat at the same table as the day before. I ordered a bottle of water and a coffee for starters. Seeing Sabir with a couple of travellers, I waved, letting him get on with his business. Rolling my first joint of the day. It was a ritual these years I sat smoking cannabis and consuming sweet watermelon, which was put on the table complementary.

Sabir came over apologizing for not meeting me that morning to go to the market. "We can go now," he offered in amends. I asked him to wait while calling on my son I went over and gave **him** a shake and he got up immediately. We immediately headed off in slow progress through the throngs of people on the back of a donkey-drawn cart. We took photos of each other laughing 'look at me with a donkey' picture before deciding that it might be quicker just to walk. Sabir took care of the cart payment and we set off on foot. I have to say our advance was not that much quicker but we did embrace the vibrant energy all around us. We pointed out the exotic and unusual or interesting. As we approached the market, we could see camels silhouetted in the distance and another feature amongst that market bustle was the uniformed Peoples Liberation Army soldiers most of the way along the route to the market centre.

It was Sabir who informed me that the people of Kashgar had some political problems with the central communist government. I was not politically minded and did not know what was going on in that region of the world but noticed his command of English sometimes surprised me. We eventually reached the market stalls by the side of the road. Most of the stuff was a cheap, Chinese copy of western styled clothing, household utensils, plastic plates, cutlery and toys. I also noticed a snow leopard skin, and furs of other endangered species, hunted, slain and skinned for a living where there are no sufficient state support systems.

The local shoemaker shops displayed an excellent variety of finest quality riding boots and would make you them to measure. Sabir took us to his friend's stall where knives were displayed almost like in a kaleidoscopic show their handles encrusted with coloured stones, the multi-purpose blades in all shapes and sizes glittering and sparkling in the sun. We browsed and bartered until late into the day buying little souvenirs.

It was time to eat and Sabir led the way.

It is a blessing to have a local befriend you and become your guide there is a fee to pay but it really does make a difference especially when you are invited into their home. Kashgar is populated with numerous ethnic minorities groups, many of them of Turkic ancestry to hear tales of legendary and historic warriors such as the Tajiks, Kazaks and the invading Tartars, not to forget the omni presence of the Han Chinese. The Islamic culture has thrived in this region of the People's Republic of China for centuries and continues to do so, despite the propaganda of the communism's atheist ideology.

Looking around me within this oasis called Kashgar. The name always evokes visions of travels through these exotic lands; where those very Harems of belly dancers, hash-filled hookahs and eating like the Kublai Khan, are colourfully depicted. This place was not exactly as the imagination might have expected, maybe in times gone by but for not any longer. I had a strange feeling in my gut like there was something missing; or that I was missing something more than material, sensational or observational -

something transcendental. Then it dawned on me that there was no music even though the atmosphere hummed as if charged with ionic magnetism.

We left the market area holding onto each other so as not to be separated. Sabir led us through a labyrinth of narrow mud lined streets baked red with the sun. When we finally reached our destination, he personally sat us around an ornate cast iron circular table. This was another garden restaurant well shaded by grape vines. Sabir ordered the food while. Scott was occupied by the rolling up of cannabis joints and my job pouring the cool wine that had been served.

We ate excellent food and laughed happy in the shade. It had been an eventful day all round and as the evening shadows crept in; we said our goodbyes to Sabir. I paid him fifteen dollars and paid the food and wine then arranged a meeting with him for the following day.

On our way back to the hotel we half stumbled into another fantastic garden bar, this time with live music and dance. This place was authentic watching in amazement as the band of musicians switched to playing on two stringed instruments during the one song yet somehow managing to keep the harmony, which hypnotically drew you into the rhythm of the accordion and percussions. A slipping smile came onto our faces whether we wanted it there or not. It was late into that morning we stumbled out, merrily, drunk and slightly hoarse, from the bar. We laughed and cried with the elation of spirit brought on by the interchange of cultures. We had been unconsciously absorbed into the rhyming of local life without expectation other than to be part of and enjoy. That was more like my visions coming to life.

One Way

After spending a week in Kashgar, we headed to Urumqi this is the capital city of the autonomous region of Xingjian. It is also the political, economic and cultural center for that entire region. We were only passing through to catch a flight to Shanghai, hopefully the following day. We checked into a twin room at the Fulan Hotel equipped with the usual red plastic thermos bottle alongside neatly wrapped green tea bags on the phone table, with no connected phone line.

Scott immediately lay down and conked out on his chosen bed. I headed out to buy tickets for our flight, being soon reminded that we were in fact in China. I was hit by a barrage of red tape - sufficient to bind an angry rhino - and I left the offices of 'China Travel Services' without tickets and the solid assurance that there would be no available flight for another week. The next stop then would have to be the train station.

I got into a taxi outside the China travel office entrance and pointed out where to go on my map. That much achieved, I managed to reach the station and buy tickets to secure the one private cabin for the following day departure. It would be a three-day journey overland through China. I knew stocking up with snacks and fruit was essential, and then returned to the hotel feeling better for my meagre accomplishment.

Scott was easy about the change of plan and accepted the news of my harrowing ordeal with a yawn. That evening we strolled down to a small restaurant I had seen whilst mobile that day. It was an outdoors barbecue sort of affair. The evening was very warm and people strolled past us with children at their side. The air was thick with the sweet scent of blossoms in full bloom many of which had fallen covering the pavements in glorious, coloured petals. A beautiful atmospheric Shangri-La, if you do not suffer from hay fever.

We sat outside with our backs to the sidewall and ordered sweet potatoes; lamb kebabs and hot freshly baked Nan bread – which was a little on the crispy side but still well appreciated. We sat by that roadside café until after midnight, just looking up at the stars and the sky stretching into infinity. Instigating a sojourn into the soul and coming up with what we then considered as momentary enlightenment, or still more justifications in the form self-delusions. The peace and tranquillity of the moment left me with the false impression that all is, and would be, well with this world.

We took a taxi to the train station the following morning. It was already crowded when we arrived two hours early. We wondered around looking for platform signs in English, but there were none. So, after showing the tickets around, we eventually found a spot to settle down to wait with our bags as backrests.

The next thing I knew was Scott urgently shaking me awake saying, "Let's go Dad. They have started boarding."

Getting my brain back into gear, I picked up my bags and began making my way towards the train unable to decipher the carriage numbers. A lanky scruff of a man eventually escorted us to our cabin. The poor soul appeared to be suffering some chronically infectious disease, so I kept my distance. The cabin was small with the collapsing table and pullout seats doubling as a bed. We unloaded our bags and sat down.

Scott said, "It looks all right here, Dad. And comfortable enough for two."

It was a treat to get away from the maddening crowd, I sat down and sighed.

Scott pulled the door closed; it was going to be a long journey and many thousand miles to cover in three dawns.

Scott took control having purchased some beer, and we had a couple to drink. I was telling the story again to Scott of how I had almost been robbed on a train traveling from Delhi to Dharam Sala to visit the Dali Lama retreat with his younger brother Lochy accompanying me. I had wrestled with the knife-wielding thug and believed him to be some kind of crazed assassin. It was hours later that I realized that the waistband of my trousers happened to be slashed exactly where the money belt and travel documents were hidden. It was the metal zipper that had saved me from being gutted and robbed.

I went on to tell him such then were the ways of the ancient Thugge's the worshipers of the terrifying Hindu goddess Kali. They would relieve weary travellers of their earthly burden with a garrotte around their necks that they may enter the kingdom of heaven unburdened. Glaswegians referred to such stolen cash as, 'Kali Dosh.' In addition, if you stole theirs you ended up in hell.

I unpacked a few things, toiletries, towel, clean underwear and socks, folded them and placed them beside my seat. There was no toilet in the cabin but there was one at either end of the carriage for sleeping berth ticket holders. Settled in, we both stared out of the window lost in our own private worlds of thought. It was the swaying of the train bringing me back to the harsh realities of Terra Firma.

Not long after the train departed, we headed for the eating area and finally found space where we could sit down amid a band of scruffy men with unkempt clothes and dirty faces. The train engineers and porters, I presumed, having ordered two beers in my limited Chinese we sat down. There was no point in looking at the menu I could not read, so instead we impolitely looked around at other tables for anything to point at but could not see anything there even remotely edible. Scott managed to get the beers opened and finally to order omelette and rice. One of the Chinese people tried to start up a conversation but the only word of English we could grasp was 'Thatcher' whatever he was on about we didn't know and couldn't have cared less.

We sat oblivious to the world outside in the buffet area for several more hours drinking beer until growing restless and returned to the berth to make a joint. I decided to stand by the window in the passageway for a change of view and was approached by the ticket collector who was pointing to his nose. I gathered he was objecting about the smell of cannabis from my joint and dropped it out of the window. He seemed happy with that and departed. Returning to tell Scott about my recklessness and close encounter, I had that uneasy feeling again. It was a dodgy situation feeling half-drunk, stoned, and sitting on 20kg of cannabis resin.

Scott looked concerned also and inquired if the person knew what I was smoking or not?

'Obviously,' I thought, but uttered uncertainty. I still felt uncomfortable. Returning to the cabin and locking our door, we unpacked the cannabis from our bags except for the suitcase that was completely sealed. We decided to sleep the night on it and if or when the knock came to the door, we would have the stuff at the ready to throw out off the window. I slept restlessly until morning.

1st August 1991

It was August 1st, 1991, a date I wouldn't forget due to what transpired on that fateful day. It was around 9am when a knock came to the cabin door. Scott was still asleep and I was not sure what to do. Not really wanting to part with my cannabis I opened the door. It was the same ticket guy, standing there going on again about God only knew what.

I produced my ticket as if that was my understanding of what he wanted and to my surprise, he took my ticket and left.

After awakening Scott, we decided to get off at the next stop then catch another train later. We repacked our bags. The cannabis that I would carry was not hidden very well to begin with, so I wrapped it inside a bath towel then put it on the top of a small daypack. Then returned to the buffet area, our bags already packed and waiting to be collected from our berth as soon as the train stopped. As the hours passed, we drank tea and discussed various options like throwing it out the window, except for the suitcase off course. Stashing it on the train to collect it another day was a feasible option. In the past I had left money and gold behind at a couple of places on my travels to later retrieve.

My ticket still had not been returned to me yet and the way things were going on in my mind, I did not want to see that porter person again anyway.

The train eventually pulled into a station called Zhi Zuo, getting off we made our way towards the exit hoping to avoid the eye of the dreaded ticket man. Having no ticket to exit with, I was stopped. Scott had produced his ticket and I told him to walk outside and wait for me, having an eye over my shoulder to see if the other ticket collector was about. I was feeling shaken and trying to be calm. After a few minutes, another railway guard took my arm and guided me to the waiting room. Scott returned with me to a large empty waiting area with high ceilings.

I immediately pushed the small daypack containing the hashish under one of the benches we sat on. We sat there for about twenty minutes occasionally getting up to peek out the door. There was an armed soldier outside and my heart raced. I realized that we were in serious danger. I had to remind myself that our problem was merely ticket related although the rising panic in me screamed otherwise. I kept expecting this ticket collector to walk through the door sniffing like a hound dog directly to my bag. The paranoia was dripping out of me. The train eventually departed and we both released an audible sigh of relief.

Then it all came on top, as is usually the case, from the least expected place. Right there in that waiting room, a woman walked out from a door behind us, went directly to where the guard who was standing outside, and started talking.

We looked around puzzled, wondering where she'd come from. Scott strode over to the open door and looked in expecting that it may have been a toilet. To our surprise, it turned out to be an office, desk, chair, and other paraphernalia including a red plastic thermos flask.

We sat back down and within a couple of minutes; the woman returned with a couple of khaki green uniformed armed men, either army or police as they all dressed the same. She strode directly over to me and pointed at the bag under the seat where I sat with my legs out-stretched, partly obscuring it from view.

I ignored her and looked bemused. One of the guards came over and pointed under my seat again. I tried to ignore his gesture but, in my heart, knew this was trouble. I started briefing Scott on what to do and what to say. Telling him, "Just keep it simple. You're traveling with your father and you know nothing about any drugs."

Scott was handling this well.

I remained silent and when the armed guard drew his gun and retrieved my bag neither Scott nor I moved nor objected.

The expression on the guard's face indicated that he had no idea what he had uncovered. A few words were spoken and one guard left the room returning a few minutes later and a few more words were exchanged. Still, we didn't know exactly what was going down until we were escorted to what could only be described as a 'torture chamber'. The ones you see in the movies with chains and manacles on bare damp brick walls.

"Fuck me! It's a fucking dungeon!" Scott exclaimed in shock looking scared as we were pushed inside.

We sat there looking at each other dreading what could be coming next. It was only a couple of hours before anything did. Three men dressed in civilian clothes entered the scene, at least one of them could speak English and introduced himself as a Public Security Bureau Officer. We were escorted from that dungeon and returned to another office in the train station.

The English-speaking police officer asked me, "Where did you acquire this substance?" pointing at the parcel.

I told him that I had it from a man in Kashgar. He asked for more details and told him I did not know the people or their names, only that one was called Danni. That was the end of our interview. To my surprise, we were escorted to a good hotel and booked in under normal hotel guest procedure except our passports were taken into the Public Security Bureau hands.

We sat around talking in the hotel lounge between interviews for most of that day. I was ready to throw my hands up in despair, bewailing my stupidity for what I had done and plead for clemency for my innocent son. Then Scott pointed out that the camera in the bag told the full story on film. I had forgotten about the video camera and had put it into the hotel baggage storeroom. If they saw that film footage Scott too would be implicated. He was on camera firing guns and posing besides tons of cannabis and other heavy-duty narcotic substances. One scene had Scott firing his gun into the air and shouting, "FREE THE GLASGOW TWO" with the two of us wearing justice campaign T-shirts emblazoned with a bloody clenched fist clutching at a barbed wire St. Andrew's cross across the chest.

The 'Glasgow Two' consisted of my younger brother, Thomas T C Campbell, and his c/o accused Joseph Steele, who were arrested and convicted of six killings in what was known as The Ice Cream Wars. Tommy maintained their innocence and their plight for justice was still ongoing at the time. It was such a national scandal with the fabricated evidence by the Scottish police force, that people were taking to the streets in protest.

If the PSB saw this film, it wouldn't look too good on my, or Scott's, resume for court. I spoke a few words with the English speaking PSB officer that I needed medicine from my bag. I was really surprised when he nodded for me to follow him down to the reception. After extracting the cassette from the camera and stashed it while picking out some toothpaste along with other little bits and pieces. I zipped up returned my heart pounding, I returned to sit with Scott. We could not go into a room together but were allowed to sit outside in a lounge space.

Lighting up a cigarette I mumbled using Glaswegian colloquial, "Give me a smother son," – asking him to cover me - then I sat for another minute heart pounding and dry mouthed before rising and strolling casually to my room, controlling the urge to make a desperate dash. I was on the verge of a panic attack – which was difficult and painful to control. It was easier going through customs than walking to that room.

With a great rush of relief, I watched the incriminating tape flush away down the toilet drain. That major problem was at least resolved, and I felt at ease again with my Kashgar story. I slept restlessly that night but at least I did sleep, my conscience pacified that Scott would be free soon from this 'house arrest' but with our bags full of cannabis downstairs that they hadn't yet discovered something would surlily arise.

.oOo.

The following morning, we were escorted to the hotel restaurant and seated with the three plain clothes PSB officers. Being served a local styled breakfast consisting of a hot congee soup with steamed bread buns and a mixture of pickled roots and vegetable, which tasted great. My appetite had not been as daunted as my present self-esteem as we ate courses of buns with juicy meat inside. It was the best breakfast we had had since leaving Kashgar. After breakfast we sat back and the cigarettes were passed around the table. We all smoked except for Scott. Having reminded the interpreter that money was needed by me to purchase cigarettes. Thus, a conversation about the best-recommended brand arose.

"I'll have to change some money also or won't have enough to pay the food or hotel bill," I continued. The interpreter agreed he would personally escort me himself to the bank after breakfast.

It was all so casual, and I could have taken off at any time, and cannot say that the urge was easy to contain. I couldn't just leave Scott to carry the proverbial can though, and in reality, there was, as the song says, "Nowhere to run, nowhere to hide". At the bank, after changing three hundred pounds, I casually slipped my passport back into my pocket in a vain hope for an oversight on my PSB guide who had let me have it to change cash. The ruse was not successful, and I reluctantly handed it back.

On return to the hotel, we stopped to purchase watermelons from a street cart by the roadside. The interpreter took every opportunity to practice his English and I encouraged him by asking questions. What he thought would happen to me when the Shanghai police arrived? In addition, why were the Shanghai police investigating us in the first place?

He smiled at that and said, "Your destination was Shanghai." He went on to say that was why Shanghai's police was involved. He was clever enough in diverting my queries, but happy to tell me about watermelons being in season. Resulting in us carrying two apiece back to the hotel.

Scott was sitting reading through a book titled, 'The Full Cycle', looking up as we entered. He asked, "Change some money, Dad?"

"Aye!" I replied simply and sat beside him.

The interpreter sent one of the other people off for a knife. Upon his return, we opened two melons and passed the slices around. They were juicy and cold and would have been pleasant if only under different circumstances other than having been arrested for possession of an illegal substance.

We were once again separated for questioning and the police tactics changed with them saying that we were both being accused of involvement in taking this cannabis to Shanghai.

"Your son has confessed," they told me.

"I knew the present Pope when he was an altar boy," I responded. This remark off course went over their head and asked me to repeat myself. I simply smiled and replied, "My son did not confess." I emphasized the word *confess* and told them the whole story again. "I met a person in Kashgar who offered to sell me some cannabis whilst sitting in a café." It was a true story after all but not the right one or the same cannabis. "He offered me a large piece for my own personal use if I took his parcel to the Seaman hotel in Shanghai where this person called Danni would call to collect it." I went on to say that I refused that offer more than one time, and that I was not tempted until a few days later when he approached me again. Finally agreeing after he would make me an increased offer of a piece weighing 300gms for personal use. Having explained that my son had no knowledge of what my doings were, telling them that my son did not smoke at all himself.

The interrogations were becoming repetitive and I would sometimes resort to sarcasm to ease the monotony using the lowest form of wit, which of course went way over their heads in their limited and humourless command of the English language. So, it achieved nothing. It was my facial expressions which revealed my contempt for their allegations about my son.

The PSB officers were very humane outside their investigation mode. I thought that they probably just wanted to practice their English, rather than admit to myself that they might even be decent people. Lee conversed tirelessly and I was never short of inquiries as to his opinion on the consequences for me regarding the *possession* of this illegal substance.

Later on, that evening, Lee accepted a drink from another bottle Scott had just opened, thus initiating our first communist party. By early evening, the beers were downed, and the liquor polished off. Lee went off and returned shortly carrying two more bottles of a powerful concoction called Mai Tai, and with another bottle opened a party atmosphere was created. Chinese and Scottish songs were sung in unity and made up my own versions as I went along. We sang The Proclaimers, *And I would walk five hundred miles*... topping my vocal range.

For a short while I forgot the dire situation we were in.

Lee ordered snacks consisting of dry shredded squid and other dishes of various kinds arriving in separate bowls. The alcohol was taking its inevitable toll. Lee's face had become reddened and his eyes looked bloodshot. By late evening, we were all ready for bed. Scott downed his glass and the other two PSB people who had not indulged in the night's booze up accompanied us to our separate rooms.

Next morning Lee informed me that the Shanghai PSB would be questioning us that afternoon. I was still hungover including a bit of a headache, and by the look of Lee and my son, they were not any better off. I showered and shaved to sober myself up a little then went for breakfast with the usual entourage. It was a beautiful sunny day. We ate at a different place that morning, soaking up the sun, eating outside, supping on delicious watermelon for a bit before returning to face the opera of our new interrogators.

Shanghai PSB

Whilst lying on top of my bed in the hotel three scruffy dressed Shanghai Public Security Bureau officers walked into my room. I sprung off the bed onto my feet.

"Sit down," the one with the rumpled double-breasted suit said, walking towards me like something out of an old black & white B movie. He had a cigarette poised in his hand millimetres from his mouth whilst busy chewing on a tooth pick.

"Hold on. What's going on here?" I inquired.

"You are under the investigation of the Shanghai Public Security Bureau," they informed me in unison.

They had commandeered office space and they manhandled me into it. All three suited agents eager to impress their professional seriousness upon my psyche. This was to be yet another ball game all together.

Scott, apparently, was being interrogated in another room and my demands to see him were ignored. I asked if I could speak with Lee, the local cop, keeping my tone civil - but that too was ignored. On the other hand, maybe the Shanghai PSB agent did not understand my English, so I repeated my request. The B movie actor simply ignored me again and introduced himself across the table. He said his name was Alan. He was in his late twenties and obviously educated on roaring 30's American movies. He started off by telling me he studied American English. Then he explained to me as if talking to a pupil, "It's easier to speak and understand."

"There is only English," I said.

"Listen to the word, it's English."

Was he having a dig at my Scots accent it crossed my mind? "So, what's this American English you're talking about?" I threw back at him. He obviously thought to take over from Lee as the more qualified interpreter but was losing face for the fact that he had never experienced an accent like mine and was having some difficulty if I choose to apply it.

The other two PSB people seated themselves, flanking me. The questions came fast. The old routine, going on and around the same repeated questions. I had been going over the same story, as told to Lee, only this time it was being recorded on tape. I asked for my cigarettes, left behind on the bedside table, in my room.

Alan cocked an eyebrow in what he must've thought depicted western cool. There was a slow arrogance to his movement as he leaned over the desk and produced a packet of 555 cigarettes. He offered one to me before placing another in the corner of his mouth, lighting it and puffing smoke in a contented show loudly into the air. I wondered if this guy was really writing his own movie script or something. I knew the story regarding foreign imported cigarettes in China they are a status symbol in many parts of Asia.

After examining the cigarette, I commented that I used to smoke that brand - which seemed to make Alan smile. He went on to tell me that he got them as part of his police rations but because they were foreign cigarettes, more expensive, he got less.

I laughed at use of the word 'rations' regarding 'cigarettes.

He looked at me, puzzled "cigarette rations"?

I touched my finger to my temple, twisting back and forth in a 'crazy' gesture - intending to indicate that the government rationing cigarettes was nuts. This unintentionally, seemed to have knocked him down a peg.

One of the others smirked, produced a packet of Marlboro Reds, and offered me one from his pack - maybe they did have a humane side after all. This first interrogation was not as bad as I had expected it would be, judging by their intrusion into my room that morning. I had expected that it might be a little more physical once they had me alone.

That evening, I met up again with Scott, this time accompanied by six Shanghai PSB to dine with. It was not the relaxed atmosphere as with the local police, so we ate in silence before heading off to bed.

Scott and I were reunited again at breakfast in the sitting lounge area eating rice soup and steamed dumplings. Scott started telling me what was going on with him but one of the PSB people said, "Don't talk".

Taken aback, we ignored his statement and I asked Scott if he had stuck to the script. Scott assured me that he had. It was getting heavier, and the pressure was taking its toll on my nerves. I still had the far greater bulk of the cannabis in the two bags that they had not discovered yet and might just stumble into at any moment. We had six PSB officers around the table with us and thoughts of 'Midnight Express' were flashing through my mind.

Perhaps "Midday Debacle" would have fitted more aptly in the situation. If they were treating us like major criminals now, what would they do if they found the rest of the cannabis stash. Alan had something to say, and the table listened. There were new conditions laid down. No more going outside to eat, no more alcohol. Also, Scott and I could only get together during meals and in the evening after interrogation sessions. We were back on the tragic round again.

The interpreter, Alan, held my passport open and flicking through the pages with a smug smile across his face. He noted the counties I visited and the time I had spent there over the years. One part of my story I told them my job was exporter and importer. Alan was not having any of that and suggested it was my involvement in international crime. How all these short visits indicated that I was part of an international smuggling network.

Alan had noted which countries I'd visited and when pointed out to me the shortness of stay at the stopovers in some places concluding that I'd smuggled drugs in or out of these countries. He was closer than he knew and too close to the bone for my liking. He was only wrong in the details. Looking at him dumbfounded in his ignorance of those places; he was effectively accusing me of the equivalent of smuggling coals to Newcastle. Alan had it a bit back to front, but I did not enlighten him on that. I was in fact a full-time smuggler but not of the ilk he proposed and not usually, nor often, with drugs, and never with class A narcotics.

.oOo.

The two PSB people accompanying me ensured that the entire luggage from the storeroom was retrieved. Thoughts had crossed my mind to simply leave it behind but that plan was off and would not have worked anyway. Feeling shaky and my nerves rattling, I would have to take that yet undetected greater bulk of cannabis with me into the Shanghai police headquarters. I might still have the chance to dump some from the train - hanging onto any hope of getting rid of the evidence. Talk about going into the lion's den - this was more like being served as the dragon's dinner.

Scott carried the suitcase with 5kg of cannabis resin professionally concealed together with his own luggage. The Shanghai PSB would carry the other captured 7.9kg as their evidence. I had the badly concealed dope with me. I only was hoping that Scott was safe and out of incriminating range, but that remained a slim hope as we carried our bags to the awaiting transit van.

My heart was in my mouth by the time we reached the train station. Then Scott freaked out, "Dad that bastard's filming us," he shouted.

Looking around me, I could not see anyone with a camera.

Scott pointed to the PSB officer behind me, "Look dad, that briefcase is a fucking camera."

Then I saw the briefcase the PSB cop was carrying, but still no camera.

The next thing I knew, Scott flew through the air and landed a Kung Fu kick on the side of the cop's chest, sending him and his briefcase spinning across the platform. Stunned, and unable to believe my eyes, I watched as all pandemonium broke out.

Two of the officers leaped on Scott. One gripping his neck in a strangle hold while the other gripped his lapel and tripped him. Scott kicked back and they all went down in a tumbling heap, rolling around the ground.

I dropped my bags instinctively, leaping into the affray, kicking and punching till sufficient space was made for me to grab hold of the PSB officer with the strangle hold on Scott. I gripped his neck. It got back into some form of order quickly and no one was touching us - so I had let go and stepped back panting.

Scott was shouting, "Who the fuck do you 'think you 'are? James Bond or something?"

Little did I know then that this was to be but the start of a perpetual battle for me and a gradual downhill slide into chaos? It was also the introduction to their reward and punishment carrot and stick system and I was not to be given any more cigarettes they informed me. Scott was also separated in an adjacent cabin.

I was directed to take the top bunk in my cabin, and I stretched out, and after an hour I asked for access to my cigarettes. It was refused.

The PSB guys had been blowing smoke in exaggerated sighs into the air – so I asked for my cigarettes again. Again, Alan refused.

"Is that right," I said sneering into their faces as in the Glasgow challenge style - depicting imminent physical confrontation. "Fuck you," I added raising my voice and my arse off the bed.

Alan mumbled something rapidly and the Marlboro man handed me a smoke. Thanking him, I laid back down to savour and enjoy that condor moment. I let my mind wonder free on a nicotine high having nowhere else to go.

During the journey, Alan had told me that we could go to jail for up to seven years. I was calculating remission in my mind, which would mean we would be free in four years maximum - still not a pleasant thought. I'd been on the road in constant travel for a long time and was growing quite alarmed and psychologically disturbed by the realization of my present predicament. It was like some kind of cosmic jet lag and I really needed to land before crashing. I meditated on my breath, trying to wind my psyche down to a minimum peep as the arrest realization landed in me with a thump.

It was lunchtime before coming back from my mind wanderings.

Scott joined us again in the crammed cabin. He was fine and we both ate heartily. The constant bump and grind of the train at every stop was mind numbing and my head was splitting. Constantly coping with the PSB did not help matters either. It was as if these people felt a need to regain lost face before reaching Shanghai. Their constant attempts at intimidation intensified as the day dragged on and on, in endless screeches, until I just wanted to scream out in pain from the steel wheel grinding on my nerves.

It was in the middle of the night before we pulled in at Shanghai station. We disembarked and stretched, grateful for the space and air.

We were escorted from the train station this time handcuffed together. We both stumbled with every step trying to manage our luggage. While yet another team of Shanghai PSB with a camera crew at hand, filmed the entire event. It was unbelievable. Something else was going on here, something we did not know about yet.

The Barracks

The road had very little traffic; the sirens wailed their universal tune, "Get off the road, we are coming." It had been raining, and the oil slick reflected colours of melancholy in my mind. We were driven to the detention cell block and seated in a large conference room. They filmed us with the cannabis at our feet.

Scott, ever undaunted, beamed a wide smile, saying to me, "Told you, Dad, we're movie stars now."

But my heart was thumping, and my mind racing — this was serious, very serious indeed. Why would so many high officials come to meet the train at this god-awful late hour of the morning? What we didn't know was that we were all over the Shanghai news as part of a gang of international smugglers, whilst Douglas Hurd the UK Secretary of State was on his trade negotiations visit to China. The Hurdy Gurdy man's himself was not singing songs of love but was here urging the Chinese authorities to clamp down on the illegal drugs trade.

My brain was bursting, mostly in fear that they would not accept Scott's story, never mind mine, and I was trying to blank out the thought that both of us would end up in jail. The fear continued to haunt me. Just picturing what his mother and all the family would be thinking about me now. They most certainly would be far from pleased. Like the towers of Babel, everyone was talking at the same time, the noise was painful to my brain and irritating to my ear. We were being ignored, except for the filming crews who kept busy on us. Not a word of English was spoken, and we had no idea what was going on. We both sat with our heads down, looking at the floor. Finally, we were escorted through a door and out onto a cobbled courtyard, which appeared like an army barracks. Two armed guards stood at each door we passed through until we entered the reception of a jail block building.

Here Scott and I were separated.

It felt like being parted from my living breath. I was escorted to the property check section, and Scott was taken elsewhere. Standing in front of the high desk, behind which sat an old officer flanked by two interpreters and one-armed guard, I had to take every item from my bag while it was noted down on an official form. I was inevitably getting closer to the bottom of my bag where the other yet undiscovered cannabis lay loosely wrapped. Eventually retrieving everything except the package, the bag partly collapsed, empty. My chest had a minor death rattle, an instinctive alarm to warn me that it was nearby. I straightened up; they had all my clothes and other items documented. Then, casually, I started putting my things back into the bag again, almost choking in my panic, folding some items and replacing them back into the bag. It felt like my whole being was transparently exposed. The interpreter told me to remove my toothbrush and soap before eventually zipping it up. To my utter disbelief and partial relief, the bag was removed and taken into storage. The sight of that bag being carried by the PSB seemed so familiar. I had seen this scene before; it was déjà vu. I just knew it would be found; I didn't know when, and it wasn't the time for contemplation nor confessions.

I was escorted back across that cobbled yard into yet another annex, through more guarded doors and finally into a large office with a film projector. They sat me down facing a group of khaki-uniformed officials. There was a lot of chatter in the room, all alien to my ear. The lights went out except for the projector; the only other light glowed from their cigarette puffs. It reminded me of the fireflies on the beach at my old place on Boracay Island in the Philippines. If ever in need of a cigarette, it was then, but just knowing nothing would be forthcoming surrounded by eight male PSB officers and one female.

I watched in disbelief as the scenes unfolded: three army trucks going down roads, the camera operators just following their route. I was unable to understand the commentary, but the message soon became clear. The trucks came to a stop at the entrance of a football stadium; the camera zoomed into the back. I saw faces of men and women, all with the same expression. It was a look of sorrowful finality in their downcast eyes. The stadium gates opened and the trucks drove inside, circling the grounds as crowds cheered. The trucks finally came to a halt outside the centre circle. Six soldiers disembarked with a prisoner bound in rope crisscrossed over their chests and held by the noose at their necks. Each prisoner had a placard on their chest with Chinese writing on them depicting their crime. These people were being humiliated before their peers as part of the punishment for their crimes before being executed. I had heard years before that it was not uncommon in China for these public mass executions. It depended on your crime; it was just the first one I had seen and not by choice.

The memory of that film will always be with me, leaving me often pondering the meaning of the word 'humane' in relation to East vs West interpretations. In China, the Government administration regularly shoots people in the head after a short period of appeal time – ten days being the quickest on serious crimes against society. It is usually within three months from passing sentence, sometimes within ten days in more controversial cases. I am not sure if twenty years on death row is more humane or cruel. I am only happy that the decisions of life or death are not mine to make. Although my instinct tells me to choose life and I would rather live. Then again, not being in that position yet, I do not know where the truth lies. The policy of public humiliation in China was yet another matter and I did not like that system. I was directed onto a wooden chair secured to the ground, like a barber's chair only with an extra arm folding over my lap to lock me down. It reminded me of an electric chair. I did not like it one bit.

The film had been shown again with English commentary by my ear. Alan, who had come into the room, was translating the Chinese placards on those people. Leaning over and saying softly, "Mr Campbell, I hope you can see the trouble you are in." He then explained that those offenders who were shot were drug dealers.

I replied quicker than I probably should have, saying, "I am not a drug dealer," and in the living reality, was already trying to talk my way out of being shot. The film had really shaken me. "What then now?" I was thinking of Scott and was trembling in outright fear.

I was escorted to a cell and told by the ancient warder, interpreted by Alan, to think on it overnight. Alan escorted me, shuffling and deflated, up two flights of stairs. The jailer was a very thin man with exposed gums and decaying teeth who smiled at me continually as the cell door was unlocked and I was pushed inside.

I stood there facing eleven seated men in an overcrowded cell. One person rose and came towards me, holding out his hand and shook mine. He stood by my side while I looked on at ten other faces. This must be a temporary holding cell, was my first thought.

The person at my side said, "Hello," and smiled.

I smiled back, then told him my name was Lockie and asked, "What is your name?"

"Mr. Cai," he said, "Sit down, please." He spoke in much-accentuated English, like a Benny Hill spoof.

The cell was about 9 feet by 12 feet with a 1 foot raised concrete platform, about one square metre in size. It had a squat toilet pan, and above that was a narrow but long barred window.

Around the walls were painted Chinese characters, which were explained to me as numbered allocation spaces for each prisoner to sit and sleep. Mr. Cai then allocated me number 12 by the door next to him and let me know he wanted to be called Charlie. The people sitting at numbers one and two were hard-looking, downcast men in leg irons. Charlie explained they were scheduled for probable execution. The others were all seated with their backs to the wall, heads down in their chests at their allocated floor space, saying nothing at all.

Once seated and not taking my eyes from the men around me, Charlie told me in his broken English that he used to work in Hong Kong. Charlie's English was limited but I had a good understanding of Asian spoken English, and I put my communication skills, and sign language, to work. I encouraged the speaker to continue confidently by smiling and nodding my head and could usually gather the gist of their meaning. Consistently going over some points until it got through to me, but still just could not take in what he was telling me. It was not his lack of communication skills but the content of what he was saying that baffled me. I sat there open-mouthed in astonishment, thinking, "This guy must be a nutcase or something."

He said that he personally had been in that detention block for the past three and a half years and hadn't been charged with anything yet. Surely, that could not be true – but I was to find that it was, and yet the worse was still to come.

As I looked around me, squinting in the dull light, I hesitated to make eye contact, I thought it very strange and unusual that nobody was speaking. Surely the sight of a foreigner had not shocked them so much. In my ignorance of the rules of detention, I tried to ask some questions. The first one being, "Do any of you speak English?"

One little guy spoke out and said, "Mr. Cai is responsible for this cell; if you want anything, you must ask him for permission."

"Permission?" I repeated, "Permission for what?"

Charlie came over beside me and said, "No speaking."

I inquired further as to why there was no talking. I had been there less than an hour and already in a verbal battle for my freedom of speech. My brain was somersaulting and was struggling to grasp his full meaning; his instructions were, "No talking unless it was to Mr. Cai. If you want to use the toilet, you have to tell Mr. Cai." He then instructed me to the towel rack and the way the towel is to be neatly folded and perfectly in line. Charlie seemed to me that he was being friendly, but still, I couldn't understand why no one else was talking, even amongst themselves.

This somehow made what Charlie was saying a little more sinister. This was not exactly what was needed under my present circumstances. Charlie pointed out the written black Chinese characters around the walls and the concept of allocation of floor space. I was thinking that couldn't be right; it is impractical, inconceivable, and impossible for people to conform to this, but the sight of these men was convincing me otherwise. They all but one had their heads and hands resting on their chests in total submission. I was not grasping why nobody spoke up, and Charlie had not told me anything that I fully understood.

Lying awake that night, my brain kept returning to rats – they would draw the police to my bag in storage. It would uncover my lie to the PSB and probably get me shot. I lay tense all night, trying to think of ways to get out of this, the last draft to hell. Hearing people getting up in the night to use the toilet kept my defences ready, in case they tried to murder me in my sleep. Twelve people in a cell size twelve feet by nine feet were only enough to lay a row of thin men sideways along the walls. There wasn't even enough room to swing a cockroach in here, never mind a cat. Looking at my situation, I couldn't even begin to feel sorry for myself, thinking of Scott and how to maintain order in an overcrowded cell.

How had all this started – cannabis instead of technology and gold that I had been smuggling before? I recalled a night out with a few smugglers in Tokyo, we were drinking hot sake at a bar called 'One Lucky' in Ikebukuro San Chome. It was a favourite hang-out with travellers, good food and cheap alcohol. The owner's novelty was taking photos of customers and had racks of photo albums dating back years for the clientele to browse through. If you returned the following day, you could see yourself in the new album and buy a copy. This particular evening was the first time that nobody in our company had any cannabis. This was something that had never happened before. The pursuit for THC was on, and we did eventually find some in the early hours of that morning in a nightclub called Club 69, a Reggae joint near Shinjuku San Chome underground station. On entry to this place, I could not believe my eyes at first. It was full of Japanese Rastafarians, dreadlocks and the whole 'Rasta man' vibration. Reggae music blaring out in that crowded smoky, wonderfully happy place. It is where also I first realised the dire expense of cannabis in that country. I had just paid the equivalent of thirty English pounds for two grams of tourist stuff you would get off the streets of Delhi or Bombay for three dollars. It was not good quality at all, and it did not take long for the mental calculator to work out the figures in the rate of exchange and for me to decide on a change of preferred commodities for my return trip back here. My first step though, was to make the connection in Japan before making the trip.

Daybreak

The sun finally dawned, redeeming the cold, harsh light of the living reality. I found myself trapped in the legendary Chinese 'Dungeons,' and they were very real. Feeling an overwhelming sense of unadulterated dread, dank, and death, I just wanted to cry out how sorry I felt. I would swear to God, with all my heart and soul, that I would never dream of doing anything wrong ever again. And I really meant it.

I could hear the sound of someone walking in the corridor outside the cell, then the sound of metal striking metal. I lifted my head and, looking around me, saw that a couple of guys had begun to sit up, myself then following suit. Whilst rubbing the sleep from my eyes, I watched the little guy who spoke to me in better English than Charlie the day before as he did some sort of breathing exercise. Standing with his legs apart, he performed some Tai Chi breathing for around five minutes until sweat dripped from his forehead. Once he finished, he immediately sat down in the squat position on the toilet. It was a six-inch-high concrete slab with a hole in the middle. For the next few minutes, the sound of his loose bowel movement and the stench of excrement fouled the air. As one person finished their bowel movement, a word from Charlie and another would squat. Then each would fold their blanket and stack them by the door wall in a perfect block shape. One by one, we got up, shat, and dressed, folded, and stacked the bedding.

The cell door had a square six-by-six-inch hatch hole cut out near the bottom where the water and food were pushed through to us. The water came in through the spout of a garden watering can, which arrived about thirty minutes later. Prisoners would fill a plastic basin, again in turn by their floor space numbers, then they laid their water basins in a row along the back wall. Charlie stood close to me, quietly mumbling in Chinese while all this was going on. Once everyone was finished, he beckoned me over and, as I had no basin, he handed me the one he hadn't used. When I had finished washing, he beckoned the others to begin. The two guys in shackles did whatever they wanted; no rules applied to them.

There was so little space to move around that without the Rota system there would bound to be chaos and violence. It was just a pity they could not organise an air filter. The stench of putrid excrement and rancid urine was thickened by the scent of sweat and fear, choking and stinging to the eyes. My head was having difficulty taking in this morning's routine; it somehow seemed like temporary accommodation following some great flood or firestorm. It was unsettling watching the two people in leg irons; it seemed so odd. They performed painstaking Houdini-like antics just to take their trousers off at night and put them on again in the morning. It was another half-hour before breakfast came through the hatch on the door. It arrived in aluminium boxes about ten inches long, three inches wide, and four high. Charlie allocated the job to one person who slid the box along the floor for each in turn to take theirs with steamed bread rolls stuffed inside. I had no cup and thus nothing to drink from. Charlie shared his cup of hot water along with the story of his arrest again with me. I listened closely, occasionally asking the other man for clarification on a meaning with Charlie's English. This quiet guy was much better, but he was obviously not very comfortable with my questioning him, and he mostly looked sidelong at Charlie for affirmation to speak.

I got up and walked around the floor, asking this Mr Charlie bloke more questions on the subject of bail procedures and such general 'need to know' issues. Charlie asked me for an explanation as to exactly what was meant by the word 'bail'. The concept of paying money to get out of jail always seemed to be interpreted as 'bribe' to Charlie.

"No!" he exclaimed, "No pay money."

It was the Tai Chi man who came to my rescue, with Charlie's permission, explaining that there was no bail system in China. I felt a strong sense of eternity right there in that cell as the chill of confinement walked through me.

Later in the afternoon, the cell door opened, and I was taken downstairs, shackled, for interrogation. I had never been shackled at the ankles before and was only glad that I had not had to sleep with these things on through the night. They were very rigid, rough, and difficult to walk with. I had seen it in the movies and noted that the prisoners always appeared to walk as if ashamed and humiliated. I realised that their appearance had nothing to do with humility or how they felt. It was more to do with how to cope with the shackles physically. You soon learned to adapt to walking with a shuffle to avoid painful tugs on the chain. You kept your head down, not out of shame, but to watch your every painful step. Having only to wear them going to and from interrogation sessions, I considered myself fortunate. Every step and every session thereafter only added to that pain. I watched the death row men; they showed me how to wrap them, but that was for those who had them on constantly.

At interrogation, I would be strapped into that chair again and shown more sequences of film: people with placards around their necks being shot for various crimes, mostly drugs. Some of these killings were very impersonal, at least because the camera made it appear so, by showing close-ups of people before a soldier raises a rifle and blasts their head.

The accusations were presented as statements of fact, and the questions as simply seeking your confirmation in confession. "No *ifs*, or *buts*, this is what you did, and this is what you are," and, "if you do not confess, you will be shot."

Confession is the only thing that can save you, in accordance with their law. All my efforts could only say that I wanted to see the British Consul, and that I was entitled to see the British consul. Trying to resist and keep my mind where I wanted it, and not in the hell where they put it. I was looking at other things and my mind was escaping into daydreams; it was the small red glows from their cigarettes taking my mind back again to a time when I often watched the fireflies dancing in the starlight on Boracay Island in the Philippines.

Then I was shocked back to my present nightmare by the popping sound of recorded gunfire. Gritting my teeth as it repeated, again and again. Then, with unintelligible babble coming from all around me, I was deeply unsettled by those gunshots-to-the-head scenes, trying to blank them out of my mind.

"Mr Campbell," a voice spoke from somewhere close to me, and a new, hard-faced PSB officer introduced himself. "I am Fan Zhiyi from the Justice Bureau," he said, gesturing to the ever-present Alan to escort me from that room to another. In that new room I was again placed into one of those restraint chairs. Fan Zhiyi exuded a powerful aura of self-confidence and iron control. He spoke clearly, almost as if with parental care to a wayward child. Not telling nor trying to convince me but simply explaining that, "True confession is the only way to gain leniency in the People's Republic of China, Mr Campbell. If you do not confess, you will be shot." His manner convinced me that he was not playing games but was simply obliged to inform me of the facts before carrying out the sentence. Like the police are obliged to do in the UK in their 'caution' before charge, only this one starts with the presumption of guilt and the sentence already passed. "You have a right to confess; if you do not wish to enforce your right, you will be punished severely. Shot dead!" His voice echoed through my mind to the popping sound of gunfire and bowed heads.

"Consul, visit," I said, repeating myself, partly mumbling, "I am entitled to see the British Consul."

Alan said that they had been informed but he expressed it in such a way as to make it seem irrelevant and impotent in the circumstances.

My heart began to beat faster than a speeding train.

"Mr Campbell," Fan Zhiyi went on to tell me, "China has suffered and been manipulated by foreign drug barons. Our national dignity has been stripped and our people trapped by addiction. You must confess now." The pitch of his voice rose considerably. "I am here to give you this chance, confess now," he insisted, summoning Alan over and speaking a few words.

Alan rifled through a desk and handed over a few sheets of A4 paper to me with a pen.

"What's this?" I inquired.

"This is for your confessions, write it down." Alan handed me the paper, and taking it from his hand, I asked for a cigarette.

They both looked at me. Alan spoke first, saying, "When you confess, you will get a cigarette."

"I've already confessed and admitted to having the cannabis," I said.

It was falling on unsympathetic ears. This was not what they wanted to hear. Handing the paper back to Alan but keeping the pen, I told him, "No written confession until my lawyer comes."

Fan barked out a spiel.

Alan interpreted: "You will confess."

Looking up at him, I asked for a cigarette again.

Alan said something, then his cigarette packet was produced, and I was given a cigarette from Alan's foreign pack, smiling up at him as he lit it for me. Inhaling the smoke like a dose of medicine, I cherished it like a badly needed fix and immediately felt more relaxed and at ease, even in the realization that this was a point of negotiation here. Yet what did I have to trade with, other than my soul in confession? Scott's soul was his own and not for me to barter with, but maybe I could spark up negotiations of my own in trade for Scott's release? I started to open up and tell Alan a bit about myself, drawing out the interrogation, playing for time, and another cigarette.

Alan had said, "The Consul has been informed," my only trump card so far, so I took the opportunity here and requested to see my son. Going on to explain the law in Scotland and the principle of the presumption of innocence and how that would entail the right to see my son.

Fan, the PSB man, however, had heard enough. He stood, pointing his finger at me like a gun, leaving me with a stern warning, "You must confess or face the consequences, Mr Campbell." So ended that day's interrogation.

I lay that night, jumping from one mad thought to another. I came to the conclusion that even in the direst of situations, your mind can still get filled with silly ideas. It must be a safety catch that instinctively kicks in and changes your perception to adjust to the present environment.

Day Two

The following day Alan had a new interrogator with him, a small person around five feet six in height and slimly built. He introduced himself as Mr Chang. I was to listen to him go over some points from Alan's notes. He asked me questions regarding how we encountered the person who gave us the cannabis. Weary, as I was of their repetitious questioning, I then retold the story of how I and not *we*, met this person Danni in Kashgar.

Chang went on to tell me China treats drug smugglers as 'counter revolutionaries' intent on undermining their government. They were not content with catching the 'courier' but more intent on the supplier as a threat to their national security. Chang had made it clear; if the buck stops with you, then you are either the main man or you are protecting him. I could not very well turn round and tell them the truth having crossed the border with it myself.

My destination was actually taking the cannabis to Japan but it was their manipulations and sly manoeuvres in trying to implicate my son that just was not going down well with me at all. At one point being so annoyed by it, I let loose with a mouthful of unpleasant Glaswegian curses. That only resulted in no more courtesy cigarettes for me. However, after signing a couple of papers from a statement I had written in English, confessing to possession of 7.9kg of cannabis. I was then returned to the cell.

Outside the cell, Chang reached down opening my leg irons whilst Alan asked me if they were painful. I ignored his comment - he knew well that these barbaric restraints caused pain. He was just having a sly dig at me below the belt in that polite and civilized oriental manner.

I entered the cell in a storm of a mood, the room was silent as usual. Everyone except Charlie was sitting with their heads bowed. I could see the look of dejection written across their faces. The cell door slammed behind me and I was still fuming as I looked around, deciding there and then I was not having any more of this subservient shit. It was only my second day there and all around were these hard-faced criminals - two opposite me, scheduled for death - and they were all afraid to talk. I simply could not fathom it at all and started pacing the remaining cell space rapidly, irate with the events of the day.

Charlie told me to sit down and the anger rose up in me. In my best impersonations of 'No!' that I could think at the time I shouted it unconsciously reverting to my natural Scots accent. "NAW!" my face up close to his, invading his space, while thumping the palm of my hand against the side of my head. I indicated plainly to Charlie that I'd had enough of this crap and would remain on my feet and continued pacing. Charlie began walking with me thus forcing the other detainees to draw their knees in closer to their chest. There just was not enough room with two people pacing the cell and I could not get into the stride nor fixed mindset.

Charlie was obstructing me by trying to walk and talk two abreast causing a lot of fidgeting and discomfort for the others. I eventually just sat down leaving him standing.

I distrusted everything there and already detested the regime and this Charlie character. I did not like the way he ran this cell. "No Talking" for example. That was the weirdest experience, locked into a cell with eleven other Chinese men and the only noise you heard was an occasional body shift. It was uncanny at times to say the least.

The afternoon meal distribution was much the same procedure as witnessed in the morning. This time when the food came through, Charlie took to dishing it out. I noticed he removed the meat from two plates before he passed their food to each in turn. Watching as everyone hunched over his bowl with no complaint or comment. The food rations were minimal at best. Charlie's plunder of these rations would leave two people hungry. It disturbed me and seeing my scowling look he handed over a piece to me and gave the remains to the other two people with shackles. I held up my hands saying, 'No Thanks' and would not tolerate any bullying or take part in the spoils. The fact was I was actually boiling with fury. I then interrupted Charlie to speak out and ask, 'Why did you take their meat? What do you think you are doing?'

Charlie explained that these two were Muslem and did not eat pork.

That shut me up. I began to realize that I had carried the trauma of the interrogation into that tiny little overcrowded universe where one person's paranoia could wreak havoc in a free reign. Grudgingly giving ground, I ate my food lost in deep dark thought. I had read the situation wrong again and resented Charlie so much for imposing this 'No talking regime' I couldn't understand how he got away with it. I wanted so much to ask these detainees so many questions. Charlie had told me none of them could speak nor understand English, but did they? What was happening to my mind? I just couldn't focus or keep a tight rein on it. There was just so much nervous energy running through me and must have radiated like a microwave.

I sat down with my back to the wall. I stretched my legs and started doing some breathing exercises. I was inhaling deeply through my nostrils trying to bring my heart rate down and calm the storms of energy threatening to explode into madness or heart attack. I put my thumbs onto my neck and massaged my muscles gently.

Charlie sat down beside me and began telling the story of his arrest again. I was not much interested in listening to his broken English for hours on end. I had my own problems preoccupying me and which needed desperately to be dealt with. Charlie chattered on with his story anyway. He and another person had set up a business importing Kodak film from Hong Kong. He went on and on about how this happened I did not really listen and was somewhere else dealing with my own worries. Then I suddenly stood up and, interrupting his story, asked if he could get me paper and a pen. I told him I needed to write notes for my lawyer.

'You no lawyer,' Charlie replied, 'I know that"

'But when one comes, I'll need some questions answered.'

Charlie told me, "You cannot have a pen or paper until the next day's interrogation."

"Everything and every communication are like an interrogation here." I left it at that sat down again and psyched myself up for another night in detention. The Shanghai Sheraton five bar hot hell was the only pit option for me that night.

I had been interrogated two times daily since my arrest. I didn't know what was really happening. I didn't know what Charlie had told me was real or not. How could it be that someone is held three years six month without being charged? I was very suspicious, and the thought of Scott going through what I was suffering haunted me all through that restless night.

.oOo.

I awoke on the morning of my seventh day feeling optimistic and hopeful that this would all soon be over. The reason for the optimism stemmed from the discovery that Scott and I were simply under investigation and would have to be charged or released ten days from our arrest in China.

I thought maybe we would not even be charged. Maybe we would simply be deported as Charlie and Tai Chi had both indicated was likely. I allowed myself to cling desperately to the illusion that it may really happen.

It was usually in the afternoons when interrogations took place, the humid temperatures rose over 120 degrees on the outside. It was more than that on the inside of this hate factory. My skin became very sensitive and sore, developing red swelling under my arms. It constantly irritated me, and I just wanted to suffer in peace but that was never allowed.

At interrogation they used the same procedure with me most days. Alan would escort me to the film room, and they would start with the execution scenes then onto accusations and demands for confessions beyond my statement. Always they tried to have me implicate my son. You would think they would have become tired of that tactic. I was certainly bone weary, sick, and brain fried by it.

The film execution message had certainly sunk deep into my psyche no matter what I tried to do to block it out. Even laying in that cell at night it would come back. That public execution at the stadium and the sound of gunshot echoed and ricocheted around my scull through each night reminding me that death remained immanent and close at hand. I felt the fear stick to my skin like sour body odour and tried to hide it. But knew I could die here - a statistic in these desperate places. The ones who knew they would die had nothing to lose. It would be enough just so long as Scott would go free.

What was happening with Scott? That question already haunted me on that hot and howling August night in Shanghai, crying in my shame and despair.

The rain battered at the prison roof that night, splashes came in through the bars, warning that the typhoon season was on its way. I lay there in that crammed cell, hot, and sore with a sticky itch. The swelling under my arm had developed into dumb boils and it felt like my brain was infected with poison puss.

The following day during interrogation sweat was running from behind my ear down my neck. This interview proceeded as usual in the barber's chair and ended up with me surrounded, yet again, by high-ranking Chinese officials.

Alan did most of the interpretation telling me these younger PSB officers were from out of town. 'They are training in Shanghai' he went on, 'Where I am proud to be born,' he said.

I thought is *this a fucking guided tour group or something.* These words screamed in my head to release the tension but remained cautiously muted as they goggled on at me. They asked me questions such as, "How much money do you earn working?" Moreover, "How much wages do policemen get in the UK?"

I gave them their place, showed interest. I answered their questions politely. Using that form of speech normally used with children. Speaking slowly and nodding encouragingly for them to continue with confidence. I could not have done too badly as along the way I had managed to get several cigarettes and a cup of coffee.

I have always enjoyed the pursuit and exploration of that twinkle of interest perceived in people's eyes. These 'out of town' PSB officers would be gone tomorrow, carrying their little tale of their confrontation with the foreign devil drug smuggler.

I was left alone again for a few minutes still locked into the Sweeny Todd barber's chair. Then in came Alan again with some X rated Red Guard renegade of the old school, he raised his voice, trying to impress me with fear again but he failed at imposing his outdated interrogation tactics upon me, shouting his anthem, "Confesses and you will be leniently treated."

Alan didn't' have to think about his translation. We both knew it by heart.

By the time the show was over I returned to my cell, my brain in melt down.

.oOo.

Then one day I was called out and, to my surprise this time, I was escorted without leg irons. Blind optimism rose in my heart again. I was led just along the landing to the guard's office, shown my chair and handed a cigarette. I was like a kid at Christmas, my smile could have split my ears.

A Chinese prisoner appeared with a red plastic thermos flask like those at the Tashgurgan Hotel and that office where the woman exposed us at the dreaded train station. The prisoner also had Nescafe, milk, sugar and smokes.

There was just the one guard who had opened the cell and one more sitting with me in the converted office cell. The guard smiled and started to talk to me, but I could only smile and nod. I felt awkward because I didn't have a clue what he was saying but did not want to interrupt his cheerful flow. Whatever it was it sounded okay with me whilst I was in receipt of this rare treat. The nicotine rush psychologically settled my head, a momentary illusionary recharge.

The guard at the door walked away, I heard another cell door opening and a Chinese prisoner came into the office and stood beside me. He too was also handed a cigarette and we were all sat around the table. They all spoke and the prisoner who had just joined us turned to me asking, "Excuse me sir, do you support football?"

He spoke in very clear English.

"Yes," I replied.

There followed the next question, "Do you support AC Milan?"

"No," I told him. Then asked him a couple of quick questions which he answered slowly but clear enough so that I felt confident to ask him if he could put my request over to the guard to see my son Scott?

There was another exchange of words. I was handed another cigarette and told, "The chief says no, you can't see your son."

I sat in silence for five minutes then was returned to the cell. Charlie wanted to know everything, especially, "Who speak English for you? You have cigarette? How many?" Then he concluded, "You go home tomorrow."

Tai Chi spoke up, "Mr Campbell you have been here ten days. Tomorrow, they will charge you or send you home."

I told them exactly what had been said in the office explaining about the coffee and cigarettes. The retelling made it sound so good, like a big day out or something.

Charlie said, "They wouldn't have been so kind if they weren't letting you go, would they?"

That night I slept in vigilance and prayer looking for a ray of light, some sign from on high to confirm that we truly would be going home tomorrow.

Routine

I roused each morning, going through my daily ablutions before anyone else was up. I sat lost in thought of what the day might bring as the 'gate fever' - the anxious excitement felt by a prisoner whose release is imminent - ran high. Could my son and I really be getting out of there? We *could* and *should* be released, maybe a fine and deportation. We had suffered more than enough for my stupidity. It was only cannabis we were talking about; it wasn't as if it were opium, heroin, cocaine or crack – so no big deal. I was thinking of all those songs and artists such as the Legendary Bob Marley and the 'Legalize it' campaigns - about the number of legal paraphernalia on sale and around the world, cannabis culture at the time was beginning to be accepted. It was openly for sale and on public display in parts of the civilized world.

I was taken from the cell early that morning without the leg irons and sat in front of Alan. This was it then, it was going down and it was looking good with the freedom of movement.

Alan spoke with a sparkling glint in his almond eyes, both his hands running over each other as if in exited expectation, "You will be charged today with possession of 7.9Kg of cannabis."

The pit of my stomach fell, digesting my futile delusions of freedom.

Alan handed over a piece of paper and told me, "Sign here."

It stuck to my sweaty hands and I uttered mournfully, "This is written in Chinese." I stared, confused and alarmed at Alan, feeling like I wanted to be sick all over this place. "What about my son?" I asked, dreading to hear the worst.

"That is another issue," said Alan. "You will be investigated next by the Prosecutor's office who is now handling the indictment procedure of your case. This is our last time seeing you until court."

Alan's statement passed over me, I could not take in the full extent of what I had just heard. My head was spinning in confused panic, "What about Scott? He's done nothing wrong."

Alan reassured me, "You will be informed of everything this afternoon." Then he again asked me to sign the papers and cooperate.

I wasn't signing any more papers until I saw and spoke with a lawyer of whom I didn't even have one yet. Alan offered me a cigarette and began asking me questions regarding my feelings about my treatment by the police. Had I been treated unfairly?

Looking directly into his eyes I answered squarely, "Yes you have treated me unfairly by not being able to see my son. You won't let me see a lawyer or phone my consul and I need to contact my family. They will be worried about Scott." I began to lose the place a little as pent-up emotions let loose. "What is going on in this fucking place?" I raved. "I'm untried, not a convicted prisoner and should be allowed to see a lawyer or make a phone call." I pointed my finger at Alan, "Do you think I do not know what you people are up to in this place? I know you're keeping guys here for years without charging them. I also know that people are shot in the back of the head for being ignorant of their crimes." I spat out a few of the horror tales I'd heard from Charlie over his years of being here.

Alan didn't look at all phased by my outburst, he simply smiled and pointed out to me that I had cooperated with the police by confessing and accepted having committed a crime from the very start. He said that I cooperated fully with the police in exchange for leniency and expressed my shame ... Listening to this, it sounded like he was mentally ticking off a list in chronological order. Like ticking off all, the right boxes for me to qualify for something, I did not exactly realize it then but that is exactly what he was doing. Being returned to the cell I handed Charlie the piece of paper which I was to sign. He read it out. I heard a few sympathetic sighs then sat down and put my hands to my face and head on my knees.

It was late in the afternoon before the cell door was opened again and I was escorted downstairs to the office. I assumed that this was because of not signing that paper given me. I was wrong again.

Two armed guards escorted me across a courtyard while Alan and another official from the prosecutor's office walked in front. I was taken into a large room, fitted throughout with a thick red pile carpet and a large wooden carved table at its centre. There were four large desks and I counted fourteen carved high back red velvet cushioned chairs. I sat there looking around me at the old flock wallpaper with the gold patterns. The ceiling had a center rose and surrounding cornice. It gave an impression of past glories but did not quite come up even near to standard. On the back wall, there hung a large, framed, painting of the Heavenly Gates and in red and gold were five stars of the Central Committee of the Communist Party.

My heart was racing as I tried to put some order to my thoughts, but everything seemed to get cross-wired and confused.

I took a deep breath and closed my eyes, willing my attention to focus on the dreadful situation we were in. Hearing their voices before seeing them I stood up excited that something had change and maybe I was finally going to have some issues sorted out or even get some inkling of our fate.

Introducing himself as from the British Consul, and offering his hand was a large well-built man in his late thirties called Ian. Then he introduced the consul interpreter as Miss Jet. We all shook hands and were seated. My first question was about Scott and his well-being. Although he had not seen him personally Ian told me that Miss Jet was with him that morning. He went on to say that Scott was fine and they would see him again later that day.

Ian was a non-smoker but did bring a packet of cigarettes with him which was very considerate. I could light up at my own pace during the visit and did not need to depend on handouts. Ian also handed me a list of lawyers.

The guard immediately intercepted this document.

Ian then asked me if I was being treated fairly and I told him about the living conditions and pointed out my arm infections. Taking notes, he next enquired whether there were any urgent messages needed passed onto my family. He produced a newspaper with the headline, 'Scotsman may face execution in China'.

I gulped, but Ian assured me this would not happen to me or Scott.

Alan leaned over to have a look but Ian pocketed it smartly.

I pursued other avenues of enquiry seeking out anything that might help gets us out of there imminently.

Ian made it clear that his office could not interfere nor be involved with judicial matters. That area would be covered by the Chinese authorities negotiating with my solicitor. I asked Ian if he could he recommend a lawyer from the list.

Ian replied that a committee of executives recommended those named. "I have no dealings with them personally. Whomever you choose will enlighten you as to what can be expected in relation to Chinese criminal law." Ian went on to say, "From what you have told me, you have made a full confession and our office has been told you have cooperated. You have not caused any trouble since being here. That should make things go easier and more smoothly."

There never seemed to be enough time but we managed to stretch the official thirty minutes into forty. Even so, I still forgot to ask a lot that I wanted to know before it was time to depart. I shook both the interpreter's and Ian's hands asking when they would return to see me again.

"Anytime in emergency," Ian replied, "ask the police to call this office." He handed me his business card, "Otherwise I'll make arrangements for another visit next month and bring you news from your family." On departing Ian called out, "Take care of yourself Lauchlan and keeps your chin up, Bye for now."

I watched them exit the building, leaving me alone in that room with that awful flock wallpaper, doodling patterns in my brain.

Living It

It had been over a week since the Consul visit with no other interrogation sessions within that time. I had not been out of the cell and still had not seen a doctor. Nor indeed, had I had a bath nor access to one since arriving there, it was all just a body wipe. I lost weight through dehydration, my skin itched and my unshaven face was irritated with the humidity. I also had a spate of boils spread under my armpit.

I asked to see a doctor when the third lump appeared. I had already asked Charlie to call through the cell door to the landing of the short-term prisoners. They were employed as the warder's goffers. Their foremost duty was to tend to the warders every instruction and every need. Then their next priority was the food and water distribution to the inmates. 'Laodong' means 'worker' in Chinese. When someone calls from their cell, he would attend to it and not the guard.

Charlie passed on my request to see the doctor.

It was evening before the cell door opened to reveal a guard accompanied by another man. He looked as if he had just been dragged out of bed and still wore his rumpled pyjama shorts and dirty string vest. His thin shoulder-length, stringy, hair straggled about his face and snagged in the wisp of a goatee beard protruding from his ever-averted face.

The guard spoke and Charlie in turn translated for me saying, "This is doctor and to show him."

I opened my shirt up and holding it there showed him. The doctor spoke a few sentences.

Charlie informed me, "You infection. Get medicine tomorrow."

"What about painkillers for now?" I asked.

More words were exchanged but, "Tomorrow," was the best he could do. I was pleased that a potential resolution might have been achieved to at least help ease the pain.

The following afternoon with no medicine forthcoming, I thought there was not much point in me accepting this situation quietly. It seemed to me that I had nothing left to lose. Getting up I began shouting through the steel door. The goffer had come on several occasions yesterday but wasn't appearing now. This pissed me off and I began shouting, "This is not acceptable. No doctor, no notepaper, no pen."

Charlie told me that the senior guard was on duty and it would be better to ask tomorrow. He pleaded, "He not like being disturbed."

"Fuck him, I want my rights," and I shouted over Charlie's head at the cell door.

The guard returned accompanied by a small flat-faced guard who asked who was making all the noise. As if he couldn't' tell my voice from the locals.

Charlie with his eyes averted down, explained about my past Consul visit and that I was told I could receive paper and a pen. He then went on to say about not having any medicine. The cell door was locked again and five minutes later, the goffer passed me a pen and one sheet of paper through the food latch.

I sat there on the floor, sticky and wet with sweat, going over repeatedly in my head exactly what I'd said during police interrogation. I had not told the real story of the cannabis, but the story I told was an accurate enough account of a similar nature. I felt satisfied that I had given a good enough account, albeit partly exempting myself from the full consequences of my actions. However, it was more important to fully exempt Scott from any responsibility. I had already admitted my crime of illegal possession of cannabis but had not accepted that I had come to China with criminal intention.

I had chosen a lawyer at random, as they were all unknown to me. Charlie and Tai Chi seemed as much in the dark regarding lawyers as me. I had also requested a legal visit, in order to get some inkling as to what my future looked like.

Charlie had mentioned a lawyer's name, 'Li Guo Ji,' but could give no contact details. Having written the name down in preparation for the next consul visit, Tai Chi added that Li Guo Ji was the best lawyer in Shanghai and that he stood up against the government.

It had been a very eventful day and I felt better for having taken things into my own hands to instigate results. I began to relax, talking more with Tai Chi, much to Charlie s obvious displeasure.

Then Charlie was called from the cell one day and Tai Chi sat closer to me telling me in perfect English that Charlie was a resident informer.

"What! How do you know this?" I asked excitedly.

He looked around nervously, saying that he was afraid to speak and that I should be very careful not to speak about my crime. Not to trust Charlie or the police, that they would trick me into confessing and then punish me severely. He told me repeatedly, "Never volunteer to speak about your crime and keep your mouth shut when dealing with the authorities."

When Charlie returned, one of the other people started speaking. I watched Charlie take off one of his thick, hard, brown, plastic shower type sandals. He walked over to Tai Chi, who had stood up with head bowed, and Charlie whacked him a full-on slap across the face with its sole. I tensed in astonishment but when he moved to deliver a second whack to the unresisting Tai Chi, I jumped to my feet and gripped Charlie by the offending arm shouting, "What is going on?"

I was promptly smothered by bodies pulling and punching at me. Pummelled under a pile of bodies I could not breathe with the overwhelming pressure upon me. I blacked out.

When opening my eyes again, I lay spread-eagled on the floor with my head resting in Charlie hands. Everyone else sat back against the wall, hands folded, heads down, eyes averted and silent. Picking myself up from the floor still breathless, I asked Charlie "What do you think you're doing?" Tapping my finger to my temple to illustrate 'craziness'.

The others stirred restlessly, some got to their feet, but with an offhand wave from Charlie they promptly sat back down again.

Tai Chi sat nursing his jaw, which had developed into a thick red welt.

In simplified speech I asked Charlie why he was an informer. Pointing around me saying, "Look at these people Charlie, why are you helping the police? You've been here for years and you should know better," Charlie merely smiled wistfully and nodded slowly; with a casual sweep said, "You no understand."

It was a clash of cultures and values. It is fundamentally wrong and erroneous to presume that one's own cultural values are universal and or morally superior. I didn't have a clue here. It was Chinese to me. It seemed to me then that Charlie was a tyrant, bully and informer and he was not denying it. Whereas, where I came from no part of any of this would be tolerated in the least. I was having difficulty getting it into my head that my standards and values were not universal and that this was, after all China.

Then the paranoia began, I wondered had I revealed anything to Charlie? Nevertheless, I knew that I had kept the secret of those kilograms of cannabis in my property so close to my chest. I was afraid to even think about it. My brain was going into overdrive again and overloading. It was so fucking hot in there that we were all were constantly wet. I lay down, which was against the rules, but I was feeling exhausted and closed my eyes.

.oOo.

Wang was a handsome bloke aged twenty-seven. He had been given the death penalty on August 26th, 1991. I thought back to when I first arrived at this cell. I had watched him do his Harry Houdini by taking off his trousers with the shackles on. He never once got flustered or irate about it but nonchalantly went about his way. He had what the Chinese consider a feature of beauty - his nose was long, rather than flat.

I had spoken a little with him, with Tai Chi interpreting for me. I learned that he had fought over a girlfriend and stabbed the other person to death. He had accepted from that moment and without complaint that he would to be executed. I called him 'Sing Song' Wang simply because he would just start singing right out of the blue. No one would ever object or complain, although I never understood a word. It was beautiful to listen to and everyone enjoyed it when he sang.

On the night before Wang went to court for sentencing to be carried out, he was handed a pen and a piece of paper to write a final farewell to his family. Tai Chi, with the tears running down his face, read Wang's letter out to everyone in the cell. It was the first emotion I had seen since coming here and it was the tears that burst the dam. Nearly everyone was crying some softly in silence and quiet dignity, while others simply sobbed their hearts out unashamedly.

Tai Chi then translated the letter content for me. Wang's letter of apology to his mother was seeking her forgiveness for the trouble and pain that he had caused her. He asked that his mother remember the days when they visited his grandparents in the countryside describing the scenery and the happy memories they shared as a family. Wang's sister should take care of Mama and not to let her work too hard.

Tai Chi said he could not translate anymore; it was too emotional. I understood well enough. I had a lump in my chest crushing me.

It was quite a surprise to hear a rustle and to see a pack of biscuits produced by one of the prisoners. Suddenly, almost like the breaking of bread and wine at the table of the last supper of Christ goodies were appearing from everywhere and passed around. Everyone moved around and chatted away freely together.

Wang himself was chatting away merrily munching biscuits as if without a care in the world. Sitting down with Tai Chi beside me, he patted me on the shoulder and smiled said, "It is a different cell today."

Tai Chi explained, "The death penalty inmate has a free day." It meant that we could talk and if Wang wanted to eat packet noodles, then the Laodong would provide the hot water for our cell.

I glanced over again, to where Wang sat, he was deep in conversation, and I felt humbled at the thought that this guy sitting opposite me would be soon dead.

Thinking of those extremes brought me to think of how little my problems where at that moment but how extreme they could become if I did not get things straightened out. I had written down all my points and queries for the lawyers' attention and would sign the contract from the list that the Consul had provided. Legal fees were to start at forty pounds sterling per hour. That was a lot of money by Chinese rates, where a monthly salary for a tradesman was thirty-pound sterling. The only other option open would be a court appointed lawyer assigned to me for a lesser fee. I decided to pay the higher fee, my reasoning being they must be very good at that sort of price.

I gradually slid down the cell wall, hot, groggy and wet with perspiration that nobody could afford to lose. My boxer shorts were tied in a knot at the waist to keep them up and were strangling my groin. Shoe laces, elastic, and belts, were all taken they even removed the metal clasp to fasten your trousers, zips and things were strictly forbidden. Probably to prevent people from hanging themselves before the authorities could get the chance to shoot them.

The Triad

It had been two days that had passed since Wangs execution although I didn't really know that young man, I felt deeply disturbed knowing he was no longer among the living. My thoughts were interrupted by the cell door opening I waited in the hope of a cool breeze that never came. I did not even bother to lift my eyes or care anymore. We were all exhausted, drained, and dehydrated. Many like me suffered from skin infections and nasty rashes in every extremity. It was the clatter of shackles that caught my attention and shook me from my stupor. I could hear the muffled grunts of pain. I quickly sat upright just as the cell door slammed shut. Jumping to my feet in shocked reflex at the sight of the badly battered and bruised man standing there at centre stage. I pointed my finger to where he could sit down and saw his jaw drop in shock at the sight of me. Perhaps it was that my beard was red and which always seemed to get a stare around that part of the world. Charlie went about telling the guy to put his things down and I went back to my attempted escape from the heat into sleep.

Later that evening Tai Chi told me that this new person was one of the 'Triad' leaders of a chapter form Northern China called the Dunbae Tigers. They were a fierce and infamous clan with a wide reputation.

This intrigued me and I asked Tai Chi to enquire further regarding the 'Tongs' and as to whether they were a big Triad mafia in China. After an exchange of just a few sentences, he answered, "We have not heard of Tongs."

I explained about the movie I had seen in Scotland as a youngster. Once more, they exchanged a few sentences. Tai Chi said the Chinese word Tong has many meanings, one of which being extortion. That sounded okay to me and I was off into some fantasy telling the people back home about my encounter with a real Tong in China. I had a feeling I would get along with the person whom I had named Triad. He also brought news of other foreigners being held there.

"How many?" I asked. Flicking open my fingers, "One, two, three?"

Tai Chi said that Triad had shared a cell with one German man who was with another man somewhere else in the building. It may seem strange and perverse but somehow it was a sense of relief to know that I was not alone. Yet it is a fate you would not wish upon anyone.

I recalled my younger brother Tommy, when he was sentenced to a ten-year incarceration for street gang related offences. He had told me about how his hands had bled as he had carved out a poem on the stone solitary cell wall with a bedspring.

Five years done, two more to do
Six months in this digger for assaulting a screw.
May get another year, may get two.
So, remember there is always someone worse off than you,
But if that's any consolation,
You are a creep.

Yes, it is true. There can be no happiness nor consolation at another suffering nor that do they suffer along beside you. To me it was just the hope of the opportunity to speaking and exchanging stories with another European who was already there.

.oOo.

The weather just got hotter and hotter along with the tempers and tensions in the cell. You could feel the violence sharpen through the thick, tepid, stale air. There was some kind of storm rising in the psychic atmosphere of this miniscule world. I could feel the static buzz crackle from one glance to another. It was becoming obvious that the clouds were about to break. I had no clue at all just what was going on. The eye of the storm appeared to stem from around Triad who seemed perfectly at ease, while unconsciously exuding an aura of natural power.

It was time for some changes to be made. Many things had been going down that I had not known about and simply could not understand from body language alone. However, it later emerged that Triad had been making moves that Tai Chi had been too frightened to mention. Charlie was receiving torrents of softly spoken abuse from Triad every time he spoke.

That evening when the food was delivered, pork fat with rice, everyone seated awaiting the go ahead from Charlie, Triad stood up and walked from his floor space to where Charlie sat. Then he calmly reached down, picked up Charlie's food container, and smashed it hard across his face.

Utter pandemonium erupted, food and blood splattered everywhere as almost everyone in the cell attacked Triad. I leapt into the affray intending to drag people off the pulverized Tong. I ended up right in amongst it. It seemed that everyone in the cell was letting loose their pent-up pain. It was terrifying, as if all hell had broken loose and I was fighting for my very survival.

I kicked with all my might and ability just to get some room around me to gasp for air. The only thought left in my head was for air to breath. Suddenly there was loud shouting and the cell door crashed opened. In pure and utter amazement, I realized that nearly everyone was sitting back in place.

Charlie had a wide-open wound on his cheek. He quickly stepped towards the cell door holding a towel to his face. He had not finished whatever it was he was saying before being frog marched out of the room.

Tai Chi then spoke up and, after a few more words the guard's face turned deadly serious with a tight-lipped expression. He pointed his finger at Triad, cackled something rapidly and slammed the door behind him. No sooner had the door slammed shut when Tai Chi said to me, "The boss wasn't happy being disturbed during dinner."

"What is going on here?" I asked. "Has everyone gone crazy or something?"

Tai Chi uttered a few words and everyone starting eating. They were still waiting to be told to eat. He then sat back down and told me, the problem started from the moment Triad had come into the cell. He had felt a deep sense of shame at being in the same cell with a government spy. The other Triads whom he associated with were known to kill informers or spies without hesitation or mercy.

Soon after we finished eating, the cell door was opened again and Tai Chi and I were called out. It had been some time since being last outside – and it felt spacious. It felt like a privilege in the weird way that sensory deprivation distorts your appreciation and perception. I was closely questioned.

They seemed more concerned with how badly hurt I was than they were with anything else. We sat there for over an hour. Tai Chi and the guard seemed to be getting along well as they sat chatting and drinking tea. Tai Chi was a non-smoker but he managed to slip a few cigarettes into my pocket before we were returned to the cell.

Tai Chi explained to me that he had been told to take charge of the cell and would interpret for me. He then went on to tell me in detail what Charlie did there at the detention cells. That he was a full-time spy. Not quite KGB or CIA. What Charlie did was to trade information with the PSB, which allowed him to be planted into whatever cell the PSB wanted to gather information. In return, he got food parcels brought in and sometimes a visit. I was to learn much more about this treacherous trade the longer I was there.

Charlie and Triad were removed from the cell giving us more space to sleep. I lay thinking about Charlie and his dastardly game then dreamt that night that I was sitting astride a massive American Bison looking onto an endless landscape. I awoke to the cold harsh light and the familiar sound of the jailer's keys.

News

I had been wasting away in that god-forsaken cell for over a month when I was escorted down to the visiting room for the second time. The Consul had come and I was looking forward to meeting him again with some relief. We sat in that same room with the outdated flock wallpaper, and I was happy enough just to be outside that dungeon.

Ian had a smile on his face upon entering the room.

"How is Scott?" I enquired immediately, anxious for news of my son.

Ian replied, "Scott has sent you £1000 from Tokyo."

I looked up, sharply, shocked and certainly surprised. Those words could only mean one thing. Scott was free and had taken the suitcase with the cannabis resin with him to Japan.

The sense of overwhelming relief almost floored me. Scott was okay and free from this hellhole - that was the main thing that had been playing on my mind for weeks. "When was he let out of here?"

"He was released on the tenth day of his imprisonment. The same day you were charged but it hadn't been confirmed when I saw you the last time."

Ian couldn't tell me how Scott had reached Japan, only that he'd flown from Shanghai to Hong Kong, after which he had no idea. We discussed a few issues, and I handed over the signed document for the hire of a lawyer. The visit passed quickly. Ian told me that he would not be returning to see me again as he was being posted back to the USA, but another Consul member would visit me soon.

We shook hands and once again and I watched them depart, and listened as the car engine fired up and they were gone. It felt like a huge weight had been lifted off my shoulders.

I was returned to the cell and sat thinking about what Ian had told me. Scott was free and in Japan, he had sent me £1000 sterling. He must have taken the case with the concealed cannabis with him – meaning I was only left with the stash in the day bag, which had not yet been found. The odds were that it might never be found at all then. I lived on hope and a prayer and slept well that night knowing Scott was okay and free.

.oOo.

The following day, things were back to the normal, stark madness and we were all out of adrenalin. Old Dong was a country bumpkin, no education, and no family to bring him anything. He usually got along by doing the local boy's laundry for miscellaneous items. He was a harmless old soul, inoffensive and always keen to oblige. So, on seeing one of the local Shanghai tough nuts slap him hard across the side of his head and sending him reeling, filled me with outrage.

I sprang to my feet instinctively reverting to my natural Glaswegian colloquial fighting talk, "Here you, fucking bam." Growling, I stepped up to him. I grabbed his hair, bent my knees to give me more spring, and head butted him with a perfectly executed *Glasgow Kiss* full on the mouth. I felt his teeth against my skull, and he was on his arse at the other side of the cell. His hands held to a bleeding mouth and spitting out teeth.

I knew he was well out of it. I was in a fucking rage but left it at that and turned away, ranting. "Who the fuck do these people think they are? Fucking Shanghai Gangsters, think they're better than everybody else, fucking bullies." The only outcome of that incident was they removed the bully to another cell.

With Charlie gone the cell was totally different. Over the weeks I had observed men like old Dong making decorative objects like lighter holders, picture frames, out of nothing but scrap paper wrappings. I watched detainees make chess pieces and playing cards from scrap paper and rice glue. The art of origami really thrived there but more as an underground movement. The chess and playing cards would be confiscated if found by the guards and would also entail a penalty imposed on the entire cell. This was set up to encourage people to inform and co-operate with the authorities. It never seemed to stop anyone in our cell and they always made a spare set. Bye Bye Charlie.

One day whilst asking help to roll some tobacco from the cigarette butts, I had saved from the guard's room and Consul Visit. However, I had no lighter to fire up.

One of the other guys took some stuffing from his quilt and spread it out roughly into a twelve-inch square. He scraped soap shavings onto it and rolled it into a cigar shape. Then he took off his shoe and forcefully rubbed the sole back and forth over the cigar shaped object. Finally, he broke it open and blew into it until smoke rose from the centre. It became tinder and our cell had a good smoke that night as we cheerfully passed around the rolled-up cigarette butts.

Another time one of the others attached a piece of cotton, rolled partially with silver paper – which he fixed to a toothbrush. Climbing up onto another's shoulders he removed the light bulb and inserted his device into the open socket and came away holding a flaming torch. What some people will do only to have a smoke! Being one of them, I was ever grateful for their ingenuity and fearlessness.

Winter 1991

The months passed and the weather grew gradually cooler as summer faded into fall then into winter – and I began to wonder if I had been forgotten.

I had just finished eating lunch when the cell door opened. I was called upon to go downstairs, expecting that it must be a Consul visit. It wasn't but I was overjoyed when it turned out to be the lawyer.

I was just glad to see somebody, until he told me that I was scheduled for court the following day. The lawyer handed me my indictment written in English. It was the first time reading my charge, 'Possession of cannabis'. Under the charge it read 'seven years maximum'. I was still confused and unsure whether to be glad or mad. I hadn't time to discuss my case before he was about to leave again.

I hurriedly went into my story, asking questions along the way about my defence. Mr Ho raised his hand to halt me in my tracks, telling me that I did not need to worry. He explained to me that I had confessed, "You are guilty, you do not need any defence," was his reply.

"Did you bring cigarettes?" I asked?

He produced a pack and lighter. Then ten minutes later Mr Ho stood up and took off on his way. I left that meeting having a strong feeling that my lawyer was a government agent. Then after listening to stories from Tai Chi, I was not sure if the lawyer was wholly working on my behalf. That night I slept fitfully, dreaming about my lawyer wearing a Judges wig as he towered above me, poised to slam the gavel down on my head.

I was up and out of bed at the usual time. I was handed a plastic disposable razor through the hole in the door to shave with but could not shave my face with this length of beard. I would need to have it cut off with scissors or electric shaver first.

Tai Chi saw the look of bewilderment in my eyes.

I asked, "Can you get scissors by any chance?"

He looked downwards as if humbled and said, "Mr Campbell, sorry you can't have those things."

"Why the fuck not?" I persisted aggressively and said, "I can't be expected to shave this off without trimming it first." Going to the door I called for the guard. The gofer came shuffling along; and could hear servility in every step.

Tai Chi interceded as the person got to the cell door, he said a few words and the gofer was off at a run again.

Finally, the slot on the cell door slid open again and a pair of manicure scissors was handed into Tai Chi. He asked me to sit by the toilet that it may then be easier to flush away the hair. There was a sudden babble of chit chat as I collected my basin. Tai Chi was having a good laugh.

"So, what's the big joke then?" I asked with a grin. "What is going on?"

"Mr Campbell," he struggled to control himself, "these countryside people want to keep your hair. Tai Chi went onto explain, "They believe it is lucky. Gold hair brings good fortune to their home and families."

I had heard of such things before but who would have thought of finding it here in this god forgotten place. Some people meditate, others in prayer implore, some people use healing stones, crystals, or quartz. Others carry a piece of cloth taken from a Shrine, Mosque or Temple. Still more bathe in the Ganges water or carry sand and stones home from the Holy Land. God is certainly great and works in wondrous ways. Who was I to object? I left the matter of my hair distribution to my barber, whom I could have garrotted that morning as he tore the face of me with a disposable razor. It doesn't matter how close you get with scissors you really need a couple of Gillette new blades to get off a beard.

The job was done though, leaving my face feeling like a well-slapped ass but I was ready for the day with great expectations of getting a smoke or two. The craving for a cigarette temporary occupied my mind more than the predicament in or what I was about to face in court. Hours that had passed before being summoned and then escorted downstairs to a large room where three other Chinese prisoners stood. Two were linked together in leg irons the other, who stood opposite me, was handcuffed.

The Chain Gang stared at me like some kind of rare species, and they started chattering excitedly. I had no clue as to what was so exciting, but they sure looked dangerous. My Scottish hackles did not rise as fear entered like a cold jag to my spine, nor did I like the odds by look of this pair. Soon we were on the move and somehow that felt safer.

I looked out of the police transit van window at busy streets full of life. It was seemingly unperturbed by the blare of sirens as we weaved through the morning traffic swerving around bicycles, and all sorts of bundle carriers. I saw stalls abundant with fruits that I would have loved to eat. I was away again into the daydream land making desperate escapes to freedom before the reality kicked back in.

We sped through the entrance of the court with the Tiananmen Square Heavenly Gates emblem on it. The People's Republic of China flag blowing in the breeze high above. I glanced at a plaque by the gate entrance 'Shanghai Intermediate People's Court. I was then escorted into the building and slammed into a small single cell about one meter square with a built-in concrete seat against the back wall where I sat down.

The guard came, handed me a cigarette, and lit it for me. I was pleased the wait for court would not be without a smoke. It probably was only some hours but it seemed like all eternity to me before entering the courtroom flanked by two PSB officers. The lawyer was there and a representative of the British Consul. Nodding to the lawyer, I was happy to see no foreign press. The court layout was similar to the British system only there was three Judges presiding there and not one.

I stood erect as the court proceedings began and remained standing until lunch. The charge against me was read out first in Chinese, then again in very poor English. "That you Lauchlan Campbell, a British national being apprehended at *(such and such a place.)* Moreover, having acknowledged your guilt, stand today charged with possession of cannabis."

It took ages for all this to be read out and it was difficult to try to keep a straight back and solemn face. I let out a few nervous coughs so that I could turn my head to look around. I noticed the full proceedings were being recorded by cameras set up at different points around the courtroom. I was direct in front of the one behind the Judges. The woman from the train station waiting room was there to identify me. The train guard ticket collector was also there, the one whom I had first encountered when foolish enough to have a joint on the train. It was that which had started this entire show rolling. Apparently, this was all standard procedure. The PSB team from Zhizou came in, and my nod to Lee was ignored. They too went through their encounter with me. Then they were asked to identify the substance, which they had found in my possession. It lay on a table in front of the Judges.

It was a painful enough experience emotionally and by lunchtime, my head was splitting, and my back was breaking with continual standing for more than three hours straight.

The court had a lunch break and once locked up in the dog box again, I requested to see the lawyer. He had not said a single word yet, but then he had not been given any opportunity to do so. The guard did not understand anything I was saying, and after ranting on for five minutes he presented me with my lunch. It was a steaming hot plate of rice with mixed vegetables. Then another dish with a whole fish covered in a sweet and sour sauce. Forgetting my headache, and forgetting my lawyer, I ate into that hot tasty food like a man possessed. This was followed by hot instant coffee and a cigarette.

I sat back sighing contentedly as the life force flowed back into me and the tension oozed out. It was all somehow not so bad again. I would probably be given a heavy fine and deported for Christmas just eleven days hence. That would be a nice gift for the family and me, I dreamed on.

The cell door was opened suddenly rousing me from my reverie as two PSB guards filled my vision to escort me back for part two of the trial process. I was left standing again while a few more witnesses were called to confirm and identify me. Then it was my lawyers turn, in plea of mitigation, he explained how I had confessed and co-operated and that the substance was a category B class, non-addictive drug. He went onto say it is often smoked and acceptable in many western countries where it had been decriminalized. I thought he was doing well and putting it across plainly. He spoke for about thirty minutes before proceedings were closed and the trial was over.

I was returned to the cell where was soon visited by the consul rep and the lawyer. The consul enquired as to my views on the fairness of the trial and I could only tell them that, as I was guilty, it did not matter and was just awaiting sentence.

The lawyer intervened to tell me, "You did very well Mr Campbell. You kept a straight back and showed no disrespect."

"So, what happens now?" I inquired anxiously.

The lawyer said that I would be called back to court within a month. Then asking what kind of sentence he thought might be meted out now that he had heard the proceedings?

His answer wasn't very reassuring, "I already told you Mr Campbell, the maximum sentence under this article is seven years, but am confident that you won't be getting that."

"What about deportation?" I asked the Consul.

The lawyer intervened, "I don't think so Mr Campbell." Then he went on to tell me about another British citizen whom he had recently represented, who had been sentenced to four years and fined £5000 when caught boarding a ship from Shanghai to Japan with cannabis. That caught my attention as this was the route I had intended to take - small world sure enough. I then thought but his charge was smuggling and he got a four-year sentence and a fine. I whereas was charged only for possession and may yet get less than four years. I would just have to live with that thinking to myself as they departed.

I sat for another hour or so until the three who arrived with me returned. Only this time two were bound with rope crossed over their chest and held firm from behind by an armed police guard. They had just been to court for the final time and were off for execution. It choked me to see that. I remembered one person in the cell making those executed men ingeniously from paper wrappers it had been this morbid pastime, which had prompted me to ask about the death sentence in more detail.

Tai Chi had explained the system to me. If you were shackled you were a potential death sentence prisoner. If you had rope bound around you then you were scheduled for execution that day. I had looked into the eyes of these two men as they were being led away on a rope leash to be shot in the back of the head. The interrogation film was one thing but to have brushed up against and sat in the same van with the condemned left indelibly marked scars deep in my psyche.

The law stated their family would be billed for the bullet that would kill their kin. The system there was for people who have committed no crime and who are often ostracized, as result of their kindred's execution. Some sick humans somewhere in the administration thought of this uncivilized procedure and everyone else had followed obediently. Whoever that was should be speedily retired if not yet long dead and that act repealed.

The lawyer was direct to the point regarding the outcome of the trial and I would just have to accept it. There was not any other choice and I would be going to jail for probably about four years.

"Fuck it," I said, horrified at the full realization.

Once back in the detention cells, I told Tai Chi the story. He was always eager for details and conversation to improve his English. We chatted until lights out. The other men rolled up cigarettes from the ones I had pocketed at court. We would keep them in store for the next couple of days then suffer withdrawals until the next puff came our way. I could not sleep for the court session running through my head like a fast forward and rewinding cassette tape. My mind leaped from one court scene to another and wouldn't slow down.

Having visions of those two people being led off to be shot made me count my blessings. I gave thanks to the Lord for showing me the sufferings of others, before dozing off into sleep at some point in the night.

The next morning, I was a little more at ease now that the massive pressure was lifted, because the trial was over. I still had that lingering hope.

The other person, the Englishman, was given four years for smuggling 7.2kg of cannabis. That is a serious international offence, and I tried to convince myself that my crime was not as serious. I was slipping back into my delusions.

That night just before lights out, another new person from Shandong Province was put into the cell. Shandong is what I called him. A very hard-faced young man and when he spoke, he looked fierce. He and his brother had been working somewhere in the city of Shanghai without the proper permit papers to allow them to stay or work. In China, you just can't up and resettle into another city without getting police registered ID card with photo. You also need permission from various other bureaucratic offices to work. The story was, one evening, some local people broke into the room Shandong was sharing with his brother and another friend from their province. The intruders were waving large, bladed knives. Fearing for their lives they defended themselves. Shandong's brother was killed and his friend badly injured, and I could see from his scar that he too was stabbed. He was thrown in jail for not having the right papers. It all just seemed a little bit over the top to me. Like as if the authorities didn't have the slightest respect for the common people and were intent only on adding to their pain and their burden. The people just seemed to take it all in their stride as if they never would have expected anything else.

Merry Xmas 1991

On December 21st, 1991, at around midday the cell door latch opened and a folded A4 envelope had been pushed through to me. I opened it with cautious apprehension, and then scanning the perfectly worded English document content carefully. I read the line again; then again to be sure was reading it properly. Case withdrawn from Public Prosecution, under Article 131 of the Chinese Criminal Procedural Act. I imagined they would take me to the immigration holding cells that afternoon and would probably spend the night there and be deported as an undesirable in the morning. It would not be a nice stamp to have on my passport but better than any alternative. Besides, that could be easily remedied.

I handed the two pages over to Tai Chi one was written in Chinese I started pacing the cell, kicking up the sand from the imaginary beaches that I'd soon be strolling on.

Tai Chi read aloud the Chinese version and soon I was being hugged and my hand shaken by the people in the cell. I wanted to laugh with relief but also to cry for those poor bastards who were all smiles and happy for me.

My emotions were chaotic, swinging from euphoric to manic sadness. Having heard so many of the prisoners tell me over these months that being a foreigner would be treated better.

"You pay money, you go free."

"British treated better you go free."

I'd found this talk gave me an uneasy feeling, difficult for me to live with. As far as I was concerned, I was treated the same. We all shit in the same hole ate the same food and shared equal cell space. I had no idea of how the Chinese system worked, it just seemed to me to be a fucking shamble. Even if only part of what I had seen and heard was real, I had realized a long time ago that corruption and bribery can often create an even balance. A bribe can give extra money and feed the families of the underpaid cops whilst simply cutting out the red tape and formal documentation of a court procedure.

I started to allocate my property to the neediest, my woollen blanket everything I possessed right down to the clothes I was wearing. I could almost smell the mold from the hash in my bag picking out my clothes for the journey ahead. By the time the evening food arrived I was mentally and emotionally drained. It was like just another of their mad Chinese puzzle games again. Every sound heard throughout that day had me up and ready in anticipation of liberation. On the other hand, was it just that ghost of freedom wailing in my brain?

By evening I knew I would not be going anywhere until morning and I reluctantly put my head down - nothing ever happened at night. I lay tossing and turning the long, lonely night away desperately willing the hours to move into day and I should be off in the morning.

Even, as guilty as sin, I began to think that I was being unlawfully and unfairly detained. Had some anonymous bureaucrat somewhere filed my release order in his overcrowded 'in' tray and had not gotten around to it yet? Didn't they know how important my life and my freedom were to me?

Holding out until lunchtime the next day when the food was being passed through, I could not contain my expectations any longer and called the guard myself.

We were taken into the office and Tai Chi asked the big question for me. "Mr Campbell wants to know when he will be going home."

They exchanged a few words. In my mind translations, the guards were saying, "Oh! Any minute now." As it turned out the actual response was that he didn't do the prosecutor's job, so how would he know? He did tell Tai Chi that the PSB were re-investigating my case and we returned to the cell with me deflated, deeply worried and scared.

The arrogance was kicked right out of me and I could not even eat lunch. I sat with my back against the wall, stretched my legs out, then pulling them up to my chest, I began to rock back and forwards. My mind was gone. My life was gone, and I was psyched up on the verge of murder. I had asked Tai Chi to explain exactly what was meant, in this country by re-investigation by the PSB.

He replied that the guard on duty did not know anything. He just shifted the responsibility to the PSB so he will not be disturbed. "Mr Campbell you are going home," Tai Chi said.

That succeeded in perking me up for about ten minutes till off again down into those dark and dangerous labyrinths of my mind. 'Gate Fever' that dreaded blues had a hold of my heart and tore at it over the next two weeks. Day by day waiting in expectation for that door to open and set me free. When they would call my name and send me home.

"Any day now, any way now, I shall be released," Bob Dylan perked up my stamina, as his song rang through my head.

Waiting for that door to open, waiting, at any time.

I would not care if it were a slow boat from China or a fucking pushbike. Just get me out of there.

I tried to relax and create the mood of Christmas. In my imagination, I invited Billy Connelly to China. We sat around the cell and he was telling the old Crucifixion yarn from the Glasgow point of view. Tai Chi was doing the translation and by the response, it was hilarious. It was great to see these people laugh everybody laughed. Chinese people do laugh yet it was a sadly rare commodity in these dire surroundings.

Xmas's day passed just like any other day. The only difference is that I sang Christian hymns and Carols, *Away in a Manger,* I sang as, *child* No crib for a bed, the little lord Jesus lay down his sweet head. The song always takes me back to the stark poverty and hunger-wrenching days of my early childhood and felt a little nostalgia choked up, but my voice did not crack. Christianity has not much pull in China not one person in that cell cared a hoot about the man who walked on water. Isn't it so true that when you are far from home and having a good time, you tend to forget everybody else? But when anything goes wrong, you expect family and friends to run to your rescue.

Boxing Day, Hogmanay, and New Year's Day are all just another ordinary day with no festivities attached. Prison truly is severe here. I couldn't let the guys in the cell down on New Year's Day so invited my family over for the day and sang a Scottish ballad with emphasis on the chorus, "For he would never dishonour the Tartan of his Clan" and even got up and did the jig with my hand on my hips holding my imaginary bagpipes blowing proudly and fiercely patriotic. Dancing around the cell like a maniac getting louder by the moment *Oh Flower of Scotland, when will we see, your likes again?* I put more emphasis on *Who fought and died for, your wee bit hill and glen, and stood against them, Proud Edwards army, and sent them homewards to think again.*

I was psyched up and ready for a fucking war with the Chinese PSB bastards but was interrupted in mid madness by the cell door opening. The room went uncannily silent, and I was called to the office and questioned as to what was wrong. Why was I shouting and disturbing everyone?

Tai Chi explained about my traditional New Year's Day celebrations. That in my country it is customary to bring in the New by singing out the Old. The guard seemed to like this idea and the cigarettes came out.

The guard asked if I had celebrated the Chinese New Year. I told him about my first encounter with those festivities in Hong Kong. The guard insisted hotly that "Hong Kong is China" as if he expected some dispute from me. I did not disagree, and never picked up on his patriotic vibe. I was rapidly discovering just how much the hatred and resentment for the British was imbedded into the Chinese psyche. The British are the top of the 'We will get you bastards back charts' in China.

I had a couple of cigarettes while Tai Chi and the guard spoke. Tai Chi said we were to be quieter once returned to our cell. Lying back that night in my cell I was still trying to fathom out what was going on. I hadn't seen my lawyer or Consul since court and felt abandoned and deserted. January had slipped into February still no lawyer, still no Consul still no one was opening the door to send me home. Still, they could be coming.

1992

Finally, they did come, bearing their new indictment which they handed me on February 7th, 1992, the charges read the same as the first one except two words. This was an upgraded and more serious charge. The use of the word *transporting* which I wondered if it was a miss translation of *smuggling*. According to their acceptance of my confession, I had never crossed any border so maybe that was why they had not used the word smuggling, nothing was ever sure. Returning to the cell still baffled, I handed Tai Chi my new indictment. He scrutinized the Chinese version before delicately pointing out to me that there were two new changes. Firstly 'Possession' was now 'Transportation, and secondly 'Cannabis' was now 'Cannabis ester.'

I had no idea what *cannabis ester* was. I could not make head nor tail of it and was just so furious that I was not going home after all.

.oOo.

The next outing from my cell came quicker than anticipated. It was February 15th and it was to see my lawyer. Cigarettes were the last thing on my mind that day. As soon as my ass got on the seat, I was boiling over with questions; I handed him the 'withdrawal from public prosecution' paper asking what it was all about. Only then did I ask if he had brought cigarettes. He produced a packet and I sat listening intensely to his explanation of the meaning of "withdrawal from public prosecution". You would think that it could only mean what it said. Not according to him. It appeared that it was no longer *public* but was now *personal* or something against the people.

It was when he read from the Statutes book exactly what the sentence for my new indictment entailed that I sacked him on the spot. "You are a treacherous bastard," I shouted at him. They had led me along the garden path only to spring their evil trap. He called the guard as my ranting raged in a torrent of vile abuse until they had to manhandle me back to the cell in a state of total manic insanity.

He had just told me that the new indictment carried the death penalty. It could not be real and I could not believe it. Sweet Jesus Christ. Standing in the cell, purple faced and cursing everything, this was my belated Christmas gift from a Godless Land. The daydreams were over with a rude awakening. This was Shit Street Shanghai Sheridan and this new indictment carried the death penalty.

There went my visions kicking up the sand on a beach. It was appearing more like pushing up the fucking daises. From the prospect of going home, to spending a few years in jail staring down steel barred corridors and concrete cubes, to staring up the cold barrel of a gun - quite a turnaround of events. I had used all my reserve just surviving, learning to accept and to cope with the day-to-day close confinement of my immediate predicament.

I had already been clinging desperately to sanity against the thought that maybe to spend even up to four long years in that dismal place of despair was better than being shot. Hearing the clanking of keys and slamming of cell doors, I could still hear the voice of the lawyer saying that the new indictment, "Carries the Death sentence, Life sentence, or Fifteen years minimum imprisonment".

I sat listlessly on the floor as the words echoed and re-vibrated through my pounding scull. It was as the cell was my head and somewhere in there was deep despair but also something else was stirring and awakening. It was some kind of outrage against the system. First to make me think I was going home by withdrawing the prosecution case against me then dragging it out until I was almost on fire with gate fever, then to tell me that was being indicted all over again. What kind of administration was it that thought it was okay to do that to anybody? In addition, why did the Chinese people tolerate it?

Despair could only give way to rebellious outrage. There was nowhere else to go. At the end of the weary day, it was my own stupid fuck up that put me there. That did not mean to say that anybody deserved to suffer that kind of torture under the system of so-called justice. I was being only charged for a bit of cannabis for goodness's sake!

The cell was silent, everyone sensing something bad had happened. I found myself in the foetus position trying to disappear into the void of nowhere ness but I couldn't escape. I did not eat that evening but just sat, staring into the far-distant space beyond the bars in front of me. My neck and head cocked to one side as if trying to find the angle to squeeze through. All the shadows churned unsettled in darkening stormy clouds not in sympathy but in disharmony with my soul.

.oOo.

I roused the following morning, automatically going through the same routine as a mindless zombie. I made inquiries about long-term prisons with Tai Chi, and he asked around the cell. The feedback neither presented relief nor hopes to cling to. It all sounded quite horrific unless you were sent to a farm. The farms, I was told, were mostly filled with criminals doing hard labour, or officials who had fallen foul of the party but still had the contacts and financial power to buy their way there. Everything was for sale there, including illicit sex. It sounded better than this Shanghai PSB – 100% party line policy puppets.

I was now waiting to be called for reinvestigation over the next few days, but it never happened. Finally, when the cell door did open for me, it was for a visit from the British Consul. They handed me another list of lawyers while I explained the latest shenanigans. The 'Withdrawal from Public Prosecution' papers and the new indictment with altered substance and wording put my head on the proverbial chopping block.

Jim Short, the new Vice Consul, wasn't exactly enthused about the procedures himself but couldn't offer assistance other than ensuring that proper legal representation would be forthcoming. Jim went on to say that he had only received notice of the second trial that morning.

I nearly swallowed the cigarette on my lip and inhaled in shock. "Second trial? When?" I asked. "20th February," Jim replied.

"But this is already the eighteenth," I stuttered in disbelief.

Jim Short had thought I was aware of the date and was quick to suggest that we could try to have it postponed under the circumstances.

We discussed that possibility, but my main worry was the conditions of confinement there, entailing reluctance to prolong that unnecessarily.

Considering the shortage of time left available, I appointed another lawyer named 'Ma Yu Min' and signed the papers for the Consul to hire him that day. Jim said to expect to see the new lawyer soon. We shook hands and said our farewells. Returning to the cell with my head thumping, by the time I had explained it all to Tai Chi, I was thoroughly exhausted and ready to bury my head in the sand. I did sleep fitfully through that night, but at least I slept.

The following morning, I couldn't get up from bed. I felt I couldn't face another day but eventually sat up with my blanket wrapped around me and covering my head like the Grim Reaper, or something like Grim Weepers, more like, with this forgotten bunch surrounding me. I was feeling deeply depressed, turning in on myself, gazing into the void that gaped before me.

I sat like that for hours until the cell door opened and a lot of shouting in Chinese shook me from my stupor rather abruptly. The guard was pulling at my bed cover, holding onto it as he pulled me to my feet.

"What's going on?" I asked, turning in confusion to Tai Chi, who explained that I had to get up and fold my blanket.

"Fuck off," was my response, and I sat back down again, huddling in my blanket.

Whatever interpretive skill Tai Chi utilized, the result was that the guard turned and left, slamming the door behind him.

"What's going on?" I asked again.

Everyone was shuffling about, fixing buttons on their jackets with excited chatter.

Tai Chi explained that sometimes a visiting committee would inspect the place and that a senior communist party member was inspecting that day and we were to clean the cell up. It was all so pathetic it was almost comical; every time any sound louder than a fart was heard, these people quickly straightened their backs and re-examined their buttons.

I couldn't make head nor tail of all the fuss and proceeded with the day as usual, not that it amounted to much more than shifting my arse into a more comfortable position. Nobody visited the cell anyway, yet these untried men remained ever-ready and dutifully upright until suppertime that evening. I had a lot to learn.

.oOo.

On the afternoon 19th February 1992, I was taken down to have a meeting with my new lawyer Ma Yu Min. We shook hands on introduction and I held on a little too long to the delicate hand of his lovely secretary.

Mr Ma then explained that the second trial would be no more than a formality. There would be no witnesses recalled.

"But I thought this was to be a retrial," I said, handing over the withdrawal from prosecution document and asking, "What is this, and why serve me with this document?" There was just so much to ask but foremost in my mind was this withdrawal document. It was doing my head in. "One minute I'm being set Scot free and the next I'm indicted with a death penalty charge. What was the difference between *Possession* to *Transporting*? It was in my possession when going from one place to another that is nothing new. So, what is going on?"

It was the way he replied that was surprising for me, he informed me that it was also his duty to disclose any information obtained from me that may help solve this crime. I could not believe my ears; this place was insane and I vented my outrage at how fucked up the system was.

Mr Ma calmly reminded me that my indictment carried the death penalty and I quickly replied, "Do not try to intimidate me, Mister. It is cannabis we are talking about here, not heroin!" I was pissed off seeing this as no more than another interrogation.

"Mr Campbell," he went on smoothly in a voice that would make a Buddha smile. "This is China and our law punishes according to the crime and how the offender cooperates with the investigating authorities knowing all that ..."

I interrupted adding that I had made a confession going into another verbal outburst of how bad the living conditions were there. "What sort of system is it, that only allows your lawyer to see you on the day before the trial? The last lawyer moved my charge from a seven-year maximum to a fifteen-year minimum with a death penalty hanging over me like it could happen. You tell me it is all a formality, all done and dusted so what am I paying you for?" Raving on I left the visit with not a bit of hope in my bones.

I was naive to expect anything else from a screwed-up system such as that and was definitely snookered. It was just a small matter of how far they wanted to blackball me.

That night's sky was quick in coming down due to the changing season. Most people sat around wrapped with a blanket. It was cold and there was no other internal heating other than the human aura as we huddled around. It was the only time we all really bonded together as a group, as if bonding together against the harshness of the winter cold chill with a smell of the grave.

I had court the next day – and it was to be a mere formality. My crime carried the death penalty but for this moment, we would have the freedom to huddle.

Appeal

My escort to court consisted only of me and three guards in a police car. I was handcuffed and placed in the back seat. The sirens wailed as if in mourning as we sped through the usual trade traffic and bustle. I lost myself in mindless daydreaming to distract from the reality of my situation. It's strange how people go about their daily routine, oblivious to other people's extremes. Would my look be as desperate and dangerous as the others I had seen, clad in chains and shuffling woefully to their death?

Our arrival at court was uneventful, almost mundane. I was put into the same box cell I'd previously occupied and again was given lit cigarettes when requesting one. I looked forward to lunch, remembering how hot and tasty the last meal there had been.

The court was finally called, and I was escorted to the rail where I had stood before. Again, I stood for hours, listening as they went on about the past trial. It was just confirming that all the facts remained the same, having accepted my guilt in confession. I was the only one left standing, and again my back ached and my mind screamed.

By lunchtime, I was close to collapse; my head was spinning amid the babble around me, which seemed to kind of taper away into the far distance. It felt as though my legs were giving way beneath me, and nobody was paying attention. Only the pain reminded me to try and stay upright and erect. I was returned to the dog box, and I let out a sigh of relief. I was eternally grateful for the small mercy of a seat and a cigarette, blowing away all my aches and pains with each glorious puff. When the food arrived, I was not disappointed either, with the same dish as served up before. I had two large steaming hot dumplings with meat stuffing. It certainly helped me relax enough to doze off for an hour of blissful oblivion.

The afternoon session was much briefer, and finally, they asked me if I had anything to say. I thought they were asking me how I pleaded and replied simply, "Guilty."

The court waited in silence, and I also wasn't sure what was going on, so I stood silent too.

My lawyer stood up and said something briefly, then produced a placard with Chinese characters written on it and explained something regarding the substance possessed.

The court was dismissed, and I was returned to the cell.

The lawyer came down to see me almost immediately and asked me why I had not spoken up, seeking the court's leniency.

I replied, "I didn't know it was expected of me to speak again, being guilty. I did not hear much by way of a plea of mitigation from your end, Mr Ma." "Mr Campbell," he said wearily, "It is my job to help you tell the truth, not to defend you or your actions."

"Come on, give me a break," I retorted, "it's your job to submit mitigating circumstances to the judges with a view toward a policy of leniency. The explanation given that, as a foreigner and not acquainted with, nor understanding Chinese law, I acted in ignorance and not out of malice or disrespect for the law and customs of this country. I already explained all this to the other lawyer and hardly had a chance to speak with you." For some reason, probably blind presumption, I just had not expected to be going over the whole thing again with this lawyer. There was no point to this anymore; it was finished and no going back to try again.

We said farewell, and he said that he would visit me again before sentencing. I couldn't have cared less what he did, having a headache and was just glad that it was over and would soon know my fate.

That night, Tai Chi and I were escorted to the office and seated facing that ever-smiling faced guard in his khaki uniform. He wanted to tell me that my case was very serious and that I should expect a prison sentence. No matter how I tried to fathom out why he would take the time to tell me this, I just could not relate to it anymore. It may be that he was trying to give me the good news that the word was not to be executed.

It all just went over my head at the time. I just nodded my head politely, as if grateful for his every word, while in fact, I was only being nice to have more time out of the cell and more cigarettes. I am not normally that shallow, but on some occasions, it is an easy escape from thinking too deeply into those darker extremes. I slept surprisingly well that night and did not awake until Tai Chi gave me a shake the next morning. We spent most of that day teaching English to the people in the cell, who would roll around in peals of laughter when I tried speaking Chinese. For the moment, at least, we had escaped into some kind of life.

.oOo.

On March 18th, 1992, I was first visited by the procurator's office. They told me to transfer my personal funds from the consulate office into my property at the detention holding cells. I asked why I should do that and was informed that it was to pay a fine. My suggestion was to pay the fine once it was imposed upon me. That comment only resulted in a stern, threatening look and a warning that non-cooperation would not bode well for me under the circumstances. Not needing another reminder that I still had the death sentence hanging over me, I wrote a short note there and then to the consulate, requesting to have my money transferred to me here at the detention holding cells.

My next visit was from the lawyer that very same day. He had me sign his legal fees bill and permission for the British Consul to pay him from my personal funds. It seemed to me that everyone was suddenly in a big hurry to grab as much of my money as they could, but before what?

I told him about the visit from the procurator's office, but he already knew. I tried to get some hint from him as to what the future might hold for me but could not get another word out of him beyond the fact that he had been paid. He merely smiled and left me with a couple of cigarettes as a consolation. Then I returned to the cell, where all were keen to hear of the latest developments.

Tai Chi translated what had just happened. This was all apparently not new and unusual in China; it was considered normal procedure.

They all babbled in speculation, still sure the money would buy an air ticket and I would be deported home. All the conclusions were positive and, in my favour, but you wouldn't really expect these poor people to conclude that the prosecution was only emptying my Western pockets before jailing me.

The consul visited me on March 22nd, and I signed the money over from their account to mine. The money had been sent via the Foreign Office by my brother Robert in London, specifically to pay legal fees. The Consul could not tell me any more about the procedures nor the possibility of a fine. Soon the visit was over, and I said thanks and goodbye.

.oOo.

The morning after my consulate visit, I was shocked to be told to get ready for court. I felt excited in the deluded hope of paying the money as a fine, which would end this horrible existence. I was escorted downstairs to the familiar rigmarole to wait. Then other detainees entered the room. I was surprised to see two Westerners with their heads bowed. I asked them which country they came from.

The smaller one of the two replied simply without looking up, "Germany."

Then a third foreigner appeared through the door. I asked where he was from and he said, "Wales."

"So, we're all from the same planet then," I joked, but nobody laughed. I was just happy to see someone and immediately started asking questions.

Within minutes, we were traveling towards the court, all handcuffed and seated together in the transit van. The guards kept telling us to be quiet, but we ignored them and talked about another British person getting four years for smuggling 7.2kg of cannabis to Japan. I was expecting the same, saying nothing about my fear of possible execution. The two Germans were charged with possession of 3kg of cannabis between them. The other British person was charged with supplying the two Germans and possession of 400 grams of cannabis and another 1kg found at his girlfriend's residence in Kashgar. I expected he would probably receive the heaviest sentence due to his charges of trafficking drugs but did not say so aloud.

The sirens sung their usual wail as we came to a halt at the court and were escorted into the building, where we were immediately separated. I could not see anyone, but we could still hear each other if we called out. I was still having difficulty with the thought of possibly having to serve up to four years imprisonment here. I kept pushing that nightmare to the back of my mind and had managed to blank out the very idea that my crime carried the death sentence. I maintained the delusion in my reasoning that, as the other guy was charged with smuggling and I wasn't, I could get a lesser sentence. I was off in some far place in my mind when the cell door opened, and it was time to face the music in court.

Standing there before the three judges, my knees were shaking as my head flashed from execution scenes to boarding a plane as a deportee. There was silence as the judge read the verdict and sentence in Chinese. I looked over at my lawyer for some indication as to what was going on. Then the court interpreter repeated it again in bad English. I didn't quite catch it all; there were the numbers fifteen and three thousand, but nothing about what that entailed. I was still very much in blissful ignorance when returned to the holding cell by two grim-faced guards.

It was only minutes later; however, the lawyer enlightened me when handing me a copy of the English version of the verdict and sentence to sign. Shanghai Intermediate People's Court Criminal Case No. 24. 1992. It was then the realization struck me like a sledgehammer – I was sentenced to fifteen years' imprisonment and $3000 dollars confiscated from me.

Fifteen years in prison. It echoed and ricocheted around my head as if trying to find a place to land or to fit. I couldn't quite take it in. It was disembodied data that did not have any real meaning and did not apply to me. Then, hearing the other detainees return, I shouted out asking what their sentences were.

The Welsh guy, who became known as Bull, shouted, "Eight and a half years and a 10,000 RMB fine."

Telling him my sentence and after a pause, he asked, "How many people did you kill?"

The two German people had received eight years and a 10,000 RMB fine each. We spoke on the way back, trying to reassure them our sentences could not stand up in the face of the other British person only getting four years for smuggling 7.2kg to Japan. I was really trying to reassure myself, trying to apply logic to how it could be that one person gets four years for smuggling 7.2kg strapped and concealed on his body, and the Germans get eight years for smuggling 3kg, and me getting fifteen years for possession or transporting 7.9kg? No way! It just could not be held up to be right; I was convincing myself.

Of course, in my ignorance, I had failed to take many other factors into account, like the kind of press received. Thanks to the Douglas Hurd mission and the press blitz in association with my brother T C Campbell's dire situation back home in Scotland. Thanks to the press, I was the head of the international crime Clan Campbell, but I was the only one here who did not know it. Not much more could be said after the initial shock set in.

We sat, lost in our own personal shattered worlds, quietly contemplating the future. We were immediately separated from each other on arrival at the detention cells. It was agreed unanimously we would all appeal against the severity of the sentence. I was taken directly into the guard's office instead of the cell and was given a cigarette. I sat for a few minutes in silence, as the guard just quietly looked me over. I felt numb.

Tai Chi entered the office and looked at me as the guard spoke. Then Tai Chi translated, saying, "Mr Campbell, the officer wants to know what you think of the sentence?"

"Fifteen years. Fifteen fucking years for a bit of cannabis, can you believe that?" I let my anger speak.

"Mr Campbell, the officer says you should return to the cell and rest now."

Once inside my cell, I felt the inmates so wanted me to get away with it so they too might also have some hope. I told them about the other foreigners; their oriental eyes opened wider with interest, and they all started babbling as if in heated debate about my news. The cell sounded like a busy marketplace where nobody listened to anybody else. The noise only stopped when a key rattled on the door.

I thought fifteen years with a five-year remission still added up to ten. It didn't make it sound any better. I was still to discover that it really and truly wasn't any better. Then I heard from Tae chi that China didn't do remission, early release schemes, or training for freedom programs.

I couldn't eat anything that night but did have a couple of smokes and began to worry about the guy popping the electric socket for a light. What if he gets electrocuted just to light an illicit smoke? Would it be me made an accessory for supplying the smokes and then dragged back to court again?

We all could certainly do without that, but it did not stop us smoking.

Tai Chi had underlined some Chinese characters on my charge and verdict. He told me that my problems all came down to the change in the naming of the substance I had been originally indicted for – 'Dama,' the Chinese word for 'Cannabis.' However, the 'Verdict Sentence' stated that I was sentenced for 'Dama Zhi,' ie, the equivalent of 'Cannabis oil.' After scrutinizing the Chinese characters underlined, I could see that they both looked the same except for one added character.

Not being able to understand this until Tai Chi explained that 'Zhi' the added character was a chemical compound in Chinese and not a natural substance. On the English version, it only used the word cannabis ie Dama yet the Chinese version differed, why? I would have to inquire about that when the next consul staff member arrived.

The next day Tai Chi unexpectedly disappeared and never returned. I enquired about him to the guard but he didn't understand what I was saying. I wondered where he had been Shanghaied to as he hadn't been given any indictment or court date.

A Dangerous Man

Everything became much more difficult without Tai Chi and his diplomatic translations. He was such a straight and intelligent person, and I really missed him. From that point onwards, everything became even more difficult and confusing, with more and more conflict arising in all areas. Another new guy arrived in shackles, scheduled for death. He named himself Fenzi, which translates as 'Crazy'. From the very moment he entered the cell, he was pointing fingers aggressively and shouting commands of some sort. Old Dong the farmer, plus a few others, mostly curled up in fear. I just sat and quietly observed.

The proverbial last straw came with the arrival of yet another two new people into the cell the following day. This brought us up to fourteen people. It was already a tight squeeze with twelve, but space was quickly allocated. I still kept my place secure at the cell door. There was no doubt in my mind that Fenzi was, in fact, crazy. I could see the desperation in his eyes, perhaps understandable since he was already scheduled for death, and he was obviously dangerous.

One of the new people, a practicing Muslim from Xinjiang, insisted on washing his hands before prayer. Fenzi, in shackles, grabbed hold of him by the neck and started to throttle him, shouting some kind of obscenities. Everybody froze. No one intervened to stop him killing this poor person.

I took action, grabbing hold of him by the neck and pulling him backwards towards me. Then, I held him in a stranglehold, forearm locked tight around his neck as he struggled to free himself from my grip. The more he struggled, the tighter my grip got, until he finally relaxed in submission. I could only speak to him in calming tones, breathing heavily close to his ear in English. Nobody had a clue what was said. "Take it easy pal, we're all in the same boat here, just settle down and you'll be fine."

When finally, I released my grip, he was keen to shake hands, but it was not long before he attacked someone else and was forcefully removed from the cell to who knows what other hell. It was strange, and particularly odd, that the cell door had not burst open the way it would when any disturbance or fighting broke out.

It was becoming apparent that we were being singled out for a hard time by the guards. On 27 March 1992, I was taken downstairs to the visiting area for a surprise meeting with my lawyer. I had not expected to see him so soon. I couldn't wait to ask about those Chinese characters that Tai Chi had underlined for me. As I spoke about this, my lawyer was quick to respond that he too had noticed that. "This substance, 'Dama Zhi' or cannabis ester is not what you possessed, Mr Campbell," he was quick and keen to agree. He went on to tell me, "There is also the quantity to consider."

So, my appeal, according to the lawyer, was to be based upon two points, firstly the erroneous renaming of the substance involved in the verdict and sentence. And secondly that there was not a clear definition in Chinese law as to what would constitute a "Large quantity" of cannabis.

The law stated those caught in possession, with 50 grams of heroin, or with 500 grams of Opium or other drugs in a *large quantity* carried the sentence of death, life imprisonment, or a minimum sentence of fifteen years. I had been indicted in English for cannabis, the Chinese word Dama. The Chinese court had sentenced me for Cannabis Oil, in Chinese *Dama Zhi*, which I did not have, and which entailed an inference of a higher concentration in the substance per weight.

As the lawyer left, he told me he would return again the next day. It was not like before the trial when I was only allowed one quick visit in all those months of waiting. This appeal visit had lasted a couple of hours, and the lawyer would return as often as needed. I returned to the cell feeling perked up and a little chirpier after our meeting. I couldn't explain to anyone what was going on without Tai Chi, but they knew as soon as the smokes came out that I'd been to a lawyer or consulate visit.

The following morning, I got up feeling good in the knowledge that I would have another visit that day and also hoped and expected to see the other foreigners at the appeal, especially as the Welsh guy was using the same lawyer as me. Being called down to the visiting rooms around two o'clock, Mr Ma was already there with a smile and a file of legal papers, smokes, chocolate, and fruit at the ready.

We went over the verdict again in more detail and realized for the first time that the money was confiscated as 'Illegal Earnings', which could be easily proven as untrue through the Foreign Office, who had made the request for legal fees to my family. This was noted.

I asked about the difference, the legal or statutory definitions and implications, between 'Transportation' and 'Possession'. For whilst the cannabis remained in my possession, whether I was going from A to B either on foot or riding a train, I still hadn't crossed any borders within China. He took notes on this for further research. Then we moved on to the main issue, the substance itself.

The lawyer had explained that the Chinese character Zhi translated as Ester in English, but that did not mean much to me. In my interpretation, he was saying that the cannabis was a chemically produced substance condensed into oil, and not a natural one. Mr Ma said he would research more into that.

The next point was how to define a *large quantity* under Chinese law. There had to be some statutory definition or case precedent references to research. I said the Englishman carried about the same or similar amount to me, but he did not come under this act. Going on to say, the quantity then must be down to the alleged condensed purity, and there has been no such evidence.

The lawyer left with a promise to be back on Monday, 31st March.

I felt alive again, something was being done to sort out this dreadful mess of administrative errors I was entangled in. I was allowed to have a pen, the lawyer had asked me to write down all the different names for cannabis, like hashish, pot, Ganja, weed, etc. I could also keep occupied with making notes for questions to ask my lawyer at the next visit.

On the 31st I was waiting impatiently in expectation for my legal visit. I listened out for every remote sound of feet coming towards my cell. It was late afternoon before the cell door eventually opened and I was off for my visit. It was such a relief to get out of that cell, even for the shortest time.

We went over a few legal points together; his manner was detached. The lawyer had already marked out the guidelines for my appeal. The main point would focus on the type of substance possessed. I gave him my notes and those on cannabis names, letting my lawyer know it is decriminalized in many countries and legalized in others. Also pointing out that it is culturally acceptable in parts of India and the West Indies and declassified downscale all over the world from B to C, whereas cannabis oil was mainly classified as A.

My next visit was on 9th April when the lawyer produced photocopies of a drug classification chart from the American Library. He had circled the words 'cannabis oil' and underlined Dama Zhi in Chinese. "This, Mr Campbell, is not what you had in your possession when you were arrested," he informed me forcefully as if I didn't already know, or as if it was my mistake for getting sentenced for the wrong thing.

Having explained all this to him at the last visit, I realized that he didn't have a clue about drugs and would not just take my word for it but would rather carry out his own impartial and objective enquiry. I asked him why my English version of the indictment stated simply cannabis, whilst the Chinese version states another substance other than that which I was arrested with.

He did not have an answer for this question but I still wanted to hear him confirm that this could only have been a deliberate deception and fraud upon me. He thought for a long time before saying that he would point that matter out in court. I asked him about the other British person who got four years and surely this was a precedent. That less than 8kg of cannabis could not be considered as a large quantity, seeing as he never came under that article on his indictment. He was able to tell me that the other British man who got eight years and six months was appealing also but would not say more than that. I shook his hand this time before saying goodbye, something I had avoided doing ever since my first encounter with the dodgy Mr Ho. However, I felt better each time discussing the appeal with this lawyer. It seemed like we were working the completely tangled mess out.

Mr Ma visited again on the 11th and 15th of April. It had all been fully discussed and the preparation for the appeal was complete. We would be ready for the Appeal Court on 21st April.

I had gotten a fresh new white shirt and tie, but for some strange reason, no change of trousers was allowed. I'd worn these ones on and off for months, and they smelled awful. This place really was red tape, Chinese Communist bureaucratic nonsense and I sought help from the consulate. I even put my plea for clean clothing in writing, but nothing was forthcoming, and finally, I had to borrow a pair of trousers from a guy in my cell. He had not long arrived and was wearing a suit.

Ready for court once more, I was taken downstairs, and it was more of a shock than a pleasant surprise. When the van door opened to admit me, there sat another Westerner. I knew this one well and could only nod in acknowledgement, keeping my eyes averted, not wanting the guards alerted that we knew each other. Like me, he was a professional and full-time smuggler. I had had a fallout with this person on more than one occasion in the past. I knew he had been busted before, so it wasn't the time to acknowledge each other. During the journey, he asked me a few questions, what sentence I had gotten, and I told him, along with news about my ongoing appeal. The guards told us to be quiet, but we continued talking until we drove into the court parking area. We were both escorted into the building and separated.

I was called within an hour of arrival and listened as much as possible as the court went through the procedure of a second hearing again. It still meant nothing to me until my lawyer took the floor.

He held up large written Chinese characters for the court to see. Then he went on to explain the difference inherent in these characters in relation to the substance possessed by me, then moving on to show the characters relating to the substance I'd been sentenced for. There was a clear error between the name of the substance sentenced for and the actual substance found in my possession. I had a natural substance, not the chemical compound as alleged on the sentence and verdict. It all came down to that. The charge should not have been upgraded for the second trial and that I should be re-sentenced under the articles of the first trial, which held a maximum of 7 years imprisonment.

This was all spoken in Chinese, as we had discussed these details and I knew what he must be saying. He did explain some of it in English for my and the consulate representative's benefit. Besides, I knew the consulate would have their own interpreter anyway and should be able to get a copy of the translation, so I had little to do but listen.

It was all over, and I was returned to the basement cells by lunchtime.

The lawyer came down to see me and told me the hearing had gone well but that we would not have the outcome for another few weeks. We shook hands and said goodbye. I had lunch at the court holding cells, before heading back to the gulag. That old acquaintance of mine, Cranky, sat opposite me.

"So, what happened at your appeal?" he asked.

I told him what the lawyer had just said. He let out an exasperated gasp, saying "Man!" as only an American can make it sound, and I knew he would be curious.

I told him the story of the case being withdrawn and the subsequent substance error to a higher charge. He had been busted with cannabis too, cannabis oil in fact, just over 2 kg inside a thermos flask. It was not the first time he had gone down with cannabis. I knew of him leaving Manila for Hong Kong and being busted with marijuana, and once again in South Korea smuggling gold.

We were in the same trade, although he had not arrived on the Asia trial until the mid-1980s. We had a mutual friend, Fred from Colorado. He was an old hand doing overland trips from Hong Kong through the Chinese mainland onto Tibet, then down into Kathmandu with gold. I did it myself a couple of times. It's a long road to travel, but when you're being paid to see parts of the world you want to visit, who could complain?

Cranky told me he had read of my arrest in the Hong Kong newspaper. "So why did you get fifteen years?" he inquired, suspicion in his voice as if disbelieving my story.

I could have said that it was because I was mistakenly charged with oil, but I simply replied with, "God, if I only knew."

It was time to say goodbye, good luck, and hope we never meet again in these circumstances. Back to the usual cell and the usual hungry eyes, the usual illicit cigarette butts, the lads got to their usual rolling; it at least felt like one more night of getting one up on the enemy.

.oOo.

I waited three weeks before my next legal visit and by then was really pissed off. I had become dependent and expected a visit at least every week. What was I paying him for? When entering the visiting room, my heart was racing in expectation that he had the result of the appeal.

I lit a cigarette, inhaled deeply, and asked, "Any news?" I was actually trembling inside.

However, the visit was only for me to sign over cash for his fees and to tell me the results were due that very week. There was nothing more to say on that, then. We sat and used up a full hour just chatting anyway. It's so good to talk in your own language in a strange land.

Mr Ma was a kind-faced old man and told me he was a Buddhist. He had not joined the communist party and was not a party member.

.oOo.

On May 18, 1992, I was called downstairs, sat between a judge and a prosecutor, and handed the appeal verdict. I read the English version and it said simply, "Appeal Refused. Verdict Upheld." Four simple words to collapse my world and blow away my deluded hopes of commonsense and justice prevailing.

What could be said? Other than, "I want to see my lawyer."

The British consulate visited the next day; they couldn't interfere with the verdict, so there was not much to talk about except to ask them to pass on information to my family. I then asked about the prison I would be going to, and if they had been there to visit the other British guy, eager for any information on what might lie ahead. They had in fact visited the other prison and commented that the conditions were appalling. I inquired as to my lawyer's whereabouts and why he had not visited. The consulate informed me that Mr Ma was no longer under contract with me. The lawyer had not told me this.

Mr Short went on to explain that once your case for appeal had reached its conclusion, you no longer had the right to legal counsel.

What if I want to petition or take my case to a higher court I said? It was neither a fair nor an accurate decision and I asked Jim Short to raise this issue with Mr Ma. Jim assured me if the lawyer delivered any news to his office, then it would be forwarded onto me.

May 1992

I had been in the same cell for ten months until May 29th, 1992, when I was escorted to the office and told that I would be moving to join the other British person from Wales. Thirty minutes later, I was in a cell that had a bath. You couldn't believe the difference from my last cell to this one – it had a bath in it! It also had a western design toilet pan and only housed four people. I sat down and exchanged stories with Bull, so named for his bullish bulk.

He told me how he had met the two Germans and it was obvious he was upset and angry with them. Bull explained that it had been them who had informed on him and his girlfriend, a local woman from Kashgar, and she was still in custody there at this same detention centre.

I told Bull my story, and he remembered seeing me in Kashgar. He told me that the PSB had shown him photos of me, asking if he knew me.

"I can recall seeing you also," I said. "One time drinking and smoking with other travellers."

We chatted easily. I was nodding my head towards the cell window and could see that this cell with a view was something special. Asking Bull how long he had been here, I was surprised to discover that he had been there since his arrest in November. He also had extra food stores and bottles of chili paste.

I just couldn't believe the contrast between this cell and the one I had just come from. I asked Bull about the two other Chinese people in the cell. One was around thirty, the other forty. The eldest was charged with dumping waste into the canal. It was shocking but not surprising that this was considered a very serious offence in China and could warrant the death penalty depending on whatever environmental damage ensued from that crime. The younger person was in for bribery. He was well-educated and spoke some English. He was expecting to go to jail but for how long he did not know, not having received his indictment yet.

I settled into my new cell by having a full body wash and enjoyed the extras offered, such as hot water to make tea or noodles etc. There was a small black and white TV It gave me a sense of suspicion, to say the least. Like, why had Bull been so much better treated than I had? What was it that I did not know? However, I never did find out nor reach any conclusions, either positive or negative, about the vast difference in treatment. It was quite a treat to be watching television and snacking on biscuits that night.

A few days later, all the Western prisoners were called to the main office and told that we should pack our things from the cell. We were moving to the main prison, Tilan Xiao.

The following day, June 2nd, 1992, Bull and I were escorted down to the area where my baggage had been stored. Hearing my heart pumping, pure paranoia ripping out of me in cold sweats in expectation of another death sentence indictment. I still didn't have any idea what bag Scott had taken with him but could only guess that they wouldn't have given him the one checked in by me, the one with the cannabis hardly hidden inside, and I could be in for big trouble, as if fifteen years wasn't enough.

That was when I saw that my son had actually taken the chance and had indeed taken my bag. I had held onto that worry for many months and finally I allowed myself to breathe again in an audible sigh of pure relief. That then only left me with the completely concealed suitcase with the last 5kg securely hidden. I wanted to cry out and shout with pride and joy, but the death sentence scenes flashed through my mind again, thus I gulped, swallowing my pride instead. Then, carrying my luggage confidently, I said to the heavens, "God bless you, my son."

.oOo.

The detention interrogation room was full; the American had joined us, his sentence being fifteen years and a $2,500 fine. We were handcuffed in twos and put onto a transit van. The jail was located in downtown Shanghai, and the police escort took us right along the waterfront, along the Shanghai Bund. It was the equivalent of driving down to Piccadilly Circus in London, only we were handcuffed in these Chinese police transit vans, taking us to God only knew where, and for how long. The drive only took about twenty minutes. We sat in silence, lost in our own thoughts. The jail entrance wasn't any different from any other prison. It had large gates and two unwelcoming military guards standing armed and ready at either side. This jail was right in the city centre, built to isolate and contain.

We were all very much in the same boat. Both Bull and were in our forties, and heading for sixty by the time we got out of here. We disembarked from the transit van, shuffling nervously inside the prison grounds. Everyone's eyes turned in our direction as we were met by an old guy, dressed in a grey prison uniform, called Jin Feng. He had blue and white stripes running down the outside leg and a stripe across the back and front of the prison jacket.

A very stern-faced guard, who stood with him, directed us into a large reception area, and we were seated. I clutched onto my suitcase as if I'd just snatched a 10-million-dollar heist. Each of us was given a prison number on a plastic card holder, pinned to our jackets. I was number 13499.

We were given a brief introduction as to what was expected of us, such as not to get out of line while going to our cell block. On the way, we passed a few very large prison blocks and could see that the exercise area was a basketball court. We entered cell block eight, being able to read the Chinese character, and walked up to the third floor. Passing some guys on the stairs, I smiled to show them I was friendly, but got no response and continued to our landing where we had a meeting.

I parked my case against the stool where I was told to sit by Jin Feng. Then I saw an English guy walking towards us, his hands outstretched. He looked as if he had just seen Man Friday as we all shook his hand. Then Cranky, Bull, and I all at once started asking him questions about the place, but he didn't get a chance to answer.

Jin Feng called us to sit down and listen. A slightly built man in his mid-thirties addressed us as Jin Feng gave us the English interpretation. "My name is Captain Yu. I am the leader of the 8th brigade third floor, and I want you to know that our system of reform is through labour. As foreigners, you will not need to work. You will be given intellectual status and a study program." He went on about Chairman Mao and how great he was. We were not to associate with the Chinese inmates. The meeting was over, Jin Feng called for us all to stand up, but the only person who did was the Englishman, the obedient lad – whom I named Grad.

.oOo.

Grad, from England, had an Oxford University degree, which he was quick to tell us. He also had a four-year sentence for smuggling 7.2kg of cannabis strapped to his body while boarding a ship bound for Japan, and he had been given a fine of forty thousand RMB, around £5000. He told us he was to be our group leader, but I didn't think so. Oxford degrees don't automatically qualify as a leader where I come from.

Walking into my cell for the first time, I lay on the floor and put my head against the back wall. Looking up, I couldn't see any electric light on the cell ceiling. Reaching out my arms, I could touch both walls, calculating that it was around 8 feet by 4 feet. No window and an iron-barred cell door. There was a wooden bucket for the toilet, which was going to be a problem – there was no way my skin was touching decades-old, damp, urine and shit stained wood. Smack in the centre of the back wall was a poster with large written Chinese characters on it. Later translated, it read:

The ten don'ts:

- Don't oppose the four cardinals.
- Don't oppose the teaching of the Cadres.
- Don't step over the warning line or leave the group.
- Don't trade in food or try to manipulate others.
- Don't fight or train kickboxing, make weapons or gamble.
- Don't conceal money, explosives, or poison.
- Don't keep contact with people outside of the prison without permission.
- Don't bully, beat, abuse, insult or frame others.
- Don't hide contraband in your cell.
- Don't sabotage production, slack off at work, or steal nor damage public property.

Whilst we all had our own cells; it was decided that the three British prisoners would share one storeroom and be allocated space there. The two Germans and Cranky would share another.

Grad informed us that if we wanted prison uniforms, we would have to write a report requesting them. He was wearing his own civilian clothes. We unanimously decided that we'd wear our own clothes, at least for now.

After securing the suitcase in the storeroom, still with a flutter in my chest, I wandered onto the landing to look around my new abode. I met the translator Jin Feng, who told me his English name was Joseph King.

"You're Joe King?" I said, laughing at my own wit, and was pleased to see Joseph laughed along with me.

"So, what shall I call you, Jin Feng or Joseph?" I asked. He said the guards wouldn't like me using his English name, but after giving it some thought, shrugged and told me to suit myself.

I asked Grad where to have a shit.

"In your cell," he replied.

I inquired as to how he managed to sit on that wood without protection, and he soon enlightened me.

Seeking out Jin Feng, I asked him to get me a set of bucket pads made. It was a simple twelve-inch-long by four-inch-wide padding, a bit like a shoe insole, one side marked to identify where to place them. With that priority sorted, I spent my first day getting to know the other tales of arrest and hearing their views on our new surroundings. We passed most of that morning exchanging stories. When telling my own, I left out several pieces, of course, omitting what Scott had done and my narrow escape thanks to him taking the dope out of the detention cells for me. Nor did I mention the case full of dope in our storeroom right beside us.

Cranky's story was a bit iffy, to say the least. According to him, his girlfriend was being held hostage in Tokyo. She'd been snatched by some guys with whom Cranky had done some deal, but it all went wrong, and he was blamed for it. The guys wanted their money, and they wanted it quick. Cranky agreed to do a run to Shanghai as part of a payback. He was to check into the Peace Hotel and pick up a parcel. If he returned with the goods, his girlfriend would be safe, and he would earn some money to clear his debt. According to him, he simply did as he was instructed but was busted picking up the parcel from a hotel room. He claimed it was a setup from the beginning and believed that the cops were just waiting for someone to show up.

When introduced to another little Chinese guy with several fingers chopped off and only stumps on his left hand, I immediately thought of a Japanese Yakuza victim for bad service to his boss. It turned out this little guy was the guards' gofer. It was his job making their tea, washing up, and doing laundry. Not a job that I fancied doing, but the Chinese prisoners didn't have a choice, especially ex-Communist Party members gone wrong, like this little guy had.

The landing was quiet when we arrived; most cons were out on work detail. We were squeezed into a tight space; the walking area was only three feet wide. I got quite a fright when an ear-shattering bell rang, and the entire area filled up with guys all shouting over each other to be heard - old men, young men, all shapes and sizes. Within minutes, they were all seated in silence.

One Chinese con stood at each table and called out something. It was headcount. Then they all started babbling again, a pandemonium of sounds, all alien to my ear, but already disturbing my mind. Watching them, you just couldn't help but be impressed by the magnitude of shared efficiency. The distribution of food was orderly. We foreigners were given stainless steel containers of piping hot food and a good portion of rice. I'd lost weight in the detention cells and was glad to see the food here wasn't as bad as I had imagined it would be. I'd expected to be served up with cockroaches if the detention cell stories were anything to go by. I had expected to be hungry every day, but instead, I slept that night with a full stomach, lying in that mini tomb in the downtown necropolis of Shanghai city in the People's Republic of China.

Wake Up Call

Day two began like a thunderstorm all you could hear was the noise of the Chinese cons rising to greet another day. Whereas I'd slept alone in my 8ft by 4ft cell, the local prisoners were three to a cell. You can imagine the clatter and organized chaos of a corridor of these cell doors opening to excrete three prisoners per cell all trying to escape the overnight cram and stench of human waste I hadn't been prepared for this, the noise it was truly brain damaging.

There was a wireless blaring off its waveband, screeching at high volume from one of the speakers' right outside my cell door. I sat up crossed legged on the thin futon mattress and began rubbing the sleep from my eyes. The sound of heavy door locks opening marched steadily towards me. Then seeing the first image of what lay ahead and for God only knew how long.

The door opened with a clatter and the large dark shadow engulfed the whole cell then click and the lock sprung open that it may not close again without a key. Keeping my focus fixed on a spot in my mind I took a deep breath. The shadow moved on.

I arose and got dressed amid the babbling clatter of hell on earth. It's beyond me to describe or fully explain the shock of waking up into pure pandemonium standing and watching as waves of Chinese prisoners passed my cell door. Every passing pair of eyes staring at me, having grown another bushy red beard. I had never felt so alienated.

Grad came to my cell and escorted me to a sink where the wash up area faced directly into another cell block housing death row prisoners. I brushed my teeth staring out of the window and saw a basketball court below. The washing and ablutions over, it was breakfast time. We were served hot steamed bread and rice gruel with pickled root and chili. After breakfast we sat around talking, it was new to all of us. We asked Grad about remission.

He diverted that question by saying that he thought that we would all be deported soon.

Cranky went along with that view.

The two Germans, Vern and Hans, didn't join the group. Suspicion crept back into me remembering what Bull had told me at the Hell Cells. Hans had apparently told the police where he bought the drugs which resulted in Bull and his girlfriend being arrested. In short Hans had informed the mutual enemy.

The day passed and dozens of officials came to stare at us. On the outside, in the streets of China, people did stare at you - westerners are so rare and unusual for them to see in real life in some rural places. Inside this prison we were a real commodity. It was the same smile we got from all the passing officials. Apparently from what Grad had said, the Cadres also wished that we go home soon. We were just so far beyond their normal routine.

The day was a long one. I wondered how many more still to go - I had lay in my cell that first night and counted from the years, counted the months and counted the weeks. I counted the days counted the stars; then counted ten thousand of the prison bars. No matter how or what way I was counting it - 15 years sounded better. Forget counting down all those days one at a time.

The first week's routine was the same, after breakfast each morning, we had a meeting. Grad suggested that we do some self-study. I was looking for something to do with work that would occupy my body and mind and just couldn't handle the sitting on my arse all day doing nothing. I asked JK, as he was called, if he could translate for me. He agreed and we went to the red line painted across the floor before you exit our landing.

JK stood and called out, "Reporting to you Captain" and waited till he was told to enter, myself in tow. JK explained that I couldn't sit doing nothing all day and needed to be occupied and wanted to work. He added that painting and decorating was my trade.

This brought a quizzical look to this guard's expression - as if he could not comprehend such a concept. He then went on to agree that labour reform was beneficial but that those foreigners detained here were not allowed to work. I asked about a study program but to no avail and left the office no further on than when I'd gone in.

.oOo.

During breakfast, Bull had been collecting the remains of our pickle ration, which was fine by all. Every morning, we were given one container to share, and Bull had been storing the leftovers in jars. Red chilies were a common part of the pickle. I wanted to collect some too and reached for the container after everyone had taken what they wanted. Bull reached for it as well, leading to a pulling struggle. Then, I headbutted him and stuck a chopstick up to his eye, which made him release the container. I was summoned to the office that morning when our leader came on duty.

Lenny from Hong Kong was doing the interpretation, he was part of the translation unit upstairs. The word was out that JK and I were becoming too friendly.

After explaining the situation regarding the pickle incident, Lenny translated, and my punishment was confinement to my cell for one week, which also included no bathing.

JK came and told me he had to write a self-criticism report.

I asked him what exactly that was. He explained that he was being accused of behaving too bourgeois. I didn't have a clue what he was on about. He went on to tell me that some inmates had handed in reports against him. I asked who, and he mumbled some curses. JK then told me to also write a self-criticism stating that my action had stepped over the line and I had overreacted in the most negative way with violence.

Looking at him, I could see he looked different and asked what he had done to his hair, as it had got darker. JK told me that was part of the reason why he had to write the self-criticism for dyeing it.

As for me writing a report, I had assured myself that I was only protecting my right to a share of the pickle. Such trivialities to fight for, you may well wonder, as I often did during that seven-day confinement. To sit all day and watch others pass your cell from morning till night, although you know they aren't going anywhere nice, you would rather be out there with them anyway.

.oOo.

On the sixteenth of June 1992, the British Consul visited the prison. I complained to them about having to sit all day without a work or study program. But what really occupied my mind was the appeal verdict, which I held in my hand.

I pointed out that my ignorance and inability to read Chinese characters had led to me being taken advantage of twice, in fact, I'd been duped. I questioned why the consul's translators hadn't picked up on this and alerted me.

JK had pointed out to me that the appeal verdict had been altered, underlining the parts he showed me. Initially, I was indicted for and tried for possession of cannabis, but that case was withdrawn. I was re-indicted for transporting cannabis oil and sentenced to 15 years.

My appeal challenged the substance I was sentenced for, which I didn't possess. The appeal paper read, "Verdict upheld for possession of cannabis," but the sentence erroneously remained unaltered. The original verdict stated, "transportation of cannabis oil," and I was sentenced to 15 years under that article. However, the appeal reverted to upholding the first charge of possession of cannabis, which carries a maximum of 7 years under that article. Yet the sentence of 15 years still remained, contrary to the law in China.

It had been doing my brain severe damage, all those altered charges. I knew it wasn't right but just didn't have the necessary knowledge to translate from the Chinese characters.

The consul, however, had the capability but could give me no explanation. So, I told the consul about lodging a petition against the altered verdict and left that visit somewhat irate.

The only consolation was that my son Scott had sent more money from Japan. "So, he is still there," I thought. "Good for him."

I signed for FEC; at that time in China, foreign travellers were expected to use these Foreign Exchange Certificates, as per the same in the diplomatic community, thus indirectly helping to create a vibrant black market. You could shop at special outlets with better quality commodities where local currency was not accepted. That's communism for you.

.oOo.

I was summoned to the office after my consul meeting and was told by the Criminal Affairs guard that I couldn't talk about my case during the visit. It wasn't JK doing the interpretation, but with Lenny's interpretative skills, he told me to "accept my guilt" and not discuss petitioning as my case was closed.

In astonished disbelief, I replied irately, stating that I could talk about whatever I wanted with my consul and that I would be lodging a petition and would need a lawyer.

Lenny, as much as he could be in the short period we had known each other, told me, "Don't speak, just listen."

I retorted, "Just do the interpretation," and went into a tirade about how the substance I was charged with was wrong and that the communist thieves had stolen my family's $3,000. The office went silent, and I was told that I had a bad attitude.

I exploded back, "No wonder!" and left the office fuming.

Grad intercepted me, asking why there was shouting in the office, and I told him what had been said. He looked at me in bewilderment and advised me to listen to the Cadres' education.

I turned and walked away, mumbling, "Cadres education? What a halfwit."

Sensing my frustration, JK eventually found me calm enough to explain how the system operated. He explained that the prison system works by reform through labour, where through labour, you can pay back your debt to society, bringing revenue for the prison upkeep, food, and guards' wages. The prison must strive to be self-sufficient and not burden the state or the people. Labour can bring remission of sentence, and success in job quotas brings added monthly bonuses to the prison guards. It's also intended to help the prisoner see the error of their ways and to repent. He said that while a prisoner does not admit his guilt, he cannot truly repent, and there is no hope for him. Further dissatisfaction and denial of guilt can result in the penalty being changed.

I contemplated trying to work on the farm, then suddenly asked JK out of the blue if the foreigners were to be sent home.

JK told me he hadn't heard such rumours and wouldn't build our hopes up on it.

I had asked because of the recent movement within the jail, the commotion about a massive transfer of prisoners.

JK assured me that I would soon know all about it, as it's televised on the prison channel. Sure enough, within a few days, we had lockdowns. The whole prison was banged up except for the kitchen, and everyone was counted. Names would be read out over the radio, doors opened, and those named had to pack. By noon, hundreds of prisoners passed by with large bundles, boarding buses to be taken to the train station in downtown Shanghai. Trains carried them to far-flung provinces like Shandong and the Xinjiang Autonomous Region, to be used as farmers or factory workers. That evening, we all watched on television as the prisoners boarded the trains to their new destinations. We had to watch; it was mandatory. The camera crews filmed the guards guiding the convicts onto the buses, at the station, and onto the trains. It was a large movement of men, about 800 in total. The prison TV station showed them on the train as they journeyed, some sleeping, some reading, all seated.

June 1992

On June 25th, 1992, I read in the China English Daily Newspaper: "Everyone makes mistakes, and the reasons for making them are varied. In the long run, it is not the mistakes themselves but the attitudes of the people towards their mistakes that are more important. Society should always provide opportunities for people to realise their errors, show repentance, mend their ways and begin lives anew. It cannot be said that a person who has had a black mark in the past won't be any good in the future. To judge people fairly, society should concentrate on their words and deeds at the present."

I had written that into my diary from a newspaper the consul brought as something to work towards.

It was Grad who had opened this door into his mind; he'd been handing in a monthly report to our leading guard. This was known as thought reform. You were to write down your thoughts about your crime but more significantly, your thoughts about others. Grad explained to us all that he'd been doing this since his arrival. We were shocked to hear this.

Cranky was quick to point out that this was a violation of his Human Rights, but when Grad told us he'd volunteered, that put an end to the story.

Grad then came out with the group leader talk again, telling us that he had been put in charge and had to put in reports on our behaviour as well.

This was becoming too much to bear. Since our arrival at this prison, we had all asked to see Grad's indictment and verdict, and he'd refused to show it to anyone. We wanted to know his charge and the kind of substance it entailed, so we could use his case as a precedent. Nobody was happy that he wouldn't say and wouldn't let us look at his indictment, confirming that something was terribly wrong.

We had been there around one month and were allowed to order food and fruit on a monthly basis. On order day, some of us wanted coffee and black tea. Grad told us there was no coffee, but Cranky persisted, stating that coffee was a cultural requirement for him. I wanted black tea and coffee if possible.

Grad suggested to Cranky that he write a report requesting coffee, and he would hand it in.

Bull suggested we just go to the office and ask, the easiest thing to do, you would imagine. So, we did. Grad, Hans, and Vern stayed behind as we marched up to the red line before the office with JK.

Cranky spoke, and when he had finished, a smile crossed the guard's face. He answered, and JK explained that our request was granted, but we could purchase only one jar per month, and it was strictly forbidden to give any to the Chinese inmates.

We thanked him and agreed about not sharing with the Chinese inmates. When we came from the office, Grad had lost some of his self-importance when coffee was added to the list.

We were handed a sheet of items we could purchase, all written in English, which JK had translated. This order was for July and was quite interesting.

My first prison order in July was as follows:

Writing paper 10 pads, Envelopes 5 packs, Notebooks 4, Soap powder 2 boxes, scrubbing brush 2, Liquid detergent 2, Toothpaste 2, Instant noodles 24, Sesame oil 1 bottle, Chili paste 1, Tinned pineapple 5, Tofu paste.

We could also order Watermelon by the kilo; we all ordered 50 kilos per person, estimating the average melon to weigh 4 to 5 kg each. The cost of this order came to £5 sterling; the cost of living was low, but so was the standard of life.

.oOo.

I had been asking at every opportunity to have a game of football and was well pleased one evening when the guard called me into the office and asked me to play. It was a warm July evening, and the guard had arranged for our brigade to play against a team from another block, a team well-known in this event, as JK told me. Along with our leading guard, whom we named Benny, and two other guys, Lee and Chan, who were prisoners and couldn't speak a word of English, we made the team.

Standing outside in the hot evening air felt good on my skin. I had been given a pair of canvas shoes by the guard, and they fitted well. As soon as the ball was passed around, they realised they had a good player, and they showed their appreciation through their expressions.

It turned out the guard and I played well together; I was laying off plenty of balls for him to finish and scoring a couple of goals myself. It was a basketball-size court, good enough for four-a-side.

Back upstairs, I washed and got ready for bed, feeling the joy of victory from the other two guys. I heard my name used many times, and it all sounded okay. I felt heavy stares at me when passing some of the Westerners, but what could be done? If they wanted to play, they could ask just like I had.

Word went around that the foreigners had a footballer, and it was arranged for all of us to have a game the following evening. Football was taking off in China; it was hot news, and although foreign players hadn't yet arrived, foreign managers, mostly from Eastern Europe, were on the scene.

As it turned out, only Bull had some skills, not much in footwork but solid in defence. Grad was hopeless, and the two Germans hadn't kicked a ball in their lives. Cranky was a basketball man and had never played football.

I had waited all day for this game; I needed to run and sweat, and to use my mind and body as one. We had a mixed game, only between guys in our unit, but the same guard and I linked up and hammered the other side. I played right into the guard's ego, jumping up triumphantly whenever he scored a goal that I had set up for him.

Benny was named so because he always told us during meetings that he was a 'good man'. Vern, who was a blues guitar player, commented after one meeting that the good man should be called Benny, after Benny Goodman, the jazz musician. Isn't it strange how you can relate one thing to another and yet be so far apart in every aspect, and it still sticks? That evening after the game, sitting with some of the Chinese guys in the guard's office, JK did the interpretations, and there was a lot of laughing at whatever the guard said.

I was praised by them all as having a good football mind. The word "Hao" was repeated often, and I learned that Hao meant good. That was two days in a row I'd had a game and felt a lot of tension going out of me. I was also informed that evening that my son Lochy was coming to visit me, and I knew what for. Besides seeing his father, he would take away the suitcase his brother Scott had left behind and finally rid me of it once and for all, as well as the worries attached to it.

The following day, Cranky, who was celebrating his 45th birthday, had asked for a special lunch of curry, chancing his hand in the hope they would go along with it, which they did. That afternoon we had a chicken curry and cream cake for dessert was something you couldn't even imagine might happen in that dark, dismal jail. But being part of the cook's brigade, our unit held a lot of sway; our guard controlled the nightshift change-over, and thus had the power to have whatever food he liked, whenever he liked.

.oOo.

My youngest son Lochy came to visit on July 5th, and we met in a small room near the prison gates. The visit was wonderful, just to see my son again. He looked fine and healthy. He told me about his journey and his plans to return to the UK.

The time just flew by, and the suitcase needed to be handed out after being itemized. Besides the clothing, I also gave him the video camera that Scott had gotten from my brother Rab. I made it clear to my son that this baggage was Scott's and that Scott had taken mine upon his release. I needed to be as clear as possible, just in case something went wrong when entering the United Kingdom with that drug-packed suitcase.

When it was time to part, I suggested another visit and told Lochy to contact the British consul to arrange it. We shook hands and hugged before saying goodbye.

Back in the cell area, I sat for a while talking with Vern, who was playing a guitar he had just received from the German Consul. I shared with him about my son's visit, and we spent an hour or so chatting. I found Vern easy to get along with; he didn't have big aspirations nor was he much of a talker, often sitting alone writing songs, some of which we would later perform.

With a lot on my mind, particularly concerning my son's welfare, I had also asked Lochy to deliver a message to the consul about arranging another visit with my lawyer. I felt confident that my son was here to help me and knew that he would get done what I had asked.

My son Lochy, at the age of seventeen, had indeed come to China to his father's rescue. That night, I slept well, relieved to have more than a load off my shoulders, and thought about the tremendous risk my son had taken.

.oOo.

It had been over a week and my son still hadn't returned to visit me, and I was losing my mind.

JK reassured me that it takes more than a week to get anything done in communist China, especially anything related with courts or jails. I needed to hear something positive and JK was older and more experienced being a local Shanghai man, he knew the script.

JK was serving a life sentence for having sex with his students. He'd been a school teacher who failed in his responsibility to society. I quizzed him on this subject thinking that it must have been a serious rape to get a life sentence. As it happened, it was his third offence, not for rape but for having sex with some of his students, aged sixteen to eighteen he told me. In China that's not allowed as the teacher has a responsibility to the family of his or her students, as well as to the students. Having already served ten years in a work farm for a past offence and still not reformed JK was doing a life sentence in a rat hole in down town Shanghai.

It was while talking with JK that I was summoned to the office this time without him as the translator.

I walked into the office where six PSB cops from the detention cells stood around. The office was overcrowded and my belly hollow and nervous; something serious was going on. Then a few words were exchanged and I was handed a telegram, thinking maybe some family member had died.

I read it and then read it again. "Lochy arrested same as you China."

I looked up and Alan whom I knew from my initial investigation said, "Mr Campbell you come downstairs with us, we have some questions to ask you."

Still in shock, *Lochy arrested same as you China,* flashed in my skull. I immediately spoke with Alan asking, "Is my son here at the Shanghai detention cells?"

"Yes," Alan replied, "He is under investigation."

I was escorted out of the office and taken to another office on the ground floor. I listened to the accusations put to me that I had knowingly passed out drugs to my son during his visit.

"I didn't give out drugs to my son. I gave him my other son's suitcase which hadn't any drugs inside it!" Stating clearly that it had been thoroughly searched when we were arrested. I asked Alan why the police hadn't found those drugs during our initial investigation at the detention cells adding, also there at the prison upon arrival. "How come it is only now that you have discovered drugs?" I raised my eyebrows questioningly.

I watched Alan take in what I was suggesting and he spoke rapidly in Shanghai dialect. It was seconds later the room erupted with high-pitched talk and a lot of staring at me as they shuffled uncomfortably around the room.

Alan stood over me and he was livid by the suggestion that the drugs may have been planted by them. I repeatedly inquired as to my son's welfare but Alan was answering none of my questions. The next route Alan perused was for me to write a statement saying that the luggage belonged to Scott.

I wasn't having any of that either but did tell Alan that I had written a letter from this prison to Scott inquiring as to why he had taken my luggage. I had done this with my first letter home covering another angle for myself if the drugs came to light, which they had.

I was escorted back up to my floor with the message ringing loud and clear in my head, we shall return tomorrow. It caused quite a stir in the jail what had just happened. I was immediately escorted back to our landing office. It was like a military-planned operation.

The khaki green uniforms all looked the same but their jobs certainly differed. It was the leader of the prison administration bureau, the criminal affairs leader, education, the Warden and several more. JK had been called and looked frightened and stood straight backed.

The questions were to the point first one being, "Did you know there were drugs in that case?

"Certainly not," and then answered a few more questions.

JK explained to me that I was in prison, the authorities here were in control of what would happen to me while there but that I might be returning to the detention cells after further inquiries.

That was certainly not something to look forward to. But then I thought the only possible good that might come from it is that I would see Lochy.

There was an uncomfortable silence, and I could see that nobody knew what more to ask.

I tried to convince them by telling them the clothes in that case were all for a young person and certainly not mine. I knew that they translated and censored my letters and reminded them of that. I knew full well and had planned this beforehand and what was written would confirm what I was telling them.

I was returned to my cell escorted by two guards and could see that the other Westerners were dying to know what was going on but couldn't tell them, not just yet.

My cell had been turned over then I was taken to the store room and asked to remove all my belongings, which I did and they were searched. All my belongings were taken to another cell in the middle of the landing cell number 31. My old cell had been 14 so here was me right in among the locals.

I then returned to the office for more inquiries. I tried to persuade the guard to let me write a letter to my son. Having pleaded with his humane side asking if he had a son or not, to which he replied proudly that he did have one son.

"My son," I continued, "is only seventeen years old and those detention cells are dangerous and dirty. Just send one letter for me please." He told me he would consult his leader then after a few more questions I was returned to my new cell.

By the time the evening meal came around, I still hadn't had enough time to sit and think this dilemma out. Instead, I had just stared vacantly at the surrounding walls.

Then when collecting my meal Grad said, "Can I ask you something?"

I nodded my head to indicate if he wanted to talk, to come and join me he didn't. I picked at my food without much desire to eat having usually looked forward to this meal at the end of the day. A good thing to be rid of for prisoners was time. I was focused on Lochy in the detention cells, caught with 5kg of cannabis concealed in a suitcase. My fault again, I'd given him the suitcase and had warned him that he must stick to one story if anything went wrong, he was collecting his brother Scott's luggage.

I searched my brain what could be done to help him? I had to stick to my story and that was, it wasn't my bag, it was Scott's. Sitting alone again, lost in troubled thought when Cranky and Bull got around me, hungry for news or scandal.

I told them about Lochy and they said at once astounded. "You had 5kg here in this jail?"

We discussed the possible outcome and they all bargained that Lochy would get at least a ten-year sentence. I lay in bed that night thinking of my son having a hard time at the hell cells and was tempted to rush into making a confession and putting myself on the firing line but decided against that.

It wouldn't help as they would be more likely to convict us both with the possibility of firing a bullet into my head.

My next-door neighbours in cell 30 were being moved out and that cell was also to be allocated to me as my storeroom. I stood looking in at my new office come storeroom. It had an old desk and chair in it. A few Chinese inmates were helping me furnish it. Asking JK what was going on and he told me that to be among the local inmates some of them would be allowed to help me settle in. The two guys who played football with me were among them. It was a sort of isolation treatment until this investigation regarding the 5kg of cannabis was resolved.

What would my ex-wife be thinking? Her two sons meet up with their dad and do not *pass go. Go straight to jail*. No bail in China. Mary would be more than angry with me. The way she'd brought those boys up, they handled themselves well. Her lads were strong, clean, and tidy and had intelligence that could be cultivated towards better things. I didn't sleep too well that night and was restless, tossing and turning, fighting off scoundrels whom Lochy was battling with over at the detention centre.

Lao Da

It wasn't long after breakfast the following day when I was called to be interrogated by the Shanghai PSB.

Alan had done most of the talking again, and I could see he had changed his approach. Now, it was more like him working out a way of ditching his responsibility and avoiding the flak for why the cannabis hadn't been discovered in the first place. He wanted me to take full responsibility. Alan pressed on relentlessly with this point, but I didn't take it up and eventually just refused point blank to answer any more questions until I could speak with my lawyer, consul, and my son. It was a quick meeting, and I was told that the PSB would return. Alan and his crew departed.

It was hot news in the jail, and as fast as jail rumours and press stories go, I was 'Lao Da' in Chinese, slang which meant 'The Boss'. Gangsters, and Mafias, whether they were Italian, Russian, or other, their names were as well-known as the Triads in China. As far as some of these Chinese convicts were concerned, I could be approached. They knew by the deed I had just done, right under the noses of every security force in China. I had unwittingly opened a door into the jail black market, which I had known would be going on somewhere. It always does. Chinese people place a lot of value on not losing face. Just by doing what I'd done had caused a lot of lost face to our mutual enemy.

I was welcomed into the fold by a small crew who were known as 'Black Jade'. JK had approached me regarding some of my clothing, asking me if I would trade something with his friend so that he could give it to his son on his birthday. Old Hun was the guy JK wanted me to help. His nickname was 'Black Fish', and he was the Triad leader in our wing. He was a good organiser and was serving a life sentence - and didn't go by the rules and regulations of the prison reform system.

I started trading, using JK as the go-between. I had received a parcel from my brother Robert in London. The contents had brought a few green-eyed monsters to the surface. My brother had sent me a dozen Lacoste polo shirts, still in their wrappers, plus another dozen T-shirts with all sorts of patterns and prints on them. I got boxes of underwear, dozens of socks, bottles of aftershave plus other body perfumes, all designer brands and costing a lot of money. I had soaps from the body shop and enough razor blades to shave for the whole sentence, even if I had to complete every day of it. I got a Walkman and over a hundred cassette tapes with a wide variety of music. I got dozens of pens; one in particular was a much-desired commodity. It had a three-in-one Red, Blue, and Black a novelty with a much-required function. I even had felt-tip pens in every colour you could possibly imagine, which was added into the parcel by an old friend, Bobby Glen from Glasgow.

It was time to make some inroads. I needed to have a letter sent out without the normal censorship. I asked JK if he could arrange that, which he did. I wrote, to my brother giving all the facts regarding the withdrawal of my case from public prosecution and the change of substance in the appeal verdict. I had placed a code word for him to reply, thus verifying its delivery.

I had given JK one Polo shirt for his services, but he didn't take it, saying he couldn't wear it here at the prison and the only person left in his family was his younger brother. JK said he had totally broken away and never came to visit due to JK having a bad reputation in their neighbourhood.

I asked him if he wanted anything else.

JK said, "I would like a three-ink pen, Mr Campbell," he said it in such a humble voice, in expectation that he had no chance of getting the desired pen. I handed him one pen, plus some blades and a new razor stick. That had been something else my brother had done. He'd put three sets of Gillette G2 razors in – they were the in-item then. I felt good that my underground letter was going on to someone who knew how to deal with such matters. My brother Tommy Campbell knew how to handle legal issues, as he was currently entangled in the biggest legal battle in Scottish history. The 'Free the Glasgow Two' campaign was turning the Scottish legal system inside out.

.oOo.

It was mid-July when my son was arrested, a very hot season but the detention cells were much worse. It was a date easy to remember, the 12th of July, when the Shanghai PSB visited me again. It was on that day when I heard the full story of Lochy's arrest. I had told him to fly into Japan to a place called Fukuoka, but Lochy decided to take the ship to Kobe instead. Alan told me the details and went on to say that if I didn't sign a confession then, my son would be charged. I again declined his offer and could see his frustration at my lack of cooperation.

It wasn't like the detention cells with me admitting to everything and signing most things. Now, having some insight into the traps and lies laid before me, I had some guidelines. Fifteen bloody years of guidelines to go by, so the smiles and the "Don't worry, you will be leniently treated," spiel weren't working this time.

I knew they wanted to shoot me, and signing one paper could have granted them their wish. I was a total embarrassment to them and the whole set-up of the investigation procedure. I knew they needed a scapegoat. I was their first choice and, rightly enough in their eyes, a father who involves his sons in crime would certainly be executed if he were local and especially drug-related.

Alan's eyes showed it all; he was going to be the one to suffer besides me. He was almost pleading with me with expressions that said, "Please confess and sign here."

I looked at him in defiance.

His eyes then spoke louder volumes, "Confess and sign here," then went on to say just, "Confess." Mr. Campbell.

I watched as he squirmed, knowing he was in trouble with his superiors. It had all gone so sweetly until then. Alan was overconfident when we first encountered each other, to the point of arrogance, and then, by a twist of fate, he was left holding a major problem. "Why didn't you confess to me in the detention cells?" Alan pursued. "Now your son will go to jail," he went on, still working out a way to get me to sign a paper that would get him off the hook and get me shot.

"It wasn't in the suitcase," I replied. I felt a little sorry for him. Then I woke up and remembered how nasty he could be. It would be his responsibility for not getting the full confession and finding the drugs during the initial investigation period. I didn't dwell too long on the sympathy feelings, having enough to worry about regarding my hellish predicament and my son's.

I never signed any papers, and I was escorted back to the wing. I had another headache coming on; I was getting too much pressure from those PSB, and the thought of my son in that hellhole wasn't helping matters either. Sitting alone in my cell, pained in mind and body, even my psychic barrier was penetrated that day, and it hurts when your love cuts cold and for real.

.oOo.

We had an unexpected visit from His Holiness the Dalai Lama, which transpired through us all being told to clean up our store room.

Whilst Cranky was clearing out, he came across a few postcards printed in Thailand with His Holiness on them. He had that calm smile and worldly face with an aura of wisdom. It was at our end-of-the-month outgoing letter hand-in time. Cranky had included one postcard to his family. It wasn't until after the evening meal had finished that we were called to sit and have a meeting.

At least three high-ranking officials were present. The postcard of His Holiness the Dalai Lama was produced. The bottom line was that our Holy friend was considered anti-communist and was trying to divide China. Cranky was criticised. Some of us just looked at each other in bewilderment.

That was a short visit by His Holiness, but he did revisit again as Crank had held firm to his stash; he never tried to send any more, but at least His Holiness was in the building. Om Mani Padme Hum.

.oOo.

The 1992 Olympic Games were coming up, creating an atmosphere for sport, and a football competition was to be arranged within the jail. In total, there would be eight teams forming two groups. This was great for me as getting out training every morning and evening took my mind away from Lochy and got me lost in the competitive aspect of the game.

I ran myself into the ground, seeking fatigue for the night's sleep ahead. I was talking with Vern one evening after playing football; Hans was having a joke with Grad, and I could hear that it was due to Grad being a vegan and not eating certain products. Hans was quick to point out that the leather coat Grad had been grooming down in anticipation of going home would have taken at least two cows to make.

"I thought you were against cruelty to animals and a vegan," Hans joked.

Grad responded with a rather bitter remark, saying that he was, "More against Nazi concentration camp products." That sounded a little below the belt but hey jail isn't a place for niceties.

It was a bit below the belt, and Hans turned away, shaking his head.

I wasn't interested in this tit-for-tat negativity and was more anxious to hear about Lochy. I asked JK to escort me to the office, which he did. I asked if a visit with my son could be arranged as he was untried. I asked if he could come here while waiting for trial. I was just trying and saying anything that came into my head, anything to get me closer to my son.

All I got was permission to write one extra letter home. As it was, we all had a one-letter-per-month ration. This incident was deemed to be important enough to warrant one more, but I could only address it to my son's mother, my ex-wife. I didn't look forward to doing it but felt obligated to do so. After writing the letter, I held onto it, rereading it, adding something here and there, and then putting it away again. I was harbouring plans to pass it over to the consul when they next visited as I didn't trust the prison mail system, especially when His Holiness the Dalai Lama was refused exit last month.

I was suffering badly from the heat, it was becoming unbearable, especially at night when the fans were switched off while I slept. It was quite an unusual sight to see that all the Chinese prisoners slept outside their cells during these hot and humid Shanghai summers; not a cell door was closed. The whole area was covered in bodies, guys slept on top of tables, and every space on the cool stone floor was used up. It would have been torture to make people share a cell in this sort of heat, and anyone who didn't abide by the rules often found themselves three to a cell, where your body is never dry.

This was the season of high tension, people freaking out, and a lot of violent eruptions occurred. The weather seemed to take over your whole life. Day and night, you were constantly wiping yourself down, fanning yourself, or drinking lots of water. Warm water, but wet enough to quench a parched thirst and prevent dehydration.

I recall one morning whilst mopping the floor outside my cell area. A large rat came out and started licking up the water. It had no fear whatsoever, its head was down, and it was thirsty. Rats were a common sight on our wing; there would always be a chase after them at one point of the day or another. I hated them, especially when they came into my cell and I could hear and feel them walking around me whilst keeping my head wrapped in a bed sheet, hiding. Or I would jump up and shout, hoping to frighten them away.

As it happens, you become accustomed to them and I just didn't encourage them by keeping food in my cell. The jail was really run down and badly in need of a whole new sanitation renovation. Being a traveller, I'd slept in places just as infested with vermin as this jail and even paid for it. One place in particular, called Sukarachi Street in Bombay, an old, dilapidated opium den housing underage girls in cages. I paid for the pipes to smoke and my dreams were not of having sex. I'm old-fashioned that way.

It was a hot summer and yet we still managed to play football, most games in the evenings, but some due to schedules were held in the heat of the day, hot and sweaty, drinking constantly to rehydrate; your feet feeling the heat through the concrete. It was worth it though, just to get out and expel energy was a godsend for me.

The Shit Patrol

I had seen the Pakistani cons most days; they were housed in the building visible from our block. My meeting up with one of them started when our yard drainage pipes got blocked. It was a job for us foreigners, as it was considered a hygiene duty and not labour. We had to carry those shit-filled buckets four at a time down three flights of stairs, walking sideways due to the narrow passage. The size and weight alone were difficult to manage. We then crossed the yard, which led us into another cellblock, then through their hall into their yard. It was an awful job.

Haled, from Rawalpindi, was serving six years for passing off counterfeit money. His associates in crime were also serving ten and seven years respectively. They were kept in other cell blocks, and I hadn't met up with them yet but knew their names to be Aktar and Butt. Haled had told me about them and about Mir, who was in cell block one, doing 10 years for a different fraud charge from them. It must have been known at this cell block that I had items for trade. Haled was looking for magazines and told me he was trading in photos of Pakistani women cut out from ones sent by his family. In the prisons in Shanghai, you weren't allowed to have photos of your wife or family, and I thought that to be an unusual regulation. I had a Thailand Calendar that was sent along with a parcel from my brother in London. The girls were exquisite and mature, their lithe bodies, small breasts firm and inviting, and skin that made you want to caress it forever. The following day I passed it over to Haled for him to do trade with, but I got it returned the next day. I couldn't believe my ears when he told me that the Chinese guys hadn't any use for other Asian girls' photos. He went on to say that they were plentiful in China.

Haled asked if I had any photos of European girls. Even in fashion magazines, he could still trade them. Haled then gave me some magazines from his country. As I slept that night, I slipped off into the land of dreams with some exotic Pakistani beauty. Allah had made women in that land a treasure to behold, and I slept that night with dreams being in Beijing forbidden city, with the Chinese actress Miss Gong Li – whom I had been infatuated with since seeing her in a movie.

I noted in my diary as I counted twelve inmates, tagged at their lapels for identification purposes, being led out from death row to be transported for execution. I could see them from our landing window below me crossing the yard of fear and inhumanity. It housed the prisoners who would never see their family again, never see anyone again. I couldn't come to terms with how little regard was given to taking another's life here. In the Chinese legal system, the death penalty was given for crimes that wouldn't warrant much more than five years in the UK, for example, river pollution or car theft. I took my mind away from that scene below and thought about my son.

The British consul had come to visit in August, and I was eager to hear about Lochy. I expected to be called first, as my anxiety was on the wellbeing of my son. The other two Brits were called and visited one at a time. I waited patiently until Grad came back, timing the visit, calculating the walk to the visiting room and back – fifty minutes. Then, Bull was called; another fifty minutes later, he returned. I was never called, and no explanation or reason was given as to why. I was furious and didn't know who was to blame. I barged into the office, crossing the red line without first calling and waiting for permission. I demanded to see the consul and was informed that I couldn't see them while my son was under investigation.

"Then I'm on a hunger protest," I stormed out of the office.

That evening, I didn't eat and followed up by missing breakfast the next morning. I was called to the office again and this time threatened that if I didn't eat, I would be force-fed.

I smiled in contempt but still didn't eat.

The following afternoon, Benny, our guard, called a meeting with the foreigners. We sat listening to the range of punishments meted out to inmates who broke the rules. Not eating was a violation of those rules. The group was asked what they thought of my action, with JK doing the translations. Grad disagreed with what I was doing and tried to persuade me to have some food. This followed suit around the table, all except Cranky spoke out with everyone making a comment advising me to eat.

I ignored them.

On the third morning, I didn't touch breakfast again, and it was becoming a headache for them. They didn't yet know how to deal with foreigners; we were still a novel enigma. That morning, around 11 o'clock, I was summoned to the office and I finally got JK to compromise that I would eat if I were allowed to send a telegram that day. This was agreed after our unit leader had made a phone call.

I left the office, drafted a short telegram letter to my family regarding my son's wellbeing, and handed it over. I was given a receipt a couple of hours later when signing for 150 Renminbi, thus verifying that my telegram had been sent. I had been looking for some way out of this no-eating stint; as it wasn't pleasant to go hungry, but I had to do it without losing face.

I knew it wouldn't solve my immediate worries, but the telegram idea had given me that out. I ate the evening meal slowly and enjoyed it. Fasting for a few days at a time was nothing new to me; I used to do it at a Yoga retreat in Kathmandu. It was not like my brother Tommy's 100-day fasts for justice, losing around 35kg in body weight, but that's TC. He's always been one seriously determined man.

.oOo.

On the summer nights we had a cooling party – so called because the jail got incredibly hot and we needed some escape from the heat.

However, this was to be a special occasion; we, the foreigners, were to visit all the prison blocks and entertain with a couple of songs. Vern, Bull, Cranky, and I had formed a little band called 'The Reformers.' Vern had the guitar and could play quite well. Cranky had got hold of a washboard, and I had a set of maracas made from empty washing liquid bottles with dried rice inside. Bull was on vocals except when I sang 'Smoky Joe's Café.' The Loudon Wainwright rendition or 'Summertime Blues' was Crank's number. We had done a little rehearsing, starting with The Beatles' number 'Help,' then onto Bob Marley's 'Baby Don't Worry,' and if we had time for another, we would do 'By the Rivers of Babylon.'

It was quite an experience going up onto a stage to perform. We couldn't see anything in front of us except lights. We were singing the chorus to 'Rivers of Babylon' and adding "Do you remember Tiananmen?" It was

Cranky who got that in first, then Bull, Vern, and we all joined in once we caught the drift. At the finish, our band was taken onto the roof of number nine blocks, which was all women. It was mind-blowing to see some of these beautiful ladies dressed in prison uniforms. Some of them showed out to us, bumping deliberately just for the touch. It was worth risking any sort of punishment for that. The closeness to so many women was painfully aching but in a pleasurable way.

That was a night to remember, performing in a downtown Shanghai city jail in the People's Republic of China. We returned to our section of the party, hot, sticky, and sweating profusely. The Chinese convicts were putting on all sorts of performances: magic acts, singing, opera, and dance groups, all in costume. We also had a group of female prisoners' dance and sing for us. It was exhausting, the excitement becoming a bit too much. A bit too much like being outside, but the main ingredient was missing: the door key.

I can honestly say it was like a dream state of mind when the ice cream was being handed out. That sweet cold vanilla flavour wrapped in chocolate, filling your mouth and cooling your throat. Here I was, singing and tapping my feet to music, feeling a lot of emotion rising in me and wanting to be with my son, and slept with him close by me, safely secure inside my head that night.

September 1992

It was the 18th of September, and the Olympic Games were over; another sports programme was in full swing for the upcoming National Day celebration. I had been picked for our block's football team. There was some dispute about whether I should be allowed to play, due to being a security risk. I got right in amongst the debate, arguing that as I was only moving within the jail and not outside of it, I should be allowed.

We had full-time sports training, so we also had volleyball, basketball, and tugs of war teams, all going outside at the same time together. The jail housed up to five thousand convicts; there were nine separate residential halls, not including the hospital, kitchen, and concert hall. Bull was in the tug-of-war team, Cranky in basketball, and me in football. The other foreigners were on the sidelines as spectators. The games were hard-fought, and although the Chinese are small in build, they are made of iron.

Time seemed to move very quickly during sports outings, but the nights were as long as two days. I had been waiting a couple of months to hear the reply to my letter sent by the underground mail service but still hadn't received any yet and was beginning to think I had been duped.

Then one day, whilst in the washing-up area, a voice called me from the landing above. Looking up the back stairs, I saw Lenny; he whispered in a hurried tone, "Take this letter, and read it, then return it to me in half an hour."

Taking the letter from him, I excitedly returned to my cell. It was from my brother confirming he had got the underground letter, thus proving that the back door mailman had fulfilled his promise. That was great news, and I felt a touch of hope creep back into me. The facts of my case needed to be told to the right people who might be able to rectify this error in law. Tommy was the man for that. I knew my brother to be an intelligent, articulate man. This was a side of his character that the scandal press had ignored and, being my brother, I could rely upon him. If need be, he could contact legal experts in Scotland and seek direction if he came up against something he couldn't verify for himself. My brother was still serving the life sentence imposed upon him for a crime he hadn't committed.

I read the letter with hungry eyes; this was my first communication in over a year from anyone outside China, except for the British consul. I had received money and a parcel, and that devastating telegram about Lochy, but this was a letter, and I needed that connection desperately. Returning the letter, I thanked Lenny profusely.

The floor above us was the translation unit. Most of the work they were doing was in English or Russian. Lenny was the English expert, as Hong Kong schooling was all carried out using the British education system. It was known throughout Asia that if you had traveled overseas for a university degree, especially to the United Kingdom or the USA, that degree held more weight than the same degree taken at universities in other parts of the world.

The Chinese prison system utilised the skills of inmates to earn money for the upkeep of the jail. This was 1992; China was moving into the world of foreign trade and hoping to join the World Trade Organisation translation work was good business. Lenny had the job of translating our outgoing and incoming mail, a job he informed me he didn't enjoy doing.

As time passed, this link with Lenny became a vital line in keeping my sanity. I was getting information beforehand about my incoming mail and had several more back door mail drops from him. Lenny was born in Hong Kong, but he had family living in London. He was serving fifteen years for money missing from the safe where he managed a five-star hotel in Shanghai.

It seemed like a long time ago that I had read that letter, waiting patiently for it to be given to me officially so that I could reply. I waited another month before being called to the office and handed it officially. God only knows how far up the party ladder it had gone before clearance. I kept a straight face when receiving it but wanted to scream. As the months went by, it appeared that there was a pattern forming. Incoming mail took so long to be sent out and delivered that we would often write again, asking why they hadn't replied to the last one. This overlapping of correspondence caused a lot of problems, not only for me but for everyone. It was a deliberate, systematic chipping away process to break down our connection with the outside world, including family.

The following month, I wrote all the details that my brother had asked for, I didn't trust sending my only copies of the indictments and verdict papers for fear they might go missing in the post. Or more to the point, not be posted at all. The mail was collected once each month, and I was feeling better those things seemed to be moving along well enough, having drafted my petition outline for Tommy to proofread and sort out the proper legal terminology.

Petition.

Gao Ji Ren Min Fa Yuan, Hong Qiao Lu 1200, Shanghai 200335.
To whom it concerns, My name is Lauchlan Campbell, I am a British national currently serving a fifteen Year sentence at Shanghai Tilanqiao prison. I am presenting this appeal petition so that it be viewed with the essential nature of Equity in mind complying with the ethics of the legal profession. My appeal petition is based on two points. My criminal case number is 24 1992.
I was sentenced to fifteen years imprisonment by the Shanghai Intermediate People's court on 1992/3/23, this resulted from being wrongly indicted by the Shanghai People's procuratorate for a substance that I did not possess. I believe there has been a violation of the Chinese Criminal Law article 136 Clause 1.
I am presenting this statement of facts for your viewing and consideration under the Chinese Procedural Law Part 3 Chapter 5 Article 149.
Sincerely, Lauchlan Campbell

.oOo.

I had a very pleasant surprise one cold autumn day when I was called to see the dentist at the hospital. I was escorted by JK without a guard. As we strolled by other blocks, JK pointed out that this block was also a baseball cap factory. That one made clothing, another block made leather footballs, and so on. I'd wanted to work rather than sit all day and mentioned that to JK; he soon assured me I wouldn't like it one little bit. He explained that the targets and tasks had to be met and very often the prisoners worked throughout the night to fulfil them - I still thought that would be better than doing nothing all day.

On arrival at the hospital, a few cons greeted JK, looking at me and then asking a barrage of questions.

"Is it true that the foreigners can have cigarettes?"

"If they pay 10,000 Yuan, can they cut off one year of their sentence?"

I thought if that were only true, then I could go home for around £14,500, including my ticket.

JK ignored most questions, and we sat outside the dentist's office. I asked JK what this was all about, but he told me he didn't know. I hadn't made any dental appointments or requests to see a doctor. This was unusual ground to be on, especially being in a hospital area. I was paranoid to say the least, walking about without a guard. The office door opened, and out came a guy holding his jaw. The dentist, a lady in her thirties, smiled and called something to JK who, in turn, beckoned me to follow him into the room. Sitting on the dental chair and still inquiring from JK as to why I was there, it was the name Lochy that perked my ears up. Then hearing it used again, I intervened, asking JK why she was using my name.

"She isn't, that's your son's name, isn't it?"

"Yes, that's correct. Why?" I asked excitedly.

The lady told JK that my son was well and healthy, and she understood how I was feeling, not being able to see him, or him me. It was when she told JK that she had arranged for Lochy to return for further treatment, this time with me in mind, that broke me up. There were tears in my eyes, and I almost cried in front of her. It was arranged that we return to the hospital on Tuesday of the next week. I wouldn't be able to meet him, but I would get to see him and was told never to mention this to anyone, as the lady would suffer the consequences. I walked across the yard back to our cellblock, my heart pumping blood with renewed faith in mankind. The Chinese legal system was new to me, but one thing was clear: you never went against the Communist Party or any authority for that matter. I was humbled by what this lady was prepared to do from her compassionate heart.

.oOo.

I had often lain awake at night thinking of killing people in my mind, putting up a fight against tyrants and dictators. I saw myself doing what was right by eliminating police and government corruption. It was just another fantasy, one I kept close to my chest for fear that I might be going insane. I was like a light switch, flickering off and on, and could easily become wired to the eyeballs by some of the tactics used against us by the authorities. They wanted us to remain distant, and due to my already somewhat isolated position, they tried me out.

One evening, after the October sports events were underway, I, along with the Chinese prisoner who normally took charge of the locals, JK, and our unit leader Benny the Goodman, were discussing matters.

Benny told me that he had heard from the local convicts that Campbell had leadership qualities and wanted to work. The Good Man went on about how labour is the best method of reform; the rewards are good if you work hand in hand with the government. I was receiving a reform spiel until he said they wanted me to take note of the other foreigners and report my findings to JK. I was gobsmacked and looked at JK as if he was a traitor.

I answered, somewhat naively, "No, I couldn't do that. Policing others is not my job," and was annoyed at the very idea of him asking me to be an informer.

Benny the Goodman had a thin smile and a confident posture. He got up from his chair and stood with his hands behind his back, and I could see that I might have upset him in some way but didn't understand how or why until after that meeting.

After leaving the office, I went directly to Cranky and Bull and told them about this reporting business. It was something you just didn't do, and if this Grad had been reporting, then we would have to be more careful about whatever we said in front of him. I left it at that and went off to get ready for bed.

JK spoke with me while I was brushing my teeth, explaining that I could not refuse to cooperate with the government.

I asked him incredulously, "What the heck are you talking about, *Not refusing to cooperate with the government*?"

JK went on to tell me that when asked to cooperate by reporting on the others, I should have agreed. I retorted, asking him if he was a spy as well.

I got the surprise of my life when he said yes and then explained that he didn't report anything useful. It was all 'glue mixing.'

His choice of words baffled me, and I had to inquire about the intended meaning of 'glue mixing.'

He explained that every month he handed in his ideological report to prove he was reforming and to gain the model prisoner award; he put in good reports on what he saw around him. This would reduce his sentence, he explained. He then went on to tell me he gave some reports on others' behaviour, which weren't good. He saw mistrust in my expression but pressed on, trying to win me over to his side again.

I would have to reassess my opinion about JK; after all, he had got my letter out. I needed to get my petition out and was already preparing it - and I knew I would need his help. I left the suggestion with JK about getting out a large document, with all translation work done by him, to be sent to the Supreme court in Beijing and another to Scotland. I could see his eyes reflect a wicked glint at the prospect of doing business with the Triads. JK liked to be involved; it gave him face and a profit.

I had been permitted to buy a small typewriter from the education department and was practising from a book on learning to type, an A to Z sort of method. Being impatient with the structure, I kept falling back on using two fingers and one thumb, and just got on with whatever job needed doing. I had drafted six pages since my chat with JK and passed them to him for translation. He wanted one thousand Yuan; that was a lot of money then, £120 at the bank exchange rate during that period. That was equal to more than three months' wages for a guard.

I asked him if he had gone crazy, but he explained that this letter was going to the Beijing court. If anyone was caught passing it out, he would be punished very severely by the party. JK went on to say, "You don't have to pay me anything for the translation; you're my friend, and the money is for this guard."

"Does he know it's for me?" I inquired.

"No," he lied.

Psychic Pain

I was closing the window opposite my cell one day when I heard a commotion in the yard below. Despite the noise, my curiosity got the better of me, and I looked down. I saw two Chinese cons pulling a basket into the yard. Hearing the wailing screams of a cat, I tried to get my head further out of the barred window to see more. The two cons appeared squarely in the yard right under me. Another con came out with a bucket full of boiling water and threw it over the cat. It was a sound that should have broken the glass. The cat screamed continuously; my teeth gritted, and my skin shrank.

A minute later, another bucket was thrown over it. This went on for what seemed like ages until the cat went silent. I then saw it being tipped out of the basket onto the ground; it looked tiny. One of the cons picked it up and tied it by the hind legs to wire mesh in the yard, then skinned it. I couldn't believe what I had just seen; it was somewhat disturbing.

Going up our corridor, I got hold of JK and told him about it. JK didn't seem in any way phased by what had happened. He told me that it would be eaten and it wasn't uncommon. I started to lose it a little and raised my voice angrily at him. It annoyed me that JK wasn't bothered. I started to spiel about animal rights then went on into a rap full of pent-up frustrations. I didn't know why, but when emotionally upset, I always returned to what I considered an injustice, whether put upon me or someone else. I would lose the plot on what started me off to begin with - the cat scenario had triggered something in me.

I returned to sit in my cell to calm down, but still wasn't happy about the incoming and outgoing mail. The snail mail was still the norm, at least one-month minimum going out. I hadn't had my petition dealt with and wanted to know why the system was all contradictory. It had effects on my psyche; there was a crack in it, and pain was seeping in when needing to get it out.

JK came over, as if by reading my mind, and explained that my petition would go out to a Chinese address first and be reposted from there. Hearing this, I felt a good sense of security and nodded my approval. The way to pay was also arranged by JK and was to have my family send money to the address JK would put in along with the petition letter. I would also pay our triad connection by buying things from the monthly shop or give some clothing or other contraband, of which I still had plenty, and was only too pleased with utilising it by finding a way out of there without censorship. A letter getting to where you want it to be is often vital.

I had already drafted my petition and handed it over to authorities there at the prison. I had sent it by registered mail and received a receipt in confirmation of when it was sent. Three months passed, and I still hadn't received any notice of whether it was received or not. I was seething with paranoia and just didn't believe a word these Chinese authorities told me. I wanted to have it sent for sure and had asked the British consul to send it for me, which they did. Then, at a later date, they received a letter from the Chinese Justice Bureau stating the petition must come from the petitioner.

It would be sent by underground mail to my son Scott. He would pass the petition to be redrafted by TC, then given to a translating company in Glasgow, and finally sent to the court in Beijing by a family member. I have also enclosed the article in Chinese law which states that a family can petition on my behalf.

It would get out, regardless of the cost. I still struggled with writing letters to the court and the British Consul seeking their help on this legal issue.

I was informed by the consul office that they could not assist further than they already had. The consul had sent me a copy of a letter which I signed at the detention cells, regarding me signing over money from their office into my possession. I had to prove that the confiscated money on my verdict wasn't illegal earnings. The fact was, the money had been sent to the consul office in Shanghai via the Foreign Office in London, by my brother Robert. It was just plain common sense that my brother's money couldn't be confiscated as he wasn't accused nor involved in any part of my crime.

My head was throbbing, and I asked JK to get me something for it. He returned minutes later and handed me one white pill, saying this would help. I swallowed the pill, lay my head down, and rested, I then awoke hours later to the sound of cons returning from work, with one headache gone and another beginning.

.oOo.

As promised, I saw Lochy from a distance on 18th November 1992 and was nearly dying not being able to shout out to him, but I kept my cool, knowing that I could get someone else into serious trouble. I could only watch him walking along the yard, going into the hospital building. I was watching from the window above. Then, once more, half an hour later, he came out again. I must have only set eyes on him for thirty seconds in total, but it was enough to let me see that he looked strong and carried his posture well. The experience of those detention cells would be causing some permanent scarring to his youthful psyche.

.oOo.

November moved into December, and we had two British MPs visit the jail. I didn't say much, other than asking if they had seen my son, to which they simply replied, "No."

I asked, "Any chance of getting me a transfer back to the UK?"

They said, "No."

I mentioned my petition, but it seemed the legal system in China was a closed shop, even to them. I couldn't get a response from my inquiries from anyone, nor get these authorities to adhere to anything, and I wasn't allowed to see my lawyer anymore because the case was closed. It was the writing and re-writing to the court, waiting, that was grinding me down. The delay was a deliberate stalling tactic, common in all despot systems the world over. Communications are the key. The first principle of control in a siege is to cut the communication and isolate from assistance to control and oppress. All the while, their prison law stated that, "Any prisoner who appeals or petitions or does not accept the verdict of the court cannot have their sentence reduced." It was a typical 'catch-22' position.

The two MPs departed with words similar to, "Well, stick in there, old boy," and left me batting for Britain, but departed with at least some insight that we were at least being fed.

I was pursuing a petition against being dealt with under the terms of the wrong article, erroneously allowing a sentence over the maximum of 7 years, and I was serving 8 years over the lawful maximum allowed. To pursue this point meant that I couldn't get remission or reduction from my sentence until withdrawing that petition. I truly thought I was entitled to at least eight years knocked off my sentence once the High Court saw the error of substance change on the appeal verdict, so I waited with the belief that one day, they would have to acknowledge my petition. After all, it is in their legal system that all inmates have the right to appeal. I still had faith then and patiently waited.

.oOo.

The next news I received was the best I'd heard since my sentence. I was visited again by Alan and the Shanghai PSB. Alan was less cocksure and seemed to have been knocked down a peg or two somewhere along the line.

It was another young guy who did the talking, and he asked me with a smile, "How are you, Mr Campbell?"

"Fine, until meeting him," nodding towards his comrade Alan, expecting more of their intimidation tactics. The humour went over his head.

He proceeded to tell me, "Your son can go home," if I would send a telegram to my family telling them to send £5000 into my account at the Consul's office. I agreed immediately to comply with that ransom demand but added the condition that I wouldn't sign any money over to them or the court unless first assured by the British consul that my son would be released.

It was a short visit, and I was given the permission to write home a letter and also to the consul office in Shanghai.

On 24th December, Christmas Eve 1992, after spending six months in the Shanghai Sheridan. My son arrived back in the United Kingdom, having paid the equivalent of £5000, and was deported. He spent Christmas day with his family and friends at home. Lochy by name, lucky by nature. That was a massive burden off my back. I had feared he would get 5 to 10 years I was just so happy he was home.

.oOo.

When the other guys heard the news about my son, instead of being happy about the outcome, some moaned and complained about the severity of their sentences in comparison with Lochy's. I could relate to what they were saying, but Lochy was the innocent party in all this; that was the difference.

I never let them know he knew the contents. He was only taking the chance to help prevent his father from possibly being shot for a piece of cannabis. As it worked out, he couldn't be held responsible and was given the substance by the prison authorities during a visit. He never opened the case and never saw the contents. The cannabis was concealed. I was thanking all the Gods and Buddha twice for taking care over my son and not letting him dwell for long in that world of prison darkness. That karma was mine.

It was quite a happy ending to 1992. All I had now was awaiting the response to my petition. Beyond that, I had nothing on my agenda to worry about now that Lochy was home safe with his family and friends and no more dope concealed.

Xmas 1992

I hadn't any complaints that day, eating Christmas dinner in this atheist country. It was a pleasant afternoon; we were at ease with one another, past conflicts put aside. It was just three British guys, two Germans, and one guy from the USA sitting around a table on Christmas day, eating Christmas dinner.

The festivities were of no consequence to the communist-run Chinese Prison system. So, it was quite a surprise when they served us a Christmas meal. We had previously got permission and got together to hang decorations supplied to us by the guard's gofers. Christmas lights and a tree were also set up. Bull and I designed a blackboard with a Christmas theme in the background using coloured paper and chalks. A round table was set up outside the guard's door where the space was biggest and could seat enough for eight people with space to move around. There was also a karaoke machine with the entire kit and caboodle to record as well.

The propaganda camera crew turned up to film us being served and treated so well. It was quite an event. Once we were all seated, we were served plates of roast turkey, roast chicken, grilled fish, roast beef, and numerous plates of vegetables adding colour to the already wonderful spread. The education guard called for silence for his little speech. He wished us all a happy Christmas and, knowing that we were far away from our homes and families, he wished that we could at least enjoy the hospitality of the Chinese People's Republic prison during our festive season. I was quite taken aback by his correctness towards the Christian festivities, as I had already experienced one guard's anger when asking about Buddha via JK. The guard only followed the principles of Mao's red book, where Gods were to be avoided.

I received two letters; one was my first correspondence from a group of very decent people forming an organisation called Prisoners Abroad. It was a newsletter, and their Christmas card photos inside were drawn by other prisoners. It was something we foreigners could relate to here, and I felt I could contribute something by writing back. It was quite an eye-opener when I read how many British are imprisoned abroad and the conditions some lived under.

You would never have expected that this little scene was inside one of the harshest prisons in Asia, known throughout China to be the cruellest, most murderous by executions, held the most prisoners, serving the longest sentences, and the prison reform programme the fiercest. They were getting more than their money's worth out of us in propaganda value, and momentarily I felt that the way things were going; I could cope well enough with prison in China.

The Christmas food lasted three days. We ate like kings and watched television; we even had a video in English and watched a film. It is cold in late December, so we sat around wrapped in thick coats with woolly scarves and hats. I had just received another parcel from my brother Robert in London. One of the clothing items was a woollen car coat-styled jacket, thick and warm. The label inside said 'London Fog'. That label would become a familiar sight the following year, mass-produced in the prison workshops. China didn't adhere to copyright laws.

It was into the New Year, 1st January 1993, and the same applied with the food again. Served up a full-on spread that would be welcome at any table on the planet. It was very clear from the start that the prison system would respect the traditions of the foreigners in their festivities. The prison department wanted the foreigners to take part in a safety play. The good food had to be repaid in some form or other. It was all good fun for a while, doing something different, but more propaganda film was being recorded.

The cameras came out whilst Bull and I did the fruit peeling scene under the banner of DO NOT LITTER. This is where someone throws a banana skin onto the floor, and that causes an accident. Cranky, Grad, and Hans were huddled together, cutting a watermelon with a jail-made knife, under the banner of FORBIDDEN KNIFE. And Vern was simulating putting his hand into a mincing machine in the kitchen while the power was still on under the banner of SWITCH OFF.

JK told us this safety play we put on would go onto the reform file, saying that several departments within the prison needed to stamp their approval before our remission papers could be sent to the court. Unlike in the UK, it wasn't one third automatic remission. In China, you had to be re-sentenced again by a judge. So that was our first clue that we might be getting something taken off our sentence. It was the prison department preparing papers for the court to prove that we were active in our reform.

As it happened, we won a prize for our performance. We were told we would all be given a certificate of merit.

JK told us that was the first step to getting our sentence reduced.

We were all delighted to hear this, having to admit my fantasy and hope of release scenes were fading fast. The illusion bubble never ever burst completely, though.

1993

The Chinese New Year was the main annual event, although they celebrated many times during the year. It was quite different from our Christmas celebrations. The Chinese New Year date differs depending on the position of the moon. When it came to setting up decorations and the laying out of food, etc, it was nothing short of spectacular.

Here was where you found out who was who, and the guys who did what needed to be done.

The Black Fish Triads were obvious, in that they smoked cigarettes in places where others would never dare, and only on holiday occasions. They also had swaggering antics and were overly loud.

Some prisoners, less financially off, had been collecting all year as a group to be able to put out a spread at this special time of year. It was their way of showing face and respect to their ancestors, gods, friends, and family. What a weird system this country had, where the communist party propagates non-religious reasoning, yet the jail was full of ancient tradition and believers.

The Chinese New Year was a very special event, and the place was rocking. It's the same the world over when Karaoke is concerned; people all think they're brilliant singers and everyone had a great time considering the venue location. Every table in the place had invited me to join them, and out of respect for them, I ate from every table.

The other Westerners were invited to one table, along with JK and the Chinese guard's gofer. I did the rounds and had a few drinks of Mai Tai, a strong alcohol spirit that Lao Hun from the Black Jade Triad had supplied. I also acquired myself two packets of 555 cigarettes and a lighter. I secured a small bottle of Mai Tai, which JK told me it was put into my storeroom along with a bottle of very cold beer.

I called Vern first, and he had a hit of spirit then a gulp of beer. Then one by one, they all did, except Cranky, who declined.

I then handed out the cigarettes as well and, because being amongst the locals, could get the guy in charge of the washroom to open up the back gate and let me use it for a smoke.

That area was my new domain, and I had to secure that space as a place to access whenever needed, especially now that Lenny had mail at times. I'd done a bit of trade with the washroom guy, giving him a bar of strawberry soap from The Body Shop, which he'd passed onto his wife at a visit, to her utter delight JK had told me about that. That washroom space was the most vital area for reading my mail without waiting a month or so before the authorities passed it out officially. So, I did more Body Shop soap trade with the washroom man in exchange for keeping contact with the world. It was also great for the change in atmosphere.

The Chinese New Year brought all sorts of colourful television shows. We played football and had basketball competitions amongst our own unit. The prison staff was at a minimum, and the parties went on until after midnight. It was getting to be just too much noise for me. The fun had gone, and all you could hear were guys shouting much too loud, Chinese chess pieces being slammed onto the board, frustrated voices, and playing cards fluttering into the air. The constant clicks of the black and white tiles used in yet another chess game. Being still new to it, I couldn't take it all in.

The New Year in Scotland is a celebration that people respect, and where the tradition is important, so I felt instinctively that the Chinese were also fiercely patriotic, and it wouldn't be wise to disrespect any of their customs or to annoy anyone during that period.

I had spoken with my new friend Lenny having told him part about JK and my dealings with him. His reply was to be careful. This guy Lenny was risking it big time for me by handing over my mail. As far as he was concerned, he came from Hong Kong and not China.

As it usually happens during a long period of inactivity, some guys get bored, and fights break out. Whilst I was going into my cell on the last night of festivities, I heard an explosion. Turning around, I saw a red plastic thermos bottle take flight. The bottle had been thumped onto the head of a guy sitting in front of the television. I saw a few guys grab at the attacker, and then punches and boots flew in. The guy was dragged into a cell, and then a blanket was thrown over his head to quieten him down; if he struggled, he would suffocate. The con was wise enough just to curl up and take his kicking.

I felt like getting involved as the odds weren't in favour of the one, but I wasn't ready to take that role on yet, though I had done in the past. I turned back from the cell and walked to where the television was and sat down. Seeing most people weren't paying any heed to the situation, we watched TV.

There was a television programme I never missed, and I sat, eyes glued to the box, on the floor in the front row in our wing, surrounded by the locals. It was about this young character, around 12 years old, called San Mao - which means 'Three Hairs' in Chinese. San Mao was an orphan living in abject poverty on the streets of Shanghai.

I didn't get to watch the other TV set, the one that had been put into the small sitting area for Western viewing only. This was due to another clash about what other channels to watch. It was a typical jail scenario where there was always someone wanting to control the channels. Cranky was the culprit this time; it was usually whoever got there first and picked up the remote. Cranky and Bull had started a monopoly with it. It was bound to happen sooner or later that two people would want to watch different channels that ran at the same time.

I, being one that seldom went to watch TV since it was all in Chinese, it didn't make sense to sit and stare at pictures, unless it was football, wildlife, or spectacular scenery. However, I did occasionally watch it, and when discovering San Mao, that was my spot. The TV workshop was also on our floor, supplying us with a 12-inch black and white set. When saying TV workshop, it really had multiple purposes. It ran back-to-back with our cells, an exact replica of our living area but turned into a money-making facility making items such as clothes and bags.

The problem arose when Bull and Cranky both wanted to watch something else, something other than San Mao. I reasoned with them that I didn't watch many programmes and I'd slotted that time. We discussed it, but nobody wanted to give way.

Bull told me to sit with the locals and watch, and Cranky agreed.

I knew they would rather just say "Bugger off" but couldn't. I got the message - it was a democracy, and they had outvoted me. Growling at Cranky, I said he was an arsehole - then smacked him a right hook on the jaw, knocking him over backwards.

Bull threw his hands up and said nothing. JK came on the scene while Cranky was shouting, "I'm taking a lawsuit against you, Campbell!"

That incident went into a written report by Cranky and Bull about how the event happened. That was the requirement; if you lodged any complaint, it had to be done in writing. I also wrote my account. The outcome was that I had to apologise to Cranky and the group, then totally split from the other foreigners. I wasn't to share any of their space and complied willingly.

Having a front-row viewing on a coloured set, and although I didn't understand what was being said, the scenes spoke for themselves. They reminded me of how I grew up - a boy in Glasgow living at George Street, one minute's walk from the centre of town, and used to run around with the arse torn out of my trousers. Sometimes having a big pair of welfare boots, but mostly none at all, a street urchin with raggedy clothes and a snotty nose, begging and thieving for my supper. My mother would be waiting for me and my brothers or sisters to bring up a cigarette, or better still, a couple of pennies.

San Mao being an orphan was close to the heart, and I really liked the characters in the Chinese period of that time, around the 1930s, when Shanghai was known as a port with multiple delights, a Shangri-La. It was while watching San Mao one of the local guys joked around with JK, and seeing JK wasn't laughing, I asked him what the problem was. I saw he was still agitated after the show ended and was surprised when he told me "Lao San Mao" was prison slang and it referred to someone within the prison system who had served their time and could go home but had to stay, like an orphan with no home to go to.

I listened to the story, and it did make sense; some people, after serving 20 plus years, didn't have any other place to go. Or their families disowned them, as JK's had. These guys who stayed on at the jail didn't have to work but did have to help out. Understanding why JK was hurting, he only had one brother, and that brother could set him free by signing a responsibility paper for him, but he wouldn't. What a Scumbag Bastard I thought.

I remember thinking that my brothers would come and serve part of my sentence for me if they could. It was from that day on that JK was adopted; by me he was my Chinese brother, and I stood by him.

1994

I was sitting on my own, looking out to nowhere on a warm June day when this new guy walked up to me with a spring in his step, stuck out his hand, and said, "Hi, my name's Dom."

He was twenty-eight and had been sentenced to two years for possession of 200 grams of cannabis. I got on with him immediately. He liked football and knew people that I knew in London. Dom was the friend of a lovely lady called Missy, who was living with my brother Robert's friend Camay. It's a small world, right enough. Dom also played the guitar, so Vern and Dom got together and did a lot of practising.

Everyone really got along well with him, maybe because he didn't drip with paranoia as I and the others did. It was typical of him to take whatever came at him, undaunted and with a smile. He would be neither intimidated nor impressed by the guards, nor their ideological reprogramming system. For example, what he wrote as his third monthly ideological report: was "I Like Pandas. "That was it Full stop.

I loved that attitude, and it was something special the way he totally cocked a snook in the faces of the prison regime. He was proof that the rest of us were all in some way tied up with the Chinese prison reform regulations, chasing the proverbial carrot but still all in self-denial of it. I was certainly counting those merit points and could see my name go up the board quicker than the other foreigners. It was a way out, and it was beginning to dawn on me that it was the only way out that I could see.

It was becoming more and more clear that no court decision was going to be reached. I had lodged the petition from every angle and avenue imaginable and still had no response as I was going into the winter of 1993. It was madness, all these officials coming from jails outside of Shanghai to see the foreigners and how we were treated. It was like playing a part in a movie. All the Chinese cons would either be at the workshop out of sight, or they would be sitting in an orderly fashion, head bowed, studying the rules and regulations which they would be quizzed on later. I had been in that jail over a year and I'd done radio interviews, wrote articles for the prison newspaper, and played more parts than a Hollywood actor. It was all to lead to nothing in my favour.

One day, I asked a passing visiting committee - who were a mixture of police, prosecutors, and Judges - why my petition to the court wasn't being dealt with? "It has been years since arriving here, "and over a year waiting for a reply.

I was assured that there was a long waiting list in the Beijing court and my petition would eventually be dealt with. I didn't care what they said, as JK had already done the job with the back door mailman.

JK came up with an idea to write a book and make cassette tapes for English study classes. All the foreigners were up for it and wanted to contribute. It was a project to help the Chinese people of any age group.

JK said it should be aimed at middle school level; no one complained. JK had written a report to the education department at the prison, going through the proper channels, first, to get permission to do the project and secondly, to be financed for the purchase of required materials to put the project into action.

Weeks passed before someone broached the subject of the English study tapes we were supposed to make. JK hadn't told any of us that he had been refused funding from the prison for his little project. It came to my notice from a smear on his character from that stumped-finger guard's gofer who was always prying into everybody else's business, and I could see from the smirk on his face he was delighted to tell me that JK was taken to the office and criticised for having too close contact with the foreigners and their ways.

I approached JK about this, and he confirmed it word for word. Having already purchased a typewriter and 10 blank 90-minute tapes and a bunch of batteries, I gave this all to JK for his use on the project. Vern added 5 more tapes and then Cranky added 5 more, so we started to write dialogues. It was a total investment of £96 sterling. JK in his element. He had a project to work on and long-term prisoners really needed projects to survive. It was a great big bubble, and I jumped right on it, floated into imaginary benefits that we would gain from this worthy project.

The book title, "Going Abroad", started out as a trip to the consul's office. It explained the proper greetings and introduction. It then went on to teaching how to go about asking for a visa application. Then helped them through the procedure, booking a ticket, airport tax, arrival, and departures. It was the basic A to Z in visa application and airport navigation.

The six of us helped out, and having different accents, added quality to the teaching that other professional teaching programmes lacked. It really did become JK's baby.

It worked wonders and continued to improve, a few guards from other buildings started to show interest in learning English. Our tapes came into demand all over the jail.

Then, when the cons wanted to learn English, it became a business. JK and Black Jade handled that. It was even rumoured a class was to be set up, and we the foreigners could work as teachers. I knew most were willing to do this, but prison politics got in the way again. The communist administration didn't mix well with Western ways.

JK's book, "Going Abroad", went underground. The bloody system didn't want you to achieve anything new.

.oOo.

It wasn't until several months later, nearing the end of 1994, that I was visited by the PSB again, along with the prison Warden and every ranking official in the prison system.

I was called to the office on our landing. As I passed up the wing, I saw eyes dart away from me. It doesn't happen often that you get the full ranks turning up to visit you personally; it had happened once in a lifetime with Lochy, but surely not twice. The office was jam-packed; I was crammed in among them. It was such a shock when the PSB guy stuck my petition in my face.

"Who sent this for you, Mr Campbell?" he inquired.

"I handed it into this office to be sent," was my reply.

There were a few sentences exchanged in Chinese, and then the PSB guy said, "This is not the same one."

A minute later, our guard Benny produced the same size and colour envelope, opened it, and retrieved my petition. I was a bit hot under the collar by being caught with my back door petition, and to add to that, the liar of a guard had just pulled my official petition from his drawer.

I said, "Hasn't that been sent yet? I sent it by registered mail and even got the receipt years ago." It then dawned on me that these people would give a receipt to a family for a bullet to your brain. What was a registered letter receipt? How naive we can become when living in a Western democracy, but this was communism it was a different ball game.

JK went on to tell me that I had violated a regulation and must confess and inform on the person who sent it for me. Replying, I said I had given it to the British consul during a visit. The PSB was quick to respond and brought to my attention that the British consul had my draft returned, along with the message that it should be sent by the petitioner. Having momentarily forgotten that I carried on regardless to say that there had been two copies in total and I had asked the consul to copy my petition and send one to my family, which in fact they had done. "It must have been sent by my son," I went on, denying any knowledge of this petition still loosely held in my hand. A few more words were spoken, then JK told me to go to my cell and collect my toothbrush and towel; on the way, he whispered that the frank on the envelope's stamps was Chinese. I had been arguing the point thinking it was sent from England.

I was taken across to another building in the hospital wing and put into a sort of white room. Being escorted by a guard besides JK and asked him what was going on.

JK told me that I had gone against the government and was a subversive and would be isolated for a while. He made it clear to me that it had to be sealed lips from my end, by his eye contact and the fear of exposure ripped from him in a way only another prisoner can sense.

I therefore went into confinement without complaint and spent my first night in a hospital like surrounding with a television in the room. Two Chinese cons did the nightshift guard duty. The following day on came the interrogation crew and kept to my story that I had given it to the consul and they had sent it onto my family. Feeling sure that of getting away with that until it was reminded to me that the petition was sent from Shanghai, the postage frank would tell what place it had come from but at least, not the person. For that information if known would cause a lot of pain for someone to suffer a lot more than just loss of remission.

I just replied that I didn't know and remained silent. Being threatened with all sorts of punishments from adding to my sentence to not having visits or sending out letters to my family was all nothing new. Meanwhile, the two Chinese cons tried to look intimidating while the guards were about, showing the party support.

JK was interpreting for them and then telling me in English, "Don't bother with them cons, they are told to do that by the guards. If you were Chinese, they would beat the shit out of you, but because you're connected to Black Fish, they wouldn't dare try." JK told me later that they had asked him if I could trade something with them. JK kept that avenue open as that section of the jail was known to be quite brutal. I even heard at the hospital the death sentence inmates had their organs removed after execution.

My sleeping pattern went haywire. It wasn't until returning that I discovered I had been away for three days, it seemed those days just disappeared. However, I did remember that my petition hadn't been sent and as soon as I got the next consul visit told them the story. I wasn't really surprised when they politely repeated their get out clause "We cannot intervene in your legal matters."

I was ready to scream, "They aren't sending my fucking legal petition." Instead, I just asked him what he personally would do in my situation.

"If you petition that means you haven't acknowledged or accepted your guilt. According to their law, whilst in that procedure, you are denied remission from your sentence. If the court doesn't or can't acknowledge your petition, then it can never be dealt with and you can never get remission from your sentence. Thus, you are stuck in a catch 22. If it was me Mr Campbell, I would look at whatever way would get me out of here the quickest."

Being the only foreigner who'd lodged a petition. The others were waiting on the outcome from mine as their outcome when they appealed would likely be the same. This way they could keep both options open for early release, whereas I had closed one of mine. The others were considered to have accepted their guilt, although nobody had put that in writing yet except Grad. On returning to the cell area that night I lay in bed thinking what the best thing to do in this situation would be. Weighing it all up, I still figured that I had been sentenced under the wrong article - so why should I back down to oppression when that very intimidation and oppression itself shows that they know that I am right? By my reckoning, I was due a minimum of 8 years cut off, under the articles of the Chinese procedural law. That's what kept me hanging on in there.

1995

I started working at the cutting table in the workshop, and by spring of 1995 we were making car coats for a company named London Fog; I had even tried some on for size. This was a Russian contractor, and I had seen the paperwork but kept these things to myself, knowing Cranky had become a collector of information. He seemed to be against everything and anything Chinese.

Some of the other foreign inmates wanted to be included in some work projects. The number board merit point system had got to them psychologically, as it had me. After being told at a meeting I was to be given the certificate of merit for my contribution to labour, we got the usual Chairman Mao lecture stating that a person can be reformed through labour and that Campbell had worked also in the evenings when required to. As far as I was concerned, it was really about getting off that narrow landing, and didn't want to sit all day looking at a wall. It was good for me to be able to work. Some of the jobs, such as Christmas time making toys, was a drag.

One particular toy drove me mad. It was when you clapped your hands the toy played a tune. The workshop was *ding-sing-a-bloody-ling* all day. I ended up smacking one guy in the jaw opposite me but kept on working. I had cracked up momentarily. It was a surreal experience just throwing a punch onto the jaw of this guy and then continuing to work as if nothing had happened.

He hadn't retaliated, maybe due to the triads at hand; it was just left as it was. It boiled down to the noise and I reckoned it did cause disturbance in my mind. In the Chinese language, there are a lot of swear words used; they are not always meant to be personal, but with my short fuse and not knowing what was said, I often just reacted impulsively.

The Shanghai word 'Na Lou' means 'foreign penises. It became commonly used, as was 'your grandmother's cunt'. Hearing those terms used daily got under my skin. It was the speech of the angry, the uneducated.

China's jails were full of those. Yet at times meeting with intellectuals and artists was also possible.

I had written a report to see the psychiatrist. In only a few days, I was called from the workshop and then escorted by Lenny over to another part of the jail. There was the sign above the door entrance in English saying, 'psychological counselling'. I entered and was taken to a small room with a window and sat down, Lenny was seated beside me.

A minute later, a guard around my age entered the room; he smiled and sat behind a desk. Lenny and the guard exchanged some conversation. The guard stood up and shook my hand, introducing himself in English, "I am Mr Wang, pleased to meet you," he said politely.

I replied giving my name in return, "Mr Campbell, and pleased to meet you too."

We were seated and he asked what my problem was. I explained about the noise, giving him several examples of when the sound penetrated my psyche and caused me to get irritated. I was also getting severe pain in the back of my neck, upper spine. It really felt like red-hot needles shot into my nervous system.

It was a pleasant surprise when he pulled out cigarettes and offered us one; Lenny was happy to have a puff of nicotine, so we accepted. It was arranged that we would see him every week and have some counselling. I had a feeling this guard wasn't like most of them I'd encountered, but we would see.

My appointments were arranged every Wednesday from 1 o'clock till 3 o'clock.

On returning to the cell block, Lenny told me to meet him on the back stairs. He had got a parcel from his sister in London and wanted to give me some chocolates. He asked for me to pass some onto Grad for him, which I could do, and did. I had started putting out more letters for Cranky and others, charging them $10 and a jar of coffee for that service – a very reasonable price for getting important letters out, and you wouldn't be sending anything underground unless you deemed it important. I didn't keep the coffee or purchases that went to Black Fish and his Triad associates.

What I did do was, tell my son Scott to photocopy the letters before sending them on. It was something I learned at a very young age, 1966, in Barlinnie prison, Glasgow, whilst waiting to be sent to Borstal – I was told never to pass on a stiff, ie an underground letter, before first reading it. So, in keeping with jail tradition had Scott photocopy, them for me. It was proof of my good work in jail, although restricted in a communist regime, that I still got messages out uncensored.

I was having less and less to do with the other foreigners, me being in the workshop all day. My life was taking new turns every other week, and I was being embraced by the locals; it had a lot of ups and as many downs. Finding out that I was just a commodity for some, a novelty to some, and a means to get something free for others. But by most, I was accepted.

1996

It was a day of happiness to see Grad pack his bag for the final time. We had watched him pack and unpack it on numerous occasions over the years.

Among the foreigners, we all had joked about Grad's antics, nicknaming him Wolf. We often watched him pace the landing vigorously, munching on fruit if he had it, or biting his nails if he hadn't. He was hungry for freedom.

It had been like this since day one really, with the foreigners not knowing what was happening with us. So many rumours went around, always related to us going home.

There was one time in particular that really got us worked up. Out of the blue one day, while in the workshop, I was told to go to the office. When I arrived, I discovered Grad, Bull, and Dom had gathered too. We were given passport application forms, which we were told to fill in that day. We were then taken over to another block and had our photos taken. We were convinced that we were going, either to another jail in the UK or going home.

Grad was excited and assured us he knew all about it beforehand, telling us that the British consul had told him that we'd all leave together. I was ready to believe that, and Bull and Dom didn't object. We reasoned that it did make more sense to send us all back together. It was a day of hope and bright expectations for all.

It still took a month or so after we'd all had those photos taken, as it turned out, it was only Grad who left. and I was pissed off with the British consul about it. At the next consul visit, I said to them that they were cruel and inconsiderate assholes to give us the passport applications to fill out, knowing well that we weren't going to get using them.

The consul assured me that they hadn't requested that we fill out any application at all, but that only Grad was to do so. The Chinese have a weird way of doing things, having us all fill out forms but not the Germans or American. They made it seem all the more realistic so that it hurt.

It was time for Grad to give out what wasn't needed and he was given a set of Chinese study tapes and books, a basic course in Chinese sent to him by the London-based organization Prisoners Abroad. Then followed the promises of things that would be done and gifts that would soon be on the way to whoever. Then he was gone.

It didn't feel any different that day, but in the days to follow, you could sense a large presence was missing. Grad was a decent man and although having a couple of clashes with him over the years, he departed giving me a firm handshake.

Serving 15 years is a long, long time in any prison, let alone a foreign one, and I could imagine after 10 years you will still clutch at straws to gain remission, even for a single year off your sentence. Because *that* year would be yours and not theirs – those jailers who had controlled your every waking moment, as you struggled in psychological chains.

One day my day would come, and no matter what they did to me, I always knew that and held onto myself, kept myself alive in the light of that.

.oOo.

I received a letter from my sister Agnes; it brought the news that my brother was released. (TC) Campbell of the *Free the Glasgow Two* campaign had finally got out of jail on a decision made by a higher court. He was to remain out of prison until his next court appeal hearing.

I thanked the Gods of justice that night; the force works in wondrous ways. Reckoning if my brother was on the street, then he would win his case. Nobody would have let such killers walk about if it was them. I wasn't living in the UK when he was originally charged, but instead was living in a paradise called Boracay Island in the Philippines, the owner of Jock's Rock School of Scuba. During my early smuggling days, having some extra cash, I had purchased some land and built my house there. It was there that the news of my brother's arrest came via a newspaper clipping sent to me at the island post office. It was the story of TC Campbell, the ice cream war monster. It had been sent by my other brother Robert, from London. No sun on any tropical island could have brightened that day but hearing that he was out of prison was another day and things were looking bright for Tommy at last. I was delighted with that news.

.oOo.

We had started to study prison law as a group at the beginning of 1996; that was the only time we would all get together, except for Christmas and New Year. That was when the authorities made the effort to show face by filming us all sitting, eating together. The handing out of letters and Christmas cards was a yearly ritual.

The new guard who came to work with us was called Captain Ma; he was filling my ears with, "Once you withdraw your petition, you will get a big reduction," telling me also a bigger reduction because I went to the workshop. It was going on four years with no sign of any petition being dealt with; it was time to move on. I had been resending my petition every year, even had the Consul send it to my family, and also the back door mailman, but nothing seemed to work.

So finally, I withdrew my petition.

.oOo.

It might have been a coincidence, but a couple of months after I sent my withdrawal - explaining that I had been wrong to petition, and also how I had now seen the error of my ways - it was in the air that the judges would be visiting the prison soon. That meant several things: there could be reductions in sentence, liberations, and most importantly, commuted death sentences to life imprisonment. When I say commuted death sentence to life imprisonment, just think about it for a moment. In China, you don't wait 20 years on death row; you know your fate within a maximum of two years. In cases where it's a public execution, you can be executed directly after court but usually within ten days.

I was feeling great getting the word from JK that the judges would arrive in the afternoon. We, the foreigners, except for Cranky, had all submitted our crime acknowledgment report.

Bull said, in excited tones, "Eighteen-month reduction at least for you." Then saying that he, Vern, and Hans would get a year off, being led to believe this from whom I considered someone in the know, ie, Captain Ma.

Late that afternoon we all went downstairs except Cranky. Bull, Vern, Hans, and I stood there in the office. There was tension in the air and still a faded hope of deportation. The four of us lined up; there were three judges sitting behind the guard's desk. The judge read from a paper for five minutes, and I could hear the Chinese word for reform being often used.

The judge finished, and JK's interpretive skills were much quicker. "You all got a ten-month reduction each," he said.

That was it, a cold hard slap of prison reform, Chinese style. I was gutted and had worked in the factory evenings and all hours. Keeping my disappointment in check, I said to Vern going upstairs, "You did the right thing, pal," on what he replied, "You studied music and bypassed the whole work for merits crap."

I was annoyed by the deception of our education's guard and could also see that the other guys weren't too happy with ten months either. Bull had voiced on our way down that they might just set us all free and keep Cranky. Of course, he was joking, yet for a second, I thought they just might. Cranky was really giving them a hard time with politics; he knew his stuff and read profusely. The only way to get back at him was to not include him in this reduction or to withhold his outgoing and incoming mail.

The back door mailman wasn't open for Cranky because we had a falling out when I had withdrawn my petition. He hadn't shown me any gratitude for having gotten out his letters to his family. He insisted at length with me, "Campbell, you're our only hope to get this Dama Zhi issue sorted out."

I argued that the petition had been in for years but still got no reply, plus it was all at my family's expense for translations and lawyers, further adding I couldn't even have a sentence reduction when petitioning. I stuck with my withdrawal and told him if he wanted to petition, he could. The others also could, as in accord to the newly promulgated prison law. I noticed none of them took up the flag. As for working anymore, I would only go to the workshop when I felt like it or to do some trading, staying more on the wing to read and study Chinese. "Fuck this working all hours' labour reform for a bullshit rubber stamp right on my forehead saying, 'No communist party, No new China.'"

I had just been indoctrinated into the melting pot of experimental reform, or as more commonly known, brainwashed. To top off the disappointment with our reduction in sentence, we had a meeting the following day; what they wanted us to do, we did it. The reason was because the system wanted you to conform. We knew if you didn't, you would suffer more.

We were to praise the authorities in writing, for showing us the path to reform. We assured them we would.

They assured us that they hoped we could go home soon; the video camera was, of course, rolling. It was taking in our fixed Mandarin smiles; we had all acquired them except Cranky, he still had the contempt, unshaven three-day growth look.

.oOo.

It was a day of happiness to see Dom leave. He had completed his full two years without any remission, which left five of us – Cranky, Bull, Vern, Hans, and me – still harbouring hopes that we would all go along with Dom. It was the same way we all thought we would go home along with Grad, but of course, it didn't happen that way.

Dom packed his bags and went around handing out bits and pieces, giving to me the book 'The Last Emperor'. I had read it, and when it came to the part in the book, the year 1959, ten years after the founding of the People's Republic of China, there was an amnesty given. The Chinese government had released political as well as war criminals to commemorate ten years of the new China under Mao Tse Tung.

Thinking to myself, 1999 would be fifty years after the founding of the PRC. Surely there could be an amnesty then, setting my sights for that date, still ever the optimist. It was 1996, so three years to go – not long when you say it fast. I had been in prison for over five years; it goes so quick when looking back but not so quick while serving it.

.oOo.

Dom wasn't gone long before two more new guys appeared.

I first saw them standing outside the office on our landing and walked towards them. I could see they were from the subcontinent and introduced myself, and they shook my hand.

The smaller of the two, built like Mike Tyson but much smaller at around 5ft 5ins, was Mustafa. The other, taller and medium-built at around 5ft 11ins, was Syed. I sat with them and heard their story.

They were both in for fraud and came from Pakistan. I was surprised that Syed could speak Chinese. Asking him how he learned, Syed explained that he had married a Chinese girl, meeting her while he was studying at a university in Beijing, then after their studies finished, he returned home to Pakistan to make her his bride. He left her there then returned to China to commit fraud.

I asked Mustafa how he had gotten here, and he explained Syed had brought him along with fake ID plus stolen cheques. It was Mustafa who was cashing them. I told them about the Pakistani guys over in the other blocks that we rarely saw these days; due to the drain being fixed, but they didn't seem concerned or interested to hear more about them.

I explained they would first have to go through briefings of the *Ten Don'ts* and get to know the prison regulations before they would get any freedom of movement. It was the system here that you got indoctrinated over a ten-day period, then after that, it meant they could go downstairs in the morning for half-hour exercise.

I was in control of the shit removal and didn't carry the buckets anymore but just stood over and watched them getting hosed down, then added the disinfectant. It makes me laugh, thinking back to that job and was glad to have it then – it was good trading ground. We all knew that the guards never came into that area, or at least very rarely.

Both Mustafa and Syed had no real interest in knowing who the other Pakistani guys were. Mustafa had linked up with Bull, who was showing interest in becoming a Muslim. I was getting feedback from Syed, who was proving to be a real arrogant bastard. He really hated communists and had gone to university in China, suffering racist verbal abuse as well as violent attacks. I could see for myself quite clearly that those Pakistani guys weren't given the respect that the Western inmates got, especially from the Chinese inmates, and sensed he would be a problem in time to come. Syed was serving five years; Mustafa was serving six years – we would see.

The 1996 Christmas festivities were the usual good food. We had plenty of pretense, and our Mandarin smiles were still full-on view. The new Muslim inmates had no complaints about the food or music. It was another Christmas with the same procedure, getting our eventual mail and eating well, all on film.

However, it was on December 29th that I got my Christmas gift.

I was told by JK that we were all moving to a brand-new jail. This was to happen the following day. He emphasised to me that it had an outdoor grass football pitch.

I was glad of any news regarding a move out of that dump. If you ask anyone who has lived a long time in a dilapidated condition, they will always exchange that in the hope of better things to come.

I spread the news around, but it wasn't accepted – we had all heard it before. Rumours were abundant when it came to foreigners.

The following morning, December 30th, 1996, we were told to pack our things. This wasn't any rumour. It was a good feeling handing out some of my possessions to Lenny upstairs, as well as some clothes and soaps to my football buddies Liang and Ho, who were still there.

JK was coming with us, an old friend who would keep me right. Then, to my surprise, all the Pakistanis were already on board a bus. I had traded with Haled and knew about Parviz and Butt, then there was another guy whom I had seen on a couple of occasions but thought he had been released.

I looked out of the bus window, swallowing the daylight like a man suffocating for air and needing to get free, harbouring a fantasy of escaping from the new jail. The road passed the airport, and a few called out, "Turn left." The humour wasn't appreciated when a guard called out for us to be quiet.

Staring out of the prison bus window, I saw that the road out of the city was bustling, and my eyes searched for God only knew what. Seeing bicycles everywhere, some scattered and discarded with buckled wheels, people swept by; it felt like a new noise for my ears, and I was soon off again into the safety net of my mind with a Pink Floyd song ringing in my ears, 'wishing away moments that make up a dull day'.

It was around a two-hour drive, mostly along a newly built highway, seeing buildings going up all around. China was under reconstruction, something we heard nearly every day from the news. Taken from my reverie when the bus eventually took off down a dirt road, I saw that we had crossed a canal, and then the surroundings of a high-wired fence arose from nowhere.

The bus was going down a country road; in the distance, buildings with a high electric fence on top came into view. Knowing I had reached my new residence, I thought hard about what might lay ahead for me and watched the large gates opening electronically, manned by two armed guards.

It was not like the old place, where the guards had to pull the gate open; seeing a lot of green grass and trees, this jail looked okay, but I would soon discover that in exchange for the impression of good surroundings, a lot would be expected in return.

.oOo.

Nearly six years in, I had spent ten months with twelve men in a cell at the detention house, some of these men being taken to be executed, which had gutted me. I had the death sentence also on my indictment but got leniency in the eyes of Chinese criminal law and was sentenced to fifteen years. After spending five years at Shanghai Tilan Xiao prison, living in a windowless cell 3ft by 8ft, living with vermin and the stink of human sweat, fear, and excrement, I, along with another British guy, two Germans, one American, and five Pakistanis, were escorted onto a prison bus. The weather was cold and the air damp.

The Pakistani guys hadn't all met up whilst in jail and immediately bonded, excitedly chatting away in Urdu. We, the Westerners, had already shared our hopes and dreams of liberation on numerous occasions over the years. I was like a paranoid android, reflecting on past confrontations with Cranky and Bull, plus the fights with local inmates, and not forgetting the guards. I wished this new jail would be less confrontational. My head was bursting, and I was going stir-crazy.

We drove through the large electric gate, we then passed a few buildings on the right, then turned left, and came to a halt. Two young guards, whom I recognized, met us; they had been introduced to us as recruits at the old jail. Another guard was coming out from the building; he looked scruffy, with trousers crumpled and his hair unkempt.

Looking around, I saw we were standing on a basketball court. There was a brand-new two-story L-shaped building. As we entered the building, we gathered on the ground floor. The new guard introduced himself as Captain Wang, and the other two were Captains Hua and Wu. There were five cells on each floor, a total of fifteen cells. We were all placed on the second floor; Bull and I were allocated cell two, Vern and Hans cell three, Khalid, Mustafa, and Cranky cell four, Parviz, Butt, and Syed into cell five. The first cell on the floor was for the four Chinese inmates; it had two bunk beds.

When I first entered our cell, I couldn't believe the contrast from the old jail. This cell was massive, around 14ft x 9ft in size, and had a bedside cabinet and a stool to sit on. The most striking feature was a veranda - a fucking veranda - with a door opening to the outside. Stepping onto this amazing feature, I stood by a bricked wall up to waist level. It had cemented fixed bars bending upwards and over my head into the wall above. The veranda alone was bigger than my cell at the old jail.

I then noticed a large electrical fence about 30 feet away from where I stood, but it was still a good feeling to be able to open a window or door and breathe clean air. It had been five years, and more, breathing in excrement gases in a windowless cell. This cell had three single beds; Bull and I took the ones with our heads facing the cell door, strategically putting us out of view from the night duty patrol. My relations with Bull had always been strained since the chopstick attack at the old jail, but we could get by, and we mostly did get along ok. We settled in and then were told to gather in the corridor with our stools. We sat in silence as the place filled with uniforms.

The head Warden, Yu Zhong Min, gave an opening speech to introduce the foreigners to Qing Pu jail; and JK was doing the interpretation. The speech unfolded, "Shanghai Qing Pu prison is a modern, civilized prison with a strong emphasis on cultural values. Culture can help you to distinguish between true and false, while art can help awaken one's conscience."

I took a mental note of those words to log into my diary.

Once the uniforms had their say and we had been told not to form gangs or pray, plus the usual spiel, "If you reform actively, you will be rewarded with a reduction in your sentence," then they departed.

Captain Wang then went on to tell us that we had to write monthly reports acknowledging our crimes. The reform through labour process was repeated; it was words we had all heard before at the old jail. The meeting was over, and walking around the new jail building, I had ideas of getting a single cell at the forefront of my mind. Then it was time to eat; we got served our food in stainless steel containers with a number on it. The container had a small inner bowl that held a lump of fish, and beneath was steamed vegetables. The rice was given out by one of the Chinese inmates. That night was a cold December one, but I still got out of bed to look out of the window and see the moon and stars.

.oOo.

I walked into cell one the following morning to speak with JK – I knew we would be given some daily hygiene duties at some point in the day and I wanted JK to put me up as head cleaner. I was thinking of ways to get around the jail and do some trade.

JK and another three Chinese guys shared cell one. It was the same as ours, only they had the bunk beds. I noticed the other three Chinese guys sitting around and hadn't spoken with them, yet my eyes were drawn to the cover of a book that lay on one of the stools. Walking over, I picked it up and was surprised when I saw the face of Bhagwan Rajneesh Shree. He is also known as Osho a renowned Indian Guru Inquiring who's owned the book, a slim, wide shouldered guy, smiled and said it belonged to him.

I immediately related with this young guy - his name was Mr Cho. He was to become known to us all as Stanley. Being somewhat suspicious though as to how could he get to read such a book. It was against the regulations to worship and you weren't supposed to pray. Listening to his use of English and could hear he was precise in his pronunciations but short of vocabulary at least his English was better than my Chinese. I struck up my first bit of trade at the new jail and would teach him English in exchange for him teaching me Chinese.

We shook hands.

Stanley was doing a fourteen-year prison sentence for his involvement in car theft relating with the Tiananmen square student uprising when it had spread from Beijing to Shanghai. Stanley was fortunate in one-way, that he had a family relation at the jail who was a high communist party official. I could see an ocean in Stan's eyes, he was in search for new knowledge and was still unquenched. Stan and I connected and told him stories about some of my travels. As that day went on, he would seek me out at every opportunity to listen to more. I enjoyed his company especially when he opened up my mind to the Chinese teachings of Lao Tzu. Spiritual healing is needed in prison and we were parched for it.

.oOo.

It is not a traditional festive date on the Chinese calendar but we knew from past experienced that New Years at the old jail would be celebrated with a great meal being put on. Hogmanay was the date to proclaim that as a Scotsman they needed to follow my traditions. I had written down several notes from that first meeting and would be using their terminology whenever submitting anything in writing and would be asking for Chinese language or cooking classes, art and calligraphy or Tai Chi Chan using the words of our great leader Warden Yu Zhong Ming statement on the importance of cultural values.

As it happened, it had been pre-arranged that we would be getting special food. The large reception room on the ground floor was allocated to us to decorate it was Bull who took over that job most years although the others did their bit. We all got special food and recreation treatment until January 3. That was a nice start to being civilized. The New Year came and went it was not as festive an atmosphere as it had been at the old jail but I was in some part glad of that.

We had plenty of Karaoke and everyone smiled when officials were present. That was something you picked up in Chinese jail, known as the

Mandarin smile, those faces with stretched lips some with gums and teeth exposed all of us foreigners thinking the same. *Fuck you*. The food was duck, chicken, fish, beef and pork. There was also an abundance of mixed vegetables and roots. It was good food and plenty of it. No complaints as of yet.

The kitchen also had a Muslem chef so no pork would be given to the followers of that faith. As usual, we had a barrage of high-ranking officials being filmed with us. They did this during dinner or presenting us with gifts ie notebooks. These 'gifts' were given for a purpose - we were informed to write our thoughts down and hand them in monthly.

We were filmed receiving letters from our family and so on and were glad to return to normal. Stir crazy normal if you know what I mean? You cannot expect to be fully functioning up top after six years in a limited space living among people who not only spoke sounds alien to your ear but also sometimes attacked you.

1997

Cranky was having a hard time and it didn't take long before he began to feel the first hint of conflict coming towards him. There was a struggle with the Pakistanis; Cranky was saying that he shouldn't have to share a cell with Muslims, and his cellmates agreed – they wanted him out. Their reasoning was that he used plates and utensils that made contact with pork products. This was not true as Cranky had a vegetarian diet.

It was the authorities who wanted to show Cranky how to play ball their way. So, Cranky remained where he was, only with one difference – he kept his utensils in a separate drawer.

It really boiled down to the fact that Cranky and Bull had secured the television remote control on the first day of arrival as they had done at the old jail. That was really the heart of it – there was friction, as the Pakistani guys wanted to watch another channel, I wanted nothing to do with it.

I was given the job as the cells and living quarters' hygiene inspector, having had JK arrange that for me. I was to select a cell each day that was looking the tidiest. By the end of the week, one cell would get merit points for winning. I talked with Vern, asking him to sort out a rota system so that over the month, each cell got equal points. The proverbial carrot was still in use at this modern, civilised prison.

Vern wrote out a rota system that ensured we were all equally rewarded throughout the month.

Bull was put in charge of the hot water container that was delivered twice a day. It was a heavy container; it needed two strong people to get the handle, one at each side, to lift it from the electric buggy that delivered it, so the giant Khalid assisted him.

Parviz was given the job of cleaning and emptying the bins in the guards' office this was considered a position of trust. Some of the inmates who didn't have a job felt left out; it was quite interesting to watch and listen to guys complain, and other inmates becoming jealous through job allocations. I had identified that emotion in myself but had not examined it closely enough yet. What were we in competition for? Some preferred not to work, like Hans and Vern, who studied most of the day; Bull was also studying and had learned to read, write, and speak Chinese.

It was down to a power struggle, and the Syed was the worst; that idiot informed on me to the authorities, telling them my hygiene setup was a fraud. He had done it after a couple of weeks of me setting up Vern's rota system. It lost me the job, and he took over from me.

Was the prison system playing the Pakistanis against the Westerners? Was it because they were more obedient? I sometimes wondered and watched closely.

I was given another job distributing the monthly food orders we could put in and pay for from our personal cash kept in our property. That put me in with the Chinese again, like the old jail workshop, and that caused quite a stir, as it was usually only the Chinese inmates who did this job.

I was constantly on my toes in this new jail, I couldn't trust myself, never mind anyone else. I was offering all sorts of assistance to Stanley to get around the jail and was being guided by him, a new friend who was pushing me to have a good position at this new unit.

We were attending meetings two or more times each day; it was obvious to me the authorities here hadn't a clue on how to occupy our time. It was an experimental unit for the Chinese authorities on how to deal with the ever-growing influx of foreign criminals. We also had new rules on how to dress; it was to be prison garb we all had to wear from now on.

We were issued two light grey cotton uniforms; we also got one darker grey, a synthetic nylon type, plus a thick dark blue cotton sweatshirt. The uniform had a blue and white stripe across the front and back of the jacket. It also ran down the outside of both trouser legs; we were also given two white short-sleeved shirts. That was to be our summer and winter attire; they again had stripes on the back and front. We were issued with ID cards, which were to be pinned to our jackets; they had our prison number and photograph on them. This foreign unit was slowly taking shape and some order. It certainly was experimental.

.oOo.

One day we were told to go outside to practice marching we had watched the Chinese inmates doing this they were housed in a building opposite the same size as ours and the only difference was, they were eight to a cell with four bunk beds. We all fell in and the charade began it was pure pandemonium. Cranky Bull and Vern turned left when it should have been right. Khalid bumped into everyone the guard was getting wound up he was used to complete discipline and order at his command. It wasn't happening here.

"Campbell," he called my name.

JK told me to go over to the guard and was told to stand at attention and say 'Duisan hao' (Good Captain) which I did. Then I was told to march around left, right, left, right, halt. The guard beamed; his lost face being partly regained by my efficient marching.

JK went on to tell everyone that's how you should march. I felt like a one-legged man at an arse-kicking party having set myself up for this by being eager to please my new turnkeys. JK and Stanley were pushing my case as being trustworthy and they needed someone who could help them run the unit. We all needed something to occupy our time having offered to work as a painter and decorator telling them that it was my trade and our building was unfinished. Having got a job for a few days was good, and I painted the windows. I was rewarded by being given a football.

Holding the new ball in my hands and smelling the leather not yet having had a kick about since arrival, that's all I wanted, just to be occupied, to be involved, and to be useful.

.oOo.

One afternoon in February, the death of Deng Xiaoping was announced. It was quite an event; a full history of his life filled the newspapers and was shown on television. The man of the open-door policies, who spearheaded China into the economic revolution. The reforms carried out by Deng gradually led China into the Global market to become one of the world's fastest-growing economies.

We, the foreigners, were instructed to write a report with our views on this great man. I still had Tony Benn's book with me, a Socialist Anthology, sent by my brother, Tommy.

Cranky still had my 'History of China' and 'Aristotle's Ethics' books from the old jail. A group of Pakistanis gathered in my cell, looking for words of wisdom to praise this great man. I can assure you that words from Emile Zola to the Suffragettes were handed in for translation, deliberately leaving out any quotes from Chairman Mao's Red Book. They were some of the best ideological reports in history, written in memory of Deng Xiaoping by foreigners held against their will in China.

.oOo.

Having had my persistent request granted at the beginning of March, the foreign unit played their first game of football against the Chinese. It was against the unit opposite us.

Bull was a solid defender and took no prisoners, to coin a phrase.

Stanley was as fast as a whippet. He was outcast by many of the Chinese, due to his position in the foreign unit, a position they wrongly believed was more relaxed than the rest of the jail. I had adopted him as my Chinese brother, letting him know clearly that he could depend on me for whatever help he needed. It was already known before I arrived that I had played in every football competition at Shanghai Tilan Xiao jail and was considered a good player by Chinese standards.

Football was taking off in China at the time, but they were still amateurs compared to Europe or South America.

Hans and Vern couldn't kick a ball straight, unusual for Germans.

Cranky was a basketball player, and the Pakistanis were cricketers.

We had a good kickabout, having a good laugh out on the basketball court. It was just fun to run and kick the ball, showing the Chinese guys how to keep the ball up. It was easy for me to roll it onto my foot, then keep it up, switch feet, onto my knee, then up to my head, and down to my foot again. Then I watched them trying to keep up the ball three to four times; nobody did it without touching the ground except one.

The guards, Captain Wang and his two assistants, Captain Hua, and Captain Wu, also joined us, eager to show their skills. Captain Wang was a better player than any of the Chinese cons we played against that day. The other two guards had never kicked a ball in their lives but knew they would have good players in other blocks. Stanley had told me about the prison team, plus each cellblock had their team. We would have ours. I knew we couldn't yet compete on the pitch with seven or eight a side, but if it was three or four a side on the basketball court, bring them on. Having received this ball in return for keeping busy with my Mandarin smile,

.oOo.

One evening, I was called into the office and met by the criminal affairs cadre, Captain Ma. He began his conversation by praising my attitude for my willingness to work. He went on to say that supporting the government benefits me and the reform of others and that I was to be commended at the end of the month and rewarded.

JK explained more about what he meant by commended and rewarded and told me the modern civilised prison story again, this time via Captain Ma. They wanted us to take part in the upcoming Chinese Spring Festival sports event.

I was to ask the other foreigners to compete in other events. They had Tug of War, sprints, and other games such as basketball, ping-pong, chess, and the card game Bridge. We were to make a list of participants, and then pass it over to JK, naming the events and who wanted to take part. I didn't see any fault with this and was enthusiastic about going to tell the others. It was always a confrontation of sorts when you had to pass on suggestions or orders, and I fucking hated it. I would never accept taking orders from another con. Getting JK to do this for me, it was mutually felt we didn't want to be playing the guards' role, but still, it was better coming from him.

It came to pass that a certificate of merit was awarded to me; it was like a small diploma in bold Chinese characters, with my name written both in Chinese and English. This was done during a meeting. It was clearly stated that if you cooperated like Campbell, you would get this reward. I wasn't the only one to get this certificate; the two Germans got one as well, also Butt and Parviz.

If you had two or more of them, you could have your sentence reduced. That was a message everybody wanted to hear, but nobody believed a fucking word of it, as the last experience proved, with all of us getting a ten-month reduction except Cranky. I knew this was for the new guys, to get them competitive, and it worked a treat. The Chinese authorities also knew my character and manipulated it sometimes. Deep within, I still clung to the illusion that this place might be different, that they might yet set us free if giving a Mandarin smile for whatever propaganda project was needed at the time.

It wasn't only me eager to get free; a couple of guys had written reform articles that got published in the jail paper. Bull had also been studying Islam for a few months and was more focused on his health and studies. He had secured the veranda of our cell for privacy when he prayed. Syed didn't accept Bull as being converted to Islam, stating that he hadn't been circumcised; Khalid was saying that the pastries from the kitchen that Bull ate had pork oil in them.

I wasn't interested in listening to all the negative reasons why Bull wasn't taking their religion seriously and had never heard anything mentioned in Bull's favour from these Pakistani guys. It wasn't like that when they first arrived, having noticed when Mustafa and Syed were only too eager to pass on words from the Holy Koran, ie, in their search for sharing Bull's monthly shopping goodies. I knew of jail converts from experience, some used it as a means to an early release, others used it to hide behind, putting themselves into the pacifist group, but I also believe some people do find their spiritual guide. In Bull's case, it was out of respect towards his girlfriend and wife-to-be from Xingjian, as she was from a Muslim family. Bull did have that thirst for knowledge.

I know the guards were rather confused when they heard that Bull prayed to Allah. It is difficult for some people to understand, but in the Chinese communist ideology, they don't believe in any God, so being a Christian convert to Islam, that had got them thinking. They were sincerely amused that we civilised Westerners could follow or believe in such unrealistic happenings that had been written about centuries ago. It wasn't permitted to pray at the prison, although it was being done privately.

Part of the problem seemed to lie in the ritual of going to wash your hands and feet five times a day. On the entrance to the washroom written in Chinese as well as English was the sign. "Water is the source of life save it." That and also the fact that they wanted to pray together. The guards didn't want to accept that Muslims could go and wash then kneel and pray as a group. It was in the regulations that you couldn't congregate in groups or form a gang.

.oOo.

It was only a few days until the Chinese New Year, and our sports training had begun a week earlier. We had a dozen Chinese people from the opposite building to train and pick a team from. We passed the ball, with me observing their moves and seeing the makings of a team. We were out on the large grass field; the pitch was about half the size of a professional pitch, but lumpy with clods of grass and ditches. Having picked a tall, slim person who had better dribbling skills than me, called Lanky.

Another player, about my height, 5ft 8 inches, but slimmer, built around 68kg. This person was twenty years younger and fast. He had another plus; he could distribute the ball quite well, he could speak some English, and like Hanley, he had family connections at the prison. He was called Shu Ming.

I picked another person from the Xingjian autonomous region in China. He was the Muslim cook, known to us as Kasha.

The night shift worker in our unit could play quite well, but he was always asleep when we needed him. Little Wang was his name, so he would be a substitute.

I needed more players and selected two people who could run fast.

The game these people played was totally disorganised. Football had really taken off nationwide and it was usually seven people a side, chasing the ball whooping all the way; when someone got it, they kicked it anywhere as hard as they could.

I got our side to at least get some passing practice. It appeared that everyone just ran about, making lots of noise. It certainly was relieving just being able to shout at the top of my voice and not be reprimanded, but I needed a team who would not just run about. Stanley, myself, Bull, and Shu Ming could easily pass the ball accurately; the goalkeeper was brave enough but had no positional skill, and the other two, they could learn while Little Wang slept. We never went to the big pitch to train unless we had a game against another cellblock, keeping our training on the basketball court.

It cut the time wasted running for miss-kicked balls.

I showed them passes using different parts of the foot. I had them shoot the ball at the goal, which was 4ft by 4ft, it was a good period, bonding well as a new team.

We played four a side for hours and we were getting fit, and I must say we were the only unit in the prison able to train as much. The Chinese in other units had to work. They would get the weekend off to train, so their games were set up for then.

It was a fair system at the big pitch; one goal, off you went, and on came the next team.

One afternoon our unit was taken over, to the big field.

In our third game, a person flew up the wing, scored and knocked us out. It was my reckoning anyways; these people should get the use of the pitch at the weekend as they worked all week. The following week we stayed at our unit basketball court, honing our skills. It was considered a big occasion by the Chinese authorities, setting up competitive sports as part of prison reform.

Bull and I were the two foreign imports representing Qing Pu modern and civilised prison in the upcoming spring festival football competition. Before the games began, we had the flag-flying ceremony and singing of the national anthem. Then there were the speeches from several ranks, and finally, the units all had a flag bearer and a group of supporters with matching outfits, marching around the track with inmates shouting all sorts. When the games began, we got off to a good start, winning our first match, but eventually, we got beaten in the semi-final. I was pleased enough with that outcome. It was not bad for our mixed team from the international foreign unit. I had to give Bull credit for taking a person down hard in that final game; this person was seriously fouling our Chinese players. Stanley, especially, was getting it. Bull had done a slide tackle on the bad guy from about twenty yards run with 80kg of power. Off went the heel hacker, not with a red card, but on a blue plastic stretcher. It was a victory at least over one bully.

The sports had come to a close, and a meeting to give out medals and cups began. We picked up a third-place flag, also 30 merit points to be shared by those who competed. Cranky had gotten a second place at the basketball throw for the whole prison, and for that, our unit was awarded 30 more points and a cup. It might have been this appreciation from the authorities of Crank's sporting skill that may have turned him from being in their face to being on their side. He was a man in transition, it seemed to me.

.oOo.

I was doing fine in this new jail, having already been awarded a certificate of merit. Then, one day, Parviz somehow got under my skin, so I head-butted him, knocking out his front tooth. There was an uprising from the Pakistanis. I was taken upstairs to the second floor, locked into cell five, and told to write an account of what had happened. After writing it down, I handed it over to JK for translation. My cell was opened after a couple of hours, and I was escorted to the office by Captain Hua. They're stood Captain Ma from the Criminal Affairs Department, alongside Captain Wang.

JK told me that I had not acknowledged the wrongdoing I had committed. He said that I had only given my reason for what had been done, which was unacceptable.

I asked JK what the guards expected me to write, he explained that I needed to take responsibility for my actions and I should write that I accept this shortcoming.

I was taken away, and locked up again, and a meeting was arranged for the following day. Stanley brought up my food and sat outside my cell door; that is the system in China if you were in the punishment cell, someone had to have you in view twenty-four hours. The night shift started at 9 pm and finished at 6 am. I lay on my bed and thought about what lay ahead tomorrow, having to acknowledge my lack of self-control. It was always someone else's fault, or so I told myself.

The night was uncomfortable, and my sleep was disturbed by the sound of passing footsteps on the concrete floor. The following afternoon, the door was unlocked, and I stood in front of everyone, reading aloud my self-criticism. I was punished by losing the certificate of merit that I had worked so hard to get, thinking that the award would bring me a reduction in my sentence next year.

I was back to square one. Everyone else at the meeting also had to write a report on what they thought of my behaviour. The diary given to us all upon arrival was for that purpose. It was during this period that many people turned against me. It was a united Muslim front because of Parviz; they stopped talking with me, except for Butt. Captain Wang gave him the job as a peacemaker and go-between.

I was investigated by the Criminal Affairs Department and told that criminal charges might well proceed. Then, it was settled that I could pay for the replacement tooth I had knocked out, which was paid immediately. Things had more or less gone back to normal after a week. However, the biggest bombshell landed from someone in my ranks.

.oOo.

The guard's desk in the office was not yet connected with a phone – it was being used more as a watch desk, as you could see up the full corridor. I was in the office with JK discussing my letters issue, when the captain was called by Hanley to go upstairs to receive a phone call, and JK followed him.

I saw Cranky's writing paper on the desk, and seeing my name, picked it up, and pocketed it. This is a copy, word for word, of the original letter that I smuggled out and kept all those years.

Attacks by 13499 Lauchlan Campbell.

Shanghai detention cells from August 1991 to June 1992 attacked and injured 5 to 7 Chinese prisoners.

June 13th, 1992, smashes 13498 in the nose with head and attempts to poke Bulls eyes out with chopsticks witnessed by Cranky, Hans Vern, and officer 31-01-427

Oct 15th, 1992, attacks 13497 twice in one day 13497 swollen knee, can't walk lay in the cell. Also attacked Grad the same day and cut his lip. Witnessed by Cranky, Bull, Hans, Vern, and Grad. 13497 had to be assisted to the hospital for three months.

Nov 16th, 1992, smashes 13497 in head cuts his cheek witnessed by same people above. 13497 has a scar on his cheek from this attack.

Feb 1993, he smashes out the window in the hospital while in a rage many witnesses.

Dec 1993 breaks 8th brigade Chinese prisoner's nose in attack. Mr Ni goes to the hospital witnessed by Bull, Grad, told by 31-01044 officers Jin that if he ever attacks anyone else, he will be given a further sentence.

1993-1994 Spits on Officer Zhu 31-01428 and Chinese inmates 7000 and 555

Oct 12th, 1994, pulls 13497 down and kicks him in face with right foot 13497 nose broken. Witnessed by Bull and Dom.

Oct 22nd, 1994, attacks Grad breaks open lip witnessed by Vern and Bull.

Feb 12th, 1995, Pushes Chinese prisoner.

Feb 18th, 1995, threatens to burn down Dom's friend's house in London gets address from translation brigade or stole it.

Jan 27th, 1997, tries to attack 13498 but stopped by Chinese prisoner Mr Liu.

Mar 25th, 1997, attacks Parvaz Akhtar. Many witnesses

When I finished reading, my heart rate jumped. My anger was going out of control. Taking a long deep breath, I thought that bastard Cranky didn't have a clue of the *why* in what he had written. My defences were up.

I did have a few fights, but how someone would never end up in a fight in this environment was beyond me. Choking with anger, and thinking the fucking wimp probably sat in corner bullied at school.

Had Cranky forgotten about the risk that was taken to get his letters out? I was disappointed to the extreme finding out that someone was taking note of me and passing it onto the guards. Looking closely at this report and justifying my actions thinking he failed to mention that the Dec 1993 attack was one that everyone was, let us say, not unhappy to hear about. The Chinese inmate known to us as *Doctor Death* was an informer and distributed us with the food rations we could order. It was clear from day one that we foreigners were at the bottom of his priority rung. If we were receiving fruit, it would be the bruised ones.

We all disliked him, and it was a regular topic of complaint between us but it was only me that took action and his shenanigans stopped after that. I was locked up but then that is the price you pay for taking the law into your own hands. The way Cranky had written it you would think I just walked up and assaulted people, and if that were true then I should have been kept in a lunatic asylum. Then in retrospect I had been sent to the hospital psychological unit at the old jail. Fuck me I thought maybe I am going crazy.

I know how damaging it can be to have people dirty your name through loose words and rumours. I had read articles in the British newspapers about my brother he was dubbed the *Ice Cream Monster*. What a tag to be put onto you. It sounded like he had been messing around stealing children's pocket money. My brother had fought heart and soul to clear his name setting up a campaign from within the prison and my brother's co-accused was a friend of the family from childhood called Joe Steel. This young man had outsmarted the police and prison authorities by escaping from them on more than one occasion. He did this and then arranged his own re-arrest thus bringing much needed publicity to their case. These were the kind of prisoners I identified myself with - not informers and wimps.

Having proof about Cranky all handwritten I knew I had uncovered an informer. I will be watching sly old Cranky from now on. It added weight to my already stir-crazy and weary head.

.oOo.

I was standing, looking onto the basketball court, wishing away the time to get out for a game of football. It was late spring, getting warm, and the guards would rather be outside. It was our arranged exercise time in the afternoon, from 4 to 5 pm.

Looking from the window, I saw a large man walking towards our unit, wearing an Arab headdress. He was in front of a little Chinese guy and a slightly overweight Asian prisoner; they were carrying luggage. I had heard a rumour that two new people were coming, but not three.

Abdul Lativ, wearing the headdress, was from Iran. The little guy, an American Chinese, was named Bo, and the third, Mir, was a Kashmiri Indian.

Lativ was a big man, 6ft 4 inches tall and powerfully built, looking around forties in age with a long, unkempt beard. Seeing the weariness on his face, I saw strength in his walk and confidence in his attire. Abdul Lativ, a jewel thief, posed a striking figure in his Arab garb.

Bo, with a full-on American accent, though born in China, was educated in the USA. His crime was related to industrial waste.

Mir had a Pakistani passport but claimed he was British, and was born in Kenya, but went by Kashmiri Indian; his crime was fraud. He would be fun to listen to, and he had already served over seven years at the old jail. Why he hadn't come along with us was a mystery often discussed. I knew that another cell would have to open to house them, and an opportunity might arise for me to have a cell move. Bull and I didn't see eye-to-eye at times; we had a couple of small incidents, mostly mouthing, and I had been trying to get a cell upstairs.

A meeting was called after about one hour of the new men's arrival. It was a short induction, only to allocate their cells. Lativ was put into cell five, along with Butt, Syed, and Parviz. Bo was housed with the two Germans, and Mir was put into cell three with Cranky, Mustafa, and Khalid. As you do when new people arrive, you get to hear their story.

Bo was charged with bringing garbage into China, something along those lines, either recycling, dumping, or some seafaring act of piracy. Bo claimed he was innocent; he seemed to be well enough educated and well-connected in the USA.

Lativ, on the other hand, said he was guilty. He was a jewel thief, cut from the cloth of Ali Baba, and I immediately took to him; he was a scammer.

Mir was a man who could not stop lying. He told me he was a multi-millionaire, had made fortunes selling anything and everything from carpets to nuclear warheads. He had fought against the Russians in Afghanistan, trained Muslims in bombing raids in the Philippines, and married a Taiwanese general's daughter. That was just for starters. Mir was fascinating to listen to; you just had to remind yourself it was just good stories like the ones you would hear from any palm reader on the many streets of India.

.oOo.

At the Muslim fasting period of Ramadan, and the issue of prayer and food hadn't quite been resolved. Bull had been practicing alone on the veranda; it was April 18th, and the fasting was over. Lativ called a meeting in his cell for a group prayer. The group got busted, causing quite a stir.

Khalid was enraged, shouting in the corridor that he would kill for his religion. The following day, we had another top brass meeting; it was decided the guard running our unit wasn't suitable or able enough. Lativ had only been in the jail for weeks when he decided to go on a protest, raising the issues of religious freedom. He was saying he was going to hunger strike if his religious rights were denied.

Advising him to use the words 'fasting for justice,' words I had read written by my brother's campaign. Lativ wasn't happy regarding the way his religion was being disrespected. It took him only one week to work out what the Pakistanis didn't want to acknowledge: that they were being treated as lesser citizens than we westerners.

The Chinese inmates looked down upon them, and some guards were open with their disrespect, recalling one occasion when a young guard from another unit, doing a shift at our block, said the Pakistanis smelled like sheep.

Cranky, Bull, and Hans openly talked about the body odour issue as well. It is true enough that body odour differs from country to country; the truth was, in all honesty, Syed, in particular, really gave off a bad smell.

All the Pakistani inmates used scented lotions. The cultural differences were beginning to cause conflict in more ways than one. It was stated in the 10 don'ts that you weren't allowed to gather in groups. You couldn't have photos of your family, idols, or any ornamentation on your walls. Abdul Lativ had a prayer rug and a wall hanging of Mecca. In the practice of Islam, visiting Mecca is every Muslim's wish, and when you do, fellow Muslims acknowledge you as Hajji. Abdul Lativ had been to the Medina. It is a mark of respect given from other Muslims if you are Hajji.

If the Christians were allowed to celebrate according to the Bible, then he, as a Muslim, would celebrate according to the Holy Koran. Abdul Lativ refused to take the wall hanging down and made his mark that day; he never ate until they fully understood his religion was more important to him than their prison reform.

The Chinese prison authorities never forgot nor forgave him for that. Lativ wasn't taking any shit from the communists. He would say to me, in all sincerity, "Campbell, how can this country not believe in God?"

From that protest by Lativ, all Muslim holidays were put onto the Qing Pu Prison calendar. After all, it was me who enlightened Lativ to the Warden's opening statement when we first arrived, *The Modern and Civilised Prison* speech. I would use that phrase time and time again, putting their words back to them and questioning the civilised prison's actions.

The Muslims would get equal treatment regarding religious beliefs; the Iranian consulate also supported their countryman's right to pray and brought him the Holy Koran during a visit. There was beginning to be a split in the Muslim camp; it was Abdul Lativ who was running the show, one Shiite as opposed to six Sunni, but only one Hajji. It was the *start of the Chinese prison Holy Jihad*; that's what Cranky would say whenever any conflict arose between them, and that was often.

.oOo.

Captain Ma from the Criminal Affairs Department visited our unit and held a short meeting. He made the statement that if any inmate could stay out of trouble for one year, they would be eligible for a reduction of sentence. This was his carrot before saying he had organised an outdoor work detail. It was retold to us how good labour is for our reform.
No one objected to that, plus the weather was really nice in May.

We were pleased when we were gathered and told we would go outside to clean up the football ground. This was observation time; we would be under scrutiny by the surrounding cameras as well as guards. The Chinese authorities used every angle they wanted to experiment with in their desire to know foreign prisoners' reactions to different situations. The sun was up, and as a group, we paced around, uprooting weeds. It didn't take long to see who formed groups and who was picking the weeds and who was taking in the sun. Knowing the system well enough, I saw this as an attitude observation, so I kept my head down most of the time. In the surrounding area of the football ground, there were another three large cell blocks, plus another under construction, and there was a smaller building that would become more familiar in the not-too-distant future. There was a massive factory building, about the size of an aircraft hangar, behind the newly constructed cell block. As we walked back to our unit after an hour or so of weeding, I felt better than it had in a long time, something about doing useful things.

.oOo.

Bull and Lativ had struck up a good friendship, as far as jail pals go. Bull still had some interest in Islam and was learning to speak Turkish. Lativ was qualified to assist in both, plus they enjoyed playing chess together.

Syed was spitting out venomous words that Bull wasn't circumcised, he was a Christian, and other verbal insults behind Bull's back. When Bull did hear rumours, they didn't seem to get under his skin.

Then, one day, Bull had the duty to clean the toilet area; it was still a rota system. He completed his job and went on with his studies.

Stanley came to Bull's cell and told him the guard wanted to see him. It was moments later that pandemonium broke out; Syed barged into the office and accused Bull of not cleaning the toilet, then kicked him. He was shouting all sorts of obscenities when two guards dragged him upstairs and locked him down. The place had an unsettled atmosphere; you could cut the air; it was thick with pent-up emotion.

Syed remained in confinement for two days, then there was a meeting called. It was the usual expected self-criticism, read from his handwritten report. However, instead Syed was cursing the guards' names. That resulted in him being locked down in what they termed *temporary confinement*, which lasted from June until September 1997 - three months! So much for the prison law on the maximum lock-up time being 30 days.

We were assured that he wasn't locked up; he was in *temporary confinement* upstairs on the top floor. This was true, but he still didn't get out to eat or exercise at all with us. There was a severe price to pay when you cursed the system.

.oOo.

One morning after breakfast, we were all gathered and taken to the hospital for a full medical check-up. The hospital had one male doctor and four female nurses, all of whom turned out to be compassionate, considerate people. I struck up a little conversation with my limited Chinese, flirting with the nurses who were still in police uniform. My Mandarin smile was full on.

The hospital building had just been recently painted, and there was still the lingering smell of it in the air. There was a bus stationed outside with X-ray equipment set up. It looked like we would be thoroughly checked up. The blood test we got gave multiple results, and nobody seemed to have any immediate medical problems. I had already had this check-up done once before at the old jail in 1992 when I first started my prison sentence over five years ago. Looking around me, all the foreign prisoners seemed overfed, and the Chinese ones underfed. Chinese inmates who worked at the factories would be hanging around the hospital, looking for any medical excuse to get them some relief from work. It was also difficult to believe that a prison holding three thousand plus inmates didn't have a dentist or dental equipment. A full medical and dental facility was needed.

It was a few weeks after those medical tests that Stanley came to me one day and said he was returning to the old jail with Cranky. He told me Cranky had an incurable disease.

Asking Stanley what it was, he told me it was Hepatitis C. The rumours soon spread that he was dying. I was told that his liver needed replacing and he would be sent home for this purpose.

Cranky complained to his consul and said he was taking out a lawsuit against the Chinese government for catching the virus while in prison. Good for him, though I would have thought he knew that wasn't even an option. However, it probably made him feel good expressing his rights. As it transpired Cranky went back to the old prison because there were better medical facilities but returned after one week.

I wanted to return home, with my health, though sometimes I had thoughts of trading my health for freedom. Coming close once in desperation over mail, with the thought of killing myself, but I struggled with my demons and continued doing my time. It would be the longest time served yet among foreign inmates in China, but I didn't know that then.

.oOo.

We got a new unit leader, Captain Qian, who was replacing the old Captain Wang. We all sat and listened to the reform education, as the Chinese prison system termed it. Captain Qian was a small man but walked with his chest out. After introducing himself, he then proceeded to introduce the "Five Goods". I had been there half a year, and every bloody month they came up with a new system on how to cause conflict about merit points. This was deliberate; this was mind games. The Shanghai Qing Pu civilized jail was experimental; they did not have a clue on how to set up a system for us.

It would have been easier if we were all treated the same, after all, we were in China. The foreigners had been told at more than one meeting that we are treated better than Chinese inmates because we do not have to work, and we have a higher budget for food rations. I was losing faith fast. The Five bloody goods, right enough.

- Acknowledge your guilt in a monthly report.
- Follow the Cadres education.
- Be active in self-study.
- Take part in the unit upkeep.
- Report any wrong doings by others.

I was spending my days designing Anti- Drug posters. This was for the upcoming UN Anti – drug day June 26th. It would be the second display of drug education we had one at the old jail when we all drew on blackboards drawing anti-drug slogans with colour chalks. It was drummed into us that if you acknowledge and accept our guilt you would be free quicker. I wrote a letter to ask the British consul to contact the Home Office for me regarding drug education which they did, and they sent me drug education information including posters.

Having also contacted an old friend of mine Davy Bryce and asked him to assist me with any ideas on drug rehabilitation. Davy was very helpful and sent me some original drawings done by schoolchildren in Scotland making me so chuffed this would add a special touch to the exhibition. True-life experience coming from a group of ex-drug addicts reformed to becoming a football team called *Calton Athletic Recovery Group (CARG)*. Davy sent me newsletters from *Cannabis to Chaos* it was all good stuff and the most important aspect of CARG was abstention from all drugs no methadone or alcohol. Davy was a hard talker and that is what made it work.

We had a good mutual friend William Burns also with CARG helping me out with good advice. It is not easy to break any addiction but I respected Wullie and Davies views that was simply *help is here but first clean up your act* and prove to yourself you want to quit. Davy always stated CARG would always embrace those who want to make the effort. Therefore, the rule was if you are on drugs don't come.

Being on a mission to prove I wanted to acknowledge my guilt and wanted to be like the lads at Calton Athletic Recovery Group. My brother Tommy sent me a few sketches and a poster about addicts sharing needles. I designed and gave out three anti-drug posters to the British Consul in June1997 these posters were to commemorate the 10th anniversary of the UN Anti-drug day of June 26th.

One was to hand over to the German consulate the other for the USA consulate. The German Consul was a Miss Fevers. This kind person sent me a photo of it hanging in the consulate office and a card of thanks. I was awarded the five *goods* for this one action of sending anti- drug posters with a clear message.

The head Prison Warden Yu Zhong Ming came to personally praise me for my good contribution to society. I took this opportunity there and then to ask him if I could put on an anti-drug exhibition there at the prison. Chinese officials are never quick to agree to anything so his reply was he would think it over.

JK later explained to me when we were alone that he had told the Warden about my already designed posters hanging on the walls at three consul offices in Shanghai. JK told me the Wardens reply was he knew JK made it sound special saying that the three foreign consulates supported the UN Anti- drug project and further added that he would help me and it would be a worthy project.

We sat and discussed ideas and decided it should be done in four parts. It was only one week later being called into the office and told to write a plan and submit it to the Warden. We sat and wrote out my plan going to use acrylic paints making the exhibition into four parts ten posters covering each topic. 40 posters in total.

JK knew all that was needed so I left it with him to make the list. Davy also enclosed the book Pain of Confinement written by a reformed prisoner from the city of Glasgow called Jimmy Boyle and it was signed. I soaked that book up and underlined parts that related with my feelings and although never meeting the author said," Thanks Jimmy."

July 1997

    The foreign inmates, especially the British, were told to write our opinions on the issue of Hong Kong returning to the motherland, the People's Republic of China. A serious assessment was wanted, and I had not realized how upset the Chinese people felt about their land being governed by Britain. Stanley had explained to me how China wanted Taiwan and Macao returned to the mainland as well.

    I never paid much attention to any of the political scenarios, other than harbouring the fantasy of being set free by amnesty on this historical occasion. The Chinese made a lot of fuss about it. It was every day in the newspaper: first, it was the history of British colonies throughout the globe, then we had the opium war rerun, then the tales of Jesuit priests drinking the menstrual blood of young Chinese country girl virgins.

    The television was also pumping out the same anti-British propaganda. On the day of the handover by Prince Charles, it was televised, and I'm sure nearly the whole country watched it. The whole jail did; it was a historical event, and the Chinese inmates were as patriotic as any others about their country. I was painting new anti-drug posters that day when the guard, Captain Qian, walked into my cell. He was a small man in height, but that did not daunt his stature; he was confident. Wang had been dismissed as unqualified to run the foreign unit, and I sensed this new guard had something to prove. I continued painting, and he started to ask me why I wasn't watching the TV as the others were. I didn't reply, and he called JK and asked him to ask me why.

    Explaining to JK that I was not interested in Chinese political affairs, saying my understanding of the Chinese language was not good enough to understand Chinese politics or decorum from a television announcer. I could see that this guard was not happy that one of his collectives was going astray. They always wanted us to do things as a group that we had no interest in, such as to study as a group. The incident was left at that, and I continued to paint until the afternoon.

The TV never got turned off that day; it was rerun, same topic, the handing over of Hong Kong to its rightful owner.

It was lunchtime and the food hadn't arrived yet; knowing the show was still on as everyone still sat there. Then I was taken by surprise when big Khalid walked into my cell and started making a loud baaing sound like a sheep. The guard came into the cell with Stanley and asked me what was going on. I told him nothing was going on.

He then asked Khalid why he was not watching the TV. Khalid actually replied, baaing like a sheep.

I started to laugh, and this brought others to the cell to have a look; it was getting out of hand, and the guard told everyone to return to their seats.

It turned out a few others had decided not to watch the remains of the handing-over ceremony; it was the first hint of collective rebellion. When you are conditioned to eat, sleep, and defecate at set times, it is taken for granted that food would be on time.

Prisons in Shanghai have a bell system; when that bell rang, you automatically knew it was time to get up out of bed, go outside for exercise, or eating time. It was an eye-opener when the bell never rang that afternoon; then the collective, as we were known, also got hungry together. It was when the food didn't arrive on time that the others got up and went to their cells, not the Chinese inmates, of course; they sat and watched obediently.

The following day, a meeting was to be held.

JK had told me that the highest authority at Qing Pu Jail was going to attend. I asked JK if he had any idea what it would be about; he said he didn't.

The following day was as JK had said; that morning we were visited by an entourage of about twenty guards of all sizes, shapes, and ranks. As we sat through five different officials having their say on how great China was, they told us that Hong Kong was returned to the mainland. I didn't give a monkey's fuck about British-Chinese relations, having had my Opium War lectures at the old jail; cannabis was never mentioned as killing the masses. I knew the heroin trade was rife worldwide and knew where to get it in the Golden Triangle or Golden Crescent. Having trekked those areas right into the remote regions of poppy land, the devil's hold in me wasn't strong enough to beat out my vision of good judgement. Heroin trafficking was a no-no on my card; I wouldn't do it ever, although I did carry it across borders when using it.

During the meeting, I wanted to shout, "I had nothing to do with the fucking opium war!" That's what I wanted to shout, but instead, I wrote this report the following day.

> *Respected Cadre.*
> *I refer to the televised program regarding the handing over of Hong Kong back to the People's Republic of China. I have been criticised for not watching this ceremony. It was a program, which I had no interest in and so continued to work on something deemed more worthy of my time. I don't like to always follow the collective as we are known through Chinese prison reform. I don't accept also this criticism at the whim of the captain in charge of me and can understand the patriotic feelings of the Chinese people watching Prince Charles go through the decorum of returning Hong Kong to China. I have no interest in the entire trumpet blowing, flag raising, marching with guns scenario. I was provoked by Captain Qian and retaliated verbally. I have been in Chinese jail now over six years. I have acknowledged my guilt by the Chinese prison law. It is my opinion this Captain's weapon is a misuse of power knowing he can control the reports that put you forward for remission of sentence. That would be in breach of Warden Yu Zhong Ming statement of being a Modern civilised prison.*
> *L. Campbell*

It wasn't long after handing in that report was called to the office and was told to sit on a stool which stood eight inches from the floor. This was a domination game that I declined to take part in, and instead, I stood.

JK was doing the interpretation for me and it unfolded that I had *gone against the government* – the use of those words always got my hackles up.

It unfolded that I had shown no respect by not watching the Hong Kong handover ceremony and was told that Britain caused a lot of misery to the Chinese people.

I replied saying, "I am Scottish."

That was a mistake. This guard knew his history and went on to explain how it was the Scots in the forefront of the Imperial Palace raid. Then he went on a bit about the Boxer rebellion and finally another Opium War spiel.

Sometimes I just felt dejected listening to this history at that moment my head was in overload and didn't want any more information about the past but had to listen.

After he finished speaking JK told me to return to my cell and think where I had gone wrong - then write a report about my findings. I did return to my cell but just continued painting my anti-drug posters. The exhibition was scheduled for the next year but it was something I had developed a passion for.

.oOo.

Parviz was the first foreign inmate to leave us since arriving at this new jail. It was always a pleasure to see someone go; we had settled our past confrontation, and we got along quite well.

Hearing all the requests coming from the Pakistani guys to visit their families and to send goods and money, it was clear their status was at stake. It depended on how much they could afford to spend each month at the jail canteen. Only Butt and Parviz had family who sent them cash. Syed had got out of his temporary confinement and had a gold chain, which he asked the prison authorities to sell for him at the current gold value. I was surprised when they did, and that money put Syed flush for at least one year.

Mustafa and Khalid didn't have any money. Mustafa's Chinese wife had filed for divorce; his family at home depended upon him to send them money back, and that wouldn't be happening from here. Parviz was leaving; those two guys would miss out on help with monthly rations, and they knew nothing would be forthcoming from Syed.

.oOo.

Another talking point, one that had been ongoing for years, was that the German consulate visited the prison every month, having done so since their three citizens were arrested. There was one German woman who had got 6 years for possession of cannabis resin. I only saw her on a couple of occasions as she passed below me, going to her unit. She was released after 3 years from the 9th brigade at the old jail's women's cellblock. The British and the American consulates visited on average five times per year. The Pakistani consulate hadn't yet visited their men at all. The regulations stated we could have two visits each month. That was fine if you were a local. It was one-upmanship for the Germans for years.

Bull had never liked the fact that Hans, especially, could have extra food from his consulate visits. The German consulate would bring smoked sausages, cheeses, mustard, good fresh baked bread, and so on. Bull had never forgiven Hans for informing on him. I didn't need special foods or such but could write and request the consul to purchase things for me. Bull's lady had been detained for quite a long time due to his arrest, all down to Hans's loose tongue.

That incident with my son was still a sore point with the authorities. It was one of those stories; news travels fast inside jail, then it moves onto other jails with prisoner transfers. My son, Lochy, and I were deeply rooted in Shanghai prison folklore by now; the story, like any other, grew as years went by. The truth of the matter was we got one over them, at a cost. I was still paying that cost by doing my time.

Bull had been arranging over the years for his lady's visa for the UK and was also getting monthly visits, and sometimes two, from her. His lady was free from detention, living and working in Shanghai. I respected her for what she did, finding a job, and being by her man. Bull said she was perfection; she dances. Bull was a more contented man during this period and I couldn't envision myself receiving any more visits, especially when my son had gotten arrested during his last visit to see me in China.

It was expected I would be having a Consul visit soon, and I had ordered paints and brushes through them. The consul visits were an uncomfortable time for me, feeling mostly totally detached. I did talk a lot, though, and it was a means of expressing my thoughts and getting feedback from people outside of jail, and I was thankful that they brought my family letters, parcels, plus art materials.

The vice-consul usually did a two-year stint then moved on; this was the third consul attaché to visit me since 1991. Jackie Barlow was a gentle, caring lady; she always brought me a small gift. She could see in my eyes the reflection of the confusion I felt; her warmth and compassion made me feel like someone out there cared.

.oOo.

The mail problem issue was ongoing; it never worked out as it should have according to the prison law. Lativ was in a rage at his incoming mail taking so long to get to him, and it was explained to him that it took time to get a translator for Persian.

"What do you need a translator for?" Lativ went on, "Do you think my wife is sending me escape plans? I am not in here for killing anyone, why do you make me and my family suffer? I can pay for a translator from the Iranian Embassy," he continued. We all knew he was correct in his views but also knew it would only delay the process of receiving his mail.

It was payback time for standing up for his religious rights during Ramadan and for refusing to shave off his beard since his arrival.

The other Muslims were clean-shaven, as they were told they couldn't get the 'five goods' awards if they had a beard.

.oOo.

The arrival of a new guy caused a stir; he was seemingly caught in possession of 10kg of heroin. This happened whilst taking North Korean diplomats to the airport. This was undoubtedly a death sentence offence. It was something that left a smell. After being in jail so long, I tried avoiding new guys' stories these days, but to no avail. Mr Ho was his name, and although born in China, his parents were North Korean by birth. It seemed Mr Ho had the job of driving a taxi. One day, he was driving North Korean diplomats from their office towards the airport. That was when the taxi was pulled over and searched, resulting in them finding of 10kg of heroin. As the other passengers were diplomats, they were released under whatever government agreements. Mr Ho, on the other hand, got a ten-year prison sentence. After hearing many stories over the years of guys claiming their innocence, I didn't pay much attention to his tale, knowing of many stories involving diplomats and their immunity to arrest. Wishing I had one diplomatic passport on hand myself. It was only another fantasy for a money-making scam in my mind.

Mr Ho needed bed space; there was a meeting held, and it was cell change time again. All the Chinese inmates, except JK, moved to the floor above. I moved into cell one with two single beds. It was a good set-up for me, and I had space to work on my anti-drug posters. JK was my new cellmate.

.oOo.

The air was full of tension; this was due to some political whisperings among the Muslim inmates. Cranky was pacing the corridor the night before after hearing news reports that some American plane had been shot down in Iraq. Bull and Cranky sat listening to the news again for further details when Syed let out a mighty laugh, saying something derogatory about America. I was standing in the background watching. Neither Cranky nor Bull responded, they were too long in the tooth for that petty provocation.

Bull got off his stool to return to his cell when Syed half-blocked him. Bull swivelled, leaving Syed leaning on the air. Seeing Bull approach Stanley and tell him about Syed and that he had better be removed or there was going to be trouble. That afternoon, we had a supply of our canteen apples arrive; the procedure was one cell went down at a time to collect. Cranky was on his way in the corridor when Syed ran out of his cell and swung a mop handle stick at him. A few other inmates were out, waiting to pick up their fruit, but Mir was the first to react and deflected the blow. It was only seconds before things were under control again; the only problem was getting Syed to shut up, which he didn't, and starting calling obscenities about America.

It didn't matter what happened in jail in China; the guards must have a report about it.

It is the duty of the Chinese inmates to gather information, that would be JK or Stanley. Bull had openly stated to the guard that Syed should be removed and also stated he would put it in writing. The foreigners all had to submit a report, giving our views on Syed's attempted assault on Cranky.

The Chinese are clever at gathering information, looking for some alternative motive in someone's report for this attack. The guard on duty didn't punish Syed that day, as there was no actual wound.

The guard had told Bull, that after a full investigation, Syed would be dealt with. Lativ didn't get along well with Cranky, but he did get along with Bull. It was a typical jail tug of war, pulling and playing mind games: are you with him or me?

I was out of the equation, that's what mattered to me.

The following morning at exercise time, Bull was running around the grounds one way as Hans ran the other. Those two hadn't spoken a word since day one. Sitting by the side of the exercise yard with Vern, we watched and chatted for a while. Hans approached after about fifteen minutes, puffing and sweating profusely. I got up and walked around, seeing Bull cooling down with a slow walk.

Then just as he was about to sit down, Syed and Khalid ran towards him, seeing Syed throwing punches and hitting Bull's arm, big Khalid had a go. Bull gave Khalid a cracking uppercut while dodging blows from Syed. I got butterflies in my stomach and wanted to join in but held back. Bull was sorting the two out himself. It was when Mustafa joined in, that I flew into the fight as well, giving Syed a right solid smack in the mouth. He then took off, grabbed a stick, and attacked Cranky.

Going after him and I started shouting, "You fucking bam, you want to use a weapon?" I grabbed him by the hair and pulled him lower, kicking him in the mouth; he never took off or got back up again.

Bull was dragged off Khalid by the Chinese inmates and was taken upstairs. I was approached by the young Guard Wu when Kashmiri Mir ran over and started punching the other Pakistani, Butt, shouting, "You are a traitor!" meaning he was on good terms with Bull.

I sidestepped the guard and walked over, landing a knockout punch on Mir; he went down. I was escorted to my cell; that was the first time I stood my ground to support Bull, but as to Cranky, I was still holding his report about me against him. We all returned to our cells and were told to write about what happened, including those not involved. It was one incident that the authorities were appalled about. It was akin to a riot in their minds.

One by one, we had to be interviewed by the Criminal Affairs Cadres. Being asked if I took part in the fight or not, I said yes and couldn't deny it but explained that I only went to Bull and Crank's defence. Using a common law point that I read from a book my brother had sent me, explaining like this: "If a little girl was drowning in a pool and a sign said to keep off the grass, would you let the girl drown or break the law by going onto the grass?"

My explanation didn't go down too well. The next line of inquiry was who started the trouble. That was easy to answer, and I told them Syed had openly attacked Bull. What about the guards, could they have prevented the incident?

I saw JK moving his eyes, trying to tell me to say no, I sometimes would answer questions in Chinese, especially when suspicious, thinking the interpreter wasn't saying what I wanted. I answered, "Yes, they could have prevented it after the attempted attack on Cranky with the brush pole."

It turned out that the following day we had another meeting, and all the brass turned up. We, the foreign prisoners, had behaved in an uncivilised manner; well, some of us had. Those of us involved got demerit points; that meant it was back to square one again for me with my five *no-fucking-goods taken from me*.

Bull was expecting to get a reduction in sentence or even be released by the end of the year; it looked like that wouldn't be happening. Syed was given temporary confinement again; we didn't know for how long.

Vern came into my cell later that evening and asked me, "Campbell, why did you get involved?"

While Iyou was down in the yard fighting, Cranky was upstairs, looking down, but I had the noble idea of thinking that the odds were against Bull and that gave me the right to take part to even things out. I was doing the right thing, as far as I was concerned. I still had a lot to learn.

December 1997

It turned cold again and everyone was wrapped up in thick woollen sweaters a heavy coat and a head cap made from the sleeves of an old sweater. The morning exercise yard was half empty as many guys preferred to stay inside rather than walk outside in that biting wind. It was after breakfast that we were called to the ground floor area assuming another meeting no doubt about reform. xxx

Bull and I had decorated that area for the upcoming Xmas festivities. We were all seated the Prison Administration Bureau boss came into the room we all stood and said, "Duisan Hao" then sat again.

It unfolded that Hans and Vern had gotten another reduction from their sentence and were told to pack their bags as they had a flight home that night. It was always like that with the Chinese authorities they never gave you any hint of coming events regarding remission. I watched Vern and Hans walking over the exercise yard carrying their luggage out from jail for the last time.

It is nice to see the back of folk especially when going out of jail.

Bull was disappointed, he felt he should have gone with them. It wasn't just felt by Bull. My complaint comparing my crime to that of the Germans and Bull. Hans and Vern had got bust for smuggling. Bull for supplying and possession. It was one of the main reform lectures never to compare your crime or sentence with others - easily said, hard to live with. I had given Vern and Hans's one oil painting apiece before they left one was of the prison band 'The Reformers' and the other a reform meeting, they were my first efforts at depicting our lives in a Chinese jail. And I wished them well as they departed.

.oOo.

I got a letter in bold type British Consul General Shanghai and in brackets 'hand delivery'.

Shanghai British Consul General
15th December 1997

Dear Lauchlan,

Many thanks for your Christmas and New Year wishes and for the card you sent. I have shown it to all my UK colleagues and will make sure that Lisa sees it too when she returns to work.

As you know, I am more than happy to support your excellent anti-drugs campaign. I have been very impressed with your work to date on it. I wish I were as creative and artistically inclined as you!

It is a bit early to start to drum up support for the exhibition but I will of course do my best a little nearer the time. Meanwhile, I have pencilled 26 June in my diary.

This letter comes by hand of David Oswald, in the absence in London of Sue. (She returns to Shanghai after the holiday period) I would like to have sent him with a bottle of Black Label for you but I am afraid it would be a no-no. I hope you enjoy the gifts we have chosen instead. Thanks for writing, Lauchlan.

Take care Kind regards, Warren.

It was a good feeling reading that letter someone out there was responding and I had the confirmation in my hand the good old British Consulate.

.oOo.

The guards had been issued with new uniforms getting rid of the ugly greenish ones and being replaced by smart navy-blue ones. They also changed the ranking system. It was silver stars and silver bars - now one bar equalled three stars. If you were a recruit you started with one star unless you had a university degree then you started with three stars moving up to one bar after completing your recruitment test. Christmas and the New Year passed that left only Cranky, Bull and me from the Westerners. It made room for another cell change and at last Cranky got to share a cell with Bull. I had been working most days on the anti-drug posters with JK, he was doing all the written Chinese characters for me.

JK had been going on for years at the old jail and telling me about how his brother was going to be his guarantee and get him out. Turning on him one day I spat out, "Your brother's a fucking dog!" Continuing on, "If it was my brother who was outside, he would be prepared to come and do half my time. That's what a fucking brother does!" I was pissed off at his illusion of freedom he had jail time of twenty plus years.

Seeing that I had hurt him, I said I was sorry for trying to take away his only lifeline of hope. I instinctively knew it was all imaginary. JK wasn't going anywhere. He had stopped dying his hair and started to look very unkempt. I had been buying him food since the first month of meeting him in 1992 and we had done a lot together. He was my elder brother, my Chinese guardian in the ways of the system. We got along well most times but I could be often fragile in mind.

1998

It was late May before completing my anti-drug poster work. It was to be exhibited from June 10th to June 26th, 1998, and had designed forty posters all with a message about the evils and perniciousness of drug use and drug trade. I had made the first poster with the UN logo on it plus the British, American, German, Russian, Belgium and Chinese flags on it and named my exhibition UN against drugs. The Chinese government were also running a campaign for the upcoming UN anti-drug day June the 26th spearheaded by Jiang Zemin the great leader of the people.

It was titled *Cherish Life, Refuse Drugs*. It was suggested that we use the government slogan, and I went along with that.

JK and I were taken over to the visiting area where the posters were set up for a preview before the exhibition. The prison film crew were there, as was the Warden and several other high-ranking officials. Warden Yu Zhong Ming told JK, I could be given a Li Gong award. That meant a direct reduction in my sentence.

In China, actively reforming criminals are given certificates of merit throughout the year, and if you accumulate two, you get a recommendation for reduction. I didn't have any at this time, after losing them through fighting. This was different, to be given a reduction for my contribution to society as promulgated in the prison law, article 58 on rewards and punishment. I had heard of guys getting a reduction for some invention or for reporting culprits of a past unsolved crime; this surely was one Chinese puzzle of reform.

I had received a letter with newspaper clippings showing my brother's co-accused, Joe Steel of the 'Free the Glasgow Two' campaign, in a crucifix posture, super-glued to Buckingham Palace gates. I was inspired to paint this image; it was a masterstroke on Joe's behalf. What better way to bring light to their case than super-gluing yourself to Her Majesty's front gate at Buckingham Palace? Well, done, Joe. I took my hat off to you that day.

It was June 2nd, 1998, and I had a consul visit, so I handed in two oil paintings to the guard to be handed out to the consul. I had done one of my brother TC Campbell, sitting in a lotus position, holding a Bible with his legs in shackles. The other was Joe Steel glued to the Buckingham Palace gate. Being called into the office before the visit, I was asked why the painting had shackles, as I don't have shackles in here. Then, I explained to them about my brother, which they already knew about, and got the newspaper clipping to show them Joe at the gates, thus letting them know it wasn't related to me in China.

The guard wasn't having any of it and told me to return the paintings to my cell.

I made the mistake by answering him in Chinese, saying, "Stick your communist thinking up your ass."

I was heckled away and stuck in the punishment block for fourteen days. I missed my consul visit, and any reduction of sentence that might have been coming was cancelled. I was sick to the back teeth and felt cheated. To rub more salt into my already aching psyche, I missed the opening game of the World Cup, Scotland vs Brazil, played on June 10th, 1998.

It was summer, and sticky heat filled the air. Here I was, lying in a cellblock in solitary confinement, trying to work out what was wrong with my mind. It was just ongoing trouble due to a lack of self-control.

I was stripped and then given a dirty prison uniform to put on, I was told to stand upright. I did this until my legs were getting tired, so I sat on the floor. The guard immediately shouted, "Stand up!"

I initially ignored him, pretending not to understand.

Shouting something else, another guard arrived with the electric cattle prod. I stood up immediately.

Later that day, it was explained to me through Stanley, who was the main translator and interpreter, that I must follow their discipline while here. Stanley sat outside my cell for observation purposes. It was a painful experience, sitting for one hour, then standing for one hour, fifteen hours a day for fourteen days. I still blamed the guard for provoking me; those paintings had nothing to do with the Chinese jail. I had to write several self-criticisms and apologise in front of the group for cursing the Chinese government. Standing there, looking at those tired and weary faces, I wondered how they manage not to lose it at times with this system. The punishment block does work, at least for a while, then you forget, well, some did.

After the meeting, I asked Bull about the consul visit, if there was mail for me; he informed me there was. I asked if they had gone to the exhibition yet. Bull told me the Consul went to view it after the last visit, but the foreigners hadn't been, although he went on to say the Chinese inmates and families could view it at their visit. My head was still in a stir, and I went to the office to ask for my letters and when we could see the exhibition. I was ready to go into a rant of, "Hey, fuckwits, it was me who created this, so demanded to see it." But I bit my tongue this time.

The guard looked at my unshaven, mosquito-bitten face and informed me that it had been arranged for the following day that the foreign inmates viewed it. "Campbell," he said, "you had better shave; some outside visitors will be viewing it also."

It just happened in the blink of an eye that my mood swung from killing these people to thanking them for exhibiting my art. I left the office and went and told Bull, who wasn't overly enthusiastic to hear such news. Then I returned to my cell, feeling elated, grabbed my bathing bag, took a shower, and shaved.

As I left the shower, the Chinese inmate Shu Ming asked me what I was doing taking a shower at that time. Ignoring him, I walked into my cell. He stood at the door and asked if I had got the captain's permission. I was ready to say, "Go fuck yourself," but bit my tongue and said, "Yes."

That was it; he left, knowing he had to do this sort of snooping around and reporting trivial stuff, but it still got my back up at times. The following afternoon, we had a meeting, and Campbell was the hero and the fool of the day. I was praised to the high heavens by the highest authority for my contribution to society. It was stated that two of my posters had been selected for prison education purposes. It felt good. Then came the criticisms, which I won't explain in detail, but all resulted in me being the fool. The Warden finished off, as usual, with an old Chinese idiom, something like, "No use crying over spilt milk."

I was thinking, "It's ok for you; it's not your milk that's spilt." We left the meeting and headed straight to the exhibition. It surprised me at how professionally they had set it up; they had made temporary walls so that the four parts could be viewed as planned, moving from part one to two, three, then four – it was a story I had painted. It was beautiful; every painting was framed, flowers and plants were placed around, and my message was colourful and clear. That was the most satisfying moment in all my time in jail to date; it really was meaningful.

I asked the guard if I could have photos taken with me at the exhibition and also of all the posters, he informed me to ask a higher authority, which I did, and got permission to have a video made of it and photographs taken. All to be given to the British Consul for safekeeping. I felt a bit sceptical about the easiness of my request being granted, but it did, and I got to return to the exhibition alone a week later and did a photo session with the education guard. The negatives were given to the Consul, along with a short video clip of my work.

July 1998

The arrival of two new prisoners from Liberia in July 1998 was a new addition to the already international jailbird collection. Wavi and Eli were both devout Christians and had committed the crime of deception. Liberia was war torn and their story was they had taken $1million from the US safety box office in their country during the civil war and needed a certain chemical to wash the ink-stained money into a usable currency. They showed the interested person a demonstration that they had expertly worked out beforehand. Another part of their story was they had a contact at the American embassy in Beijing or wherever they did a scam and he could get the supposed chemical but at a price. Sometimes they would catch a greedy investor and con them. It worked a treat at times and the more money you give to them to buy the chemical the more you are promised to get back. It was a good con and nobody got hurt.

The authorities moved us again. Cell five was to be the induction cell. This had never been done before and both guys were the first to have this imposed upon them. I went to their cell every evening and sat with them still not fully quenched in my thirst of meeting new and exotic looking people.

Wavi told me his father was a police inspector and his house was attacked. He went on to tell me that he had to take up arms at a young age he was twenty-six and had escaped Liberia, eventually getting to the Ivory coast where he was kept at a refugee camp waiting to be sent to America to link up with his family. It was there he met up with Eli and decided to make their own way to America, so they left the camp and went onto Ghana where they got fake documents and passports. They were both street wise men and Eli spoke French and had gone to college whereas Wavi couldn't read or write (which, for me, threw suspicion on his story of being a police inspector's son.)

.oOo.

By August the weather was hot and getting humid, there was excitement in the Pakistani camp as one of them was going home and could take messages to families and pleas of financial help.

Khalid had got a three-year sentence for fraud and he served every day of it. When Parviz had went home, he kept in touch with Butt sending him the occasional parcel. I couldn't see Khalid doing the same as his three-year was without monthly ration purchases due to his economic status. It had been Butt and Lativ who had been getting him fruits and toiletries from their monthly purchase as there was no limit on how much you could spend on such items. We purchased everything from the prison canteen including our socks, underwear, sports shoes pens paper and stamps. I was neither sad nor glad to see the back of Khalid he was a sort of simpleton and could be dangerous at times.

.oOo.

JK had not been well. He had been staying in bed most of the month of July with me thinking the old codger was just resting due to the excessive heat. He had been taken to the old jail hospital at Tilan Xiao in August and I was shattered when getting the news that he had died there.

I lay on top of my bed thinking about him, saddened that he never got to publish his English teaching book that Grad, Bull, Cranky myself and the two Germans had helped him with at the old jail.

I said a silent farewell and reminisced about all the little scams we had done together. I loved JK and would miss him dearly.

.oOo.

Cranky was for sure an informer and had also read a report written by Bull about me related to an electric organ that Vern had left behind. The organ had lay in the storeroom for months unused when one day Mustafa asked me who it belonged to and told him Vern had left it behind, he asked if he could use it, I said sure why not. It was a couple of days later being called into the office and asked did I give Mustafa the organ and replied yes. I was told that it wasn't my property to give out but replied that it was my property and that Vern had given it to me before he left – I was lying but I also knew they didn't know that.

As it worked out the organ was returned to the storeroom and nobody could use it thanks to Bulls report.

That's how it was at this jail you couldn't trust anyone and I thanked the communist party for instilling the wisdom of silence into me. In short keep your thoughts to yourself.

.oOo.

The arrival of another new guard, Captain Jiang, at the end of September was the third guard change since our arrival here. The foreign unit always had conflict usually trivial and mostly verbal. Besides being in a foreign jail, the cultural mix among the foreigners was often clashing. I couldn't relate sometimes with the cultural difference it was difficult to bridge.

The Muslim inmates were saying they didn't do any work on Fridays.

I offered to do Lativ's share of the building cleaning on Fridays if he could do mine on a Monday - but what of the others. These sorts of issues often came up who gets the hot water first in the morning, which cell should be first in line for canteen and on it went.

Captain Jiang was a man who wanted order and discipline he was slight in build and short in stature.

Stanley had asked me to help him keep this guard happy so as to make sure he himself wasn't transferred to the workshop for not helping to run our unit smoothly.

It didn't take long for this guard to show his colours. Captain Jiang would often walk into our cells and try to catch us lying on the bed. The regulations stated you should sit at your table and study or read. It had become a ritual for Jiang to try and catch Lativ who always lay on the bed. Most of us did at times throughout the day, as we had no jobs to do it was a boring existence for most.

I had written to the prison education department asking for a Chinese language teacher to start classes having done this on numerous reports regarding equal treatment. Putting forward that the Chinese inmates had avenues for study. The next avenue pursued was writing to the British consul with a request to buy me an oil paints easel palette brushes and canvas to which they complied and am eternally grateful for that service. I had finished the anti-drug paintings and was looking to be useful. Needing to be active with my restless spirit. The equipment was brought to me at the next visit and got to setting up my workshop on the veranda in my cell and started my first oil painting. I copied a face from a magazine thinking of myself as the undiscovered Rembrandt.

I didn't find it that difficult to paint that first face - in fact it reminded me of my ex-wife Mary - and enjoyed that first encounter with oil on canvas. It did give me a feeling of achievement.

One day Lativ said to me, "Campbell, we need to cover the toilets."

We had three squat toilets in the corridor and there were no doors on them. In my eyes this toilet was a big improvement on the old jail and hadn't thought of being behind a closed door whilst having a shit. I guess having to do my daily toilet functions in a cell with twelve men at the detention cells - then with the slight improvement of being able to shit in a bucket alone in my cell - this was a great leap forward.

Lativ asked me to get him some material from the workshop as I had a connection there through Stanley.

It took a couple of days then Stanley got several meters of dark plastic sheeting and Lativ cut out three door-size panels and stitched a piece of string to them - and nailed the whole thing over the toilet sitting area. It was the following day that we heard a lot of commotion coming from Lativ's cell but I didn't go to inquire as to why. As it transpired the guard had told Stanley to remove the curtain from the toilet and that had thrown Lativ into a rage. It was something you learned in jail to mind your affairs. It was my experience on more than one occasion that when trying to solve certain issues it usually ended up with me getting involved and into trouble.

.oOo.

It was Christmas Day that year when it was time for the year-end meeting. We had all gathered in the great Hall of the People, and there must have been at least 500 inmates in attendance. On stage, the usual high brass sat with their giant microphones, while guards sat strategically throughout the hall. I loathed these meetings—hours of repetitive gabble about reform. Bull half expected to be released, similar to how two Germans had been the previous Christmas. I expected nothing, which was precisely what transpired.

Bull, on the other hand, was rewarded with a reform activist award, entitling him to a sentence reduction. However, when this would happen and how much time would be deducted remained a mystery. Before Christmas, the Criminal Affairs guard had visited us, taking our photos with the promise of sending some to our families. He returned after the New Year, wanting some of us to interview for the prison newspaper, hinting that without our cooperation, we wouldn't get the photos.

The following morning, I was called downstairs and told I had a visitor. I hadn't even shaved, but I didn't want to keep my visitor waiting, and I didn't care about my appearance.

Nervously entering the visiting room, I saw my brother, relaxed as if he were at home. He stood, and we embraced. Rab immediately spoke in colloquial Glaswegian, offering me hash or cash. I told him to put the money into my property and instructed him on what to do with the hash. The visit flew by. Rab showed me photos of his family and a gold Buddha he had bought. He had arranged for two visits, so when he left, he gave the guard £1000 for my property. We shook hands, and he promised to return the next week. It was the best surprise in nearly a decade.

In the unit, Bull asked about the visit. I replied it was good but unexpected. He had been receiving regular visits from his wife and was eager to leave. Despite not getting along well with Bull, we had an understanding of mutual support.

Bull once reassured me in the new jail that there was nothing to worry about; we were all going nowhere, stuck in the donkey carrot trick. I agreed but held a glimmer of hope for early release.

Eight days later, my brother Robert returned, slightly inebriated, with McDonald's for us both. He told me he had left a parcel with the consul, as he couldn't carry it. We hugged, and he gave the guards money for my property. Our goodbye was extended, and I felt fortunate to have such caring brothers. That week, I was in a euphoric state, buoyed by Rab's visit and news about my brother and the 'Free the Glasgow Two' campaign.

.oOo.

I couldn't handle all the back biting this Captain Jiang was doing he was seriously demented which might have been the outcome of a motorbike crash he had just weeks after his arrival to our unit. He had been off sick for one month and he looked sluggish constantly. I had been watching Captain Jiang closely sneaking up on inmates when they stayed in their cell. He was a nutcase jumping in your cell after tiptoeing up to it. If he caught you, he would deduct 0.5 merit points from you and that was a lot to the carrot chasers to keep you on edge. Half a point was a lot to lose.

In one month if all was good, you got 6 to 8 points which if amounted to 90 at the end of the year would entitle you to a reward? Several inmates came to tell me all sorts of stories about what Jiang had said about me. It was soon discovered that he had been telling stories not only about me but many others as well. He certainly was of bad character this man.

.oOo.

It was Chinese New Year coming up again and there was a sports competition being put on. This was to be the biggest event so far with all cellblocks taking part also two other jails were coming to join the event. We had football, basketball; and the 100m 200m up to 400m sprints and 1500 meters for the final race.

It was a cool spring day and everyone was excited at the upcoming outing. The grounds were crowded all brigades had their own colours in sportswear. Still being a bit curious looking around trying to identify with anyone from the old jail but never saw anyone and proceeded to mingle a little.

The prison reform lecture was broadcast from a stage with the usual high-ranking officials being filmed while giving a speech. The flag rising and national anthem had been completed.

It was time to start and the 100m was the first race on the card. The crowds chanted encouragement to their cellblock and we did likewise.

The starting pistol fired the race was off and Wavi went on and won the 100m and 200m races easily. Stanley had a place in the 400m it was Bull who was running next.

As the firing gun went off, Bull was left standing. He looked like a dummy as the Chinese runners sprinted off. We were all shouting, "Move it! Come on Bull. Don't let the troops down!" But he lagged behind still as he came around for the second time.

Cranky was on his feet and was shouting encouragement as Bull passed. Then when the bell rang for the final round, we all jumped and cheered Bull on as he overtook one after another and sprinted over the finishing line in first place.

I was happy to see Bull silence his critics (namely the Pakistani contingent). It was the following day that our football games were to begin and we went on to win that final. It was sheer determination from all the foreign participants to win, even at ping-pong and cards.

Cranky was not shooting ball anymore though, after being diagnosed with Hepatitis C he just stopped caring for himself and started getting fat.

1999

It was the first week of April 1999 and I felt sick one night lying on my bed sweating profusely. The following morning, I put my name down to see the doctor and was given a couple of pills but did not take them. I was told to rest because I had a little fever.

That night the same thing happened. I awakened totally soaked and started to get paranoid.

It was Eli and Wavi who started the ongoing story that Cranky was practicing black magic. One day during the exercise, period Wavi called me upstairs to look down at Cranky walking around the yard. He pointed out to me that Cranky dragged one of his feet. Wavi said that was the sign.

I told him the story of Cranky damaging his leg at the old jail and Wavi immediately replied that was his other leg.

That sudden reply knocked the wind out of me, as I didn't remember which leg he had damaged.

Wavi went on to tell me he had also seen a snake in the shower after Bull had come out. This was becoming too much. The Africans were in constant huddle with stories of the dead from Egypt to Nigeria and along the Ivory Coast. I had read parts of a book written by a Nigerian person about spirits and ghosts, it seemed all becoming real.

For me the icing on the cake was when going into the cell I now shared with Stanley and found nail cuttings on the floor next to my bed. I immediately rushed to get Wavi and told him. I had read somewhere that nail cuttings were a voodoo means of getting to you.

Wavi examined the nails looking them over and he said, "Toenails it is for making a strong spell."

"Who the fuck put them there!" I asked.

"It was a big person, look at their size," Wavi replied.

I did look but did not touch them and just screwed up my nose and looked at Wavi. "Cranky or Bull?" I asked.

"Bull," Wavi replied.

.oOo.

There was a certain stir in the air suggesting that Bull would soon be leaving; it was a common occurrence in Chinese jails, known as a 'tail cut'. A tail cut involves a slight reduction in jail time before one's release date. Typically, it ranges from one month to six months, and every day of remission counts as a final bite at the proverbial carrot – an unexpected bonus you can easily convince yourself that you deserve.

Having returned to the hospital again after another bout of the sweats, I wasn't given any medication. Instead, I was provided with a couple of paper packets with no label on them. I was told it was a powder mix for rehydration and instructed to take one after the evening meal.

I recall having supper that evening, then drinking the hot rehydration drink I was given at the hospital.

The next I knew I awoke after ten in the next morning. I hadn't slept that late in eight years, and we weren't allowed too anyway. Upon waking, found that two more inmates, Butt from Pakistan and Bull from the UK, had gone home. Several hours later, I began to feel muscle tightness in my body – the medicinal pollution had taken effect.

It dawned on me that I had been drugged. Realising my mind was off-balance, I had become caught up in the belief that Black Magic was causing my condition but the bastards had been drugging me. Was it their way of making it easier for me, being the only British national left imprisoned in China? More likely, they thought I would stir up trouble. I had been rather volatile and unpredictable over the years. Thus, I concluded that they didn't want me to witness a British national leaving causing stress for my longing for home. With two more gone, another cell reshuffle was imminent.

Whether I would stay put or demand a single cell was my next consideration.

.oOo.

With two inmates gone, the next day two more new people arrived. Both came from Africa one from the Ivory Coast the other Cameroon. They had been working as a team selling white paper. It was the same swindle that landed Wavi and Eli here the only difference was the amount swindled.

Prince Jean Marie Happy came from Ivory Coast and was the same age as me then forty-nine. He had a bushy head of pure white hair and white beard to match; he was overweight and around 175cm tall.

Joe his partner was a big well-built guy around 184cm. They both spoke in French as well as English and Eli spoke French so that was the beginning of the Qing Pu Jail African union with Jean Marie Happy at the head.

It turned out that Happy had also been on Hajji and he and Lativ struck up a friendship. They also brought news of other foreigners locked up at the detention cells - other Pakistanis, Japanese, and Koreans.

The unit was running without much incident until Jiang went on the hunt again. Jiang did not like Muslims and Lativ was still getting hassle from him.

The two Hajjis got more respect from the other followers of that faith, and Jiang did and did not like it at all. Jiang had called a meeting just a week after their arrival. He wanted to expose Happy for taking stamps on credit from other inmates. This was true and I had given him stamps because he needed them to write to his family letting them know about his welfare and whereabouts - and to request money to be sent to him.

It was Jiang up to his mind games again this time Happy was his victim. It turned out to be a glorious outcome for Jiang. During the meeting, Happy frustratingly asked to have the storeroom door opened which Jiang called the other guard to comply.

Then Happy returned upstairs with $300 in crisp $100 bills waving in his hand. He said, "Don't you insult Africans we are not beggars as you call us."

That started it. The search was on for more money and another $29,700 was uncovered lying in the bottom of Happy's bag. The pauper to Prince and back to pauper again had unfolded right in front of our eyes.

The meeting came to an abrupt end and we were all locked up then the place was filled with uniforms. The storeroom was quarantined and each inmate was called one by one and identified their belongings, which they then watched being searched.

I got a flash of what my sons Scott, Lochy, and I had gotten away with that maybe gave them the idea to look closer at us all plus with $30,000 already uncovered it gave them a good incentive.

Happy had declared the money was in his bag since arrest and had assumed the guards knew about it at the detention cells. The money was confiscated and that left Happy in the same boat as before he opened his bag.

What a fucking halfwit I thought $30k would have set him up for going home. I spoke to him later and suggested all sorts of ways he could have gotten it out but as usual, no one wanted to hear it.

He certainly didn't and neither do I when people try to tell me what I should have done with the cannabis eight years down the line.

.oOo.

The unit had been running smoothly which should have been a warning sign. I had just received art books from a good Scottish friend in London called Ralph Maclaren and was sitting reading them when Mr Ho came into the cell and asked to have a look as he also painted in oils.

I was sharing a cell with Mustafa due to conflict he had with Mir before he had left in January. Stanley had told me beforehand that Captain Jiang wanted me to share a cell with Mustafa and told me not to agree and to say it isn't culturally acceptable and to use Cranky as an example how conflict could arise between us.

I ignored Stanley's advice and agreed to share a cell with Mustafa.

Stanley knew much more than he let on – particularly about Jiang - and often confided in me to be careful or to not get involved with what Jiang was brewing.

It was made clear to me that trouble would arise, so I was to watch out. One thought came to my mind was Mir had told me that Jiang had commented he "Will swat Campbell like a mosquito when the time comes."

The time had come.

It transpired that Captain Jiang, still riding on his high horse with talk of promotion at finding the money, had managed to convince Mustafa that I disrespected his religion.

Mustafa informed me that I had shown Mr Ho his shrine when he came to our cell to look at the art books. There was a meeting held and I was smack in the middle. Jiang had set me up and had fallen straight into his trap.

It was too late as Stanley's words rang in my ears do not change cell.

I ended up losing the plot as usual, and started to curse the communist party, which resulted in another fourteen-day, confinement cell experience. Whilst being carted away still shouting abuse at Jiang.

There was me lying in a mosquito-filled cell naked with a rough and dirty hairy blanket that made your skin creep. Whilst in confinement you have to write self-criticisms and this was my first submission.

Dear Sir.
I am a foreign national in Shanghai I am a prisoner under the Chinese prison reform system and have been educated at the prison to express my thoughts honestly and to write a monthly ideological report under the prison reform demands. I am a sensitive person and attentive to certain comments made by others and also articles read in the China Daily newspaper.
It has been my experience that the China Daily newspaper does not waste space in printing sensationalism. I write this report requesting that you follow up on my accusations by doing some investigation and want to expose the wrongdoing of one man in particular.
Throughout the years whilst serving my sentence has experienced many racial comments towards foreigners even today still hear them. I recall this caused much conflict between the foreigners and Chinese at Tilan Xiao jail. We were often offended and at times angry.
As time went by began to realise that most of the racial slurs were said parrot fashion due to the inmate's lack of worldly knowledge knowing that every language uses words that are uncouth and are often spoken without malice or intentional disrespect. At the end of the year 1998 while having my daily exercise was shocked when a guard spoke to me using racial slurs against two African inmates. I walked away in disgust at this guard's use of words. After the exercise period was finished was called to the office and asked why I showed

contempt by walking away from this guard during exercise. I answered his question through the interpreter Mr Chon that did not want to listen to the captain's racial views about other people or their countries. I could clearly see that this guard was not pleased with my outspokenness. On another occasion whilst walking with the inmate Mustafa Iqbal when this same guard joined us and interrupted our conversation by making the statement in a racial tone about the Iranian inmate Lativ manner of dress. Mustafa Iqbal changed the conversation by saying the weather was nice for sport today and asked the guard to arrange some events. Once more on another occasion, the same guard approached me and again started using racial slurs against the Cameroonian inmate Nesiwe. I immediately stepped up my pace mumbling idiot and forcing my psyche to get the message through to him. When I returned to my cell Mustafa came to me with quite animated eyes, he told me that his religion teaches that people who talk that way are evil. I agreed with him and began to distance myself from this guard's presence telling this guard not to come to my cell unless he was with an interpreter. I have no respect for this type of bigot. What finally determined me to write this report was the meeting held on 1999/3/24 during that meeting the guard openly humiliated the African inmate Jean Marie Happy. The guard openly exposed this man's private affairs in a mocking disrespectful manner which had no relevance to reform or the meeting.

The guard revealed matters regarding his and Neiwe personal property openly stating that these two Africans had no property which later proved to be a lie the guard had told. The guard even stated during that meeting that the Warden of Qing Pu Jail wasn't qualified to talk to Prince Jean Marie only the Justice Minister was qualified. The whole meeting was humiliating and racially biased. If this type of talk is tolerated one day it will get out of hand.

STOP RACIAL DISCRIMINATION AT QING PU JAIL

L Campbell

.oOo.

When released from confinement I was just a red blob of mosquito bites literally hundreds if not thousands covered my face and body. Feeling shattered my mental state was suspect. Revenge was on my mind and started my one-man campaign. I was telling no one that my plans were, that was always a mistake some of us made, thinking you can tell someone. I had made copies of the report and sent one to the British Consul also one to the Prison procurator and one into the Wardens box and thought, 'Let's see what transpires!'

It did not take long. The following day after handing in the consul letter I was called to the office by Captain Ma of the criminal affairs department and asked to not send this letter. I asked why. In addition, went on to explain it is my right to correspond with my consul, telling Captain Ma that one had already been put into the Warden's box.

He frowned.

The foreign inmates knew by experience that the guards in our unit kept the problems away from the ears of the higher authorities. By going over the head of Captain Jiang he was not going to be happy about it.

It was Stanley who was doing the interpretations and said to me slyly, "Do not push it and withdraw that letter please."

I left the office still undecided but with a promise from Captain Ma that he would look closely at my accusations.

The following day the prison procurator visited me and had a surprise in store for them. Syed also wrote a report accusing Jiang of discrimination. Syed signed it for me - this was the sort of leverage needed and I thanked him for his support - knowing he only did this because he also knew he wasn't getting any remission moreover; he was just happy to stir it up.

The prison procurator listened to my story and then also asked me to retrieve the letter being sent to the consul. They assured me that it would be resolved within the prison.

I told them about past promises from the Prison Administration Bureau that if I withdrew my petition I would be paroled. I made it very clear to them that whilst Jiang was running the unit my life was a misery.

It was left at that and I never retrieved my letter.

The following day in the afternoon Captain Ma called a meeting telling us to rearrange our cells as four new inmates from Japan were arriving the following day.

The unit then consisted of four Africans, two Pakistanis, two Americans, one Iranian, one North Korean, and me from the UK. The Chinese inmates were Stanley in charge another new guy we called Eddie plus two nightshift workers Toto and little Wang.

I got hold of Captain Ma before he escaped downstairs and had Stanley at the ready to ask my question and took him by surprise when asking for a single cell on the top floor. To my surprise, he immediately replied, "Yes."

This was a first from him. They always said, 'let me think it over' and never got back to you.

I asked, "Can you inform Captain Jiang of your decision?"

Stanley intervened and said to me, "It will be done, Lockie. Jiang won't dare go over Captain Ma's decision." I was so excited to be having a single cell again but knew it would stir things up with some others and knew that Stanley would be coming to me over the next couple of days and try to persuade me to retract my letter to the Consul.

.oOo.

The four new Japanese inmates arrived the following day as was told to us at the meeting. They got out of the prison van carrying bags and bowing as they walked. They were imprisoned for arranging visas for women from China to get into Japan. The sex trade was as ancient as China itself and a big business in Japan for Chinese beauties.

Mr Funahashi - sentenced to four years - was a man of slim build, height around 174cm, head slightly bowed and was around 46. Mr Kamimura – sentenced to four years - was overweight around 178cm, aged 42, and always walked with chest out. Mr Matsuda – sentenced to two years - was slim and fit, his age 30, around 173cm and appeared withdrawn. Lastly there was young Josikawa age 19, sentenced to two years, who was Mr Funahashi's nephew.

They had been sending the women under many guises some as students with fake college documents others as tourists with set up bank accounts in addition, return tickets. It was known as the oldest trade in the world and is still being applied by one of the most cultured and civilized nations – ie Japan.

I had already moved into a single cell on the top floor and the cell layout had improved since the four new guys arrived. They opened all of the upstairs. The two-night shift guys moved to cell one also with Elah and Wavi in cell two the four Japanese in cell three and me alone in cell four. Cell Five was our storeroom.

I was getting a consul to visit the following day and had my letter at the ready nothing had been done about Jiang and his shenanigans he was still creeping up to cells and catching guys laying on their beds and only too happy to deduct 0.5 merit points.

.oOo.

At my consul visit I arrived with my letter stashed down my briefs. I walked briskly to the visiting room, we first crossed our yard, then passed the hospital unit and then into the main building.

To my surprise, the consul showed great concern about my welfare - not that they did not usually - but that day was different. Then out came a clipping from a UK newspaper with an article about the rough treatment that I had not so long ago undergone.

The consul read this article out to me as passing correspondence at visits was forbidden. I was elated for more than one reason it proved to me my underground mail system still worked as had given a letter to someone at a risk of putting myself straight back into the mosquito farm (and him to the torture seat). The article stated most of the facts that I had sent out ie being left handcuffed on my tiptoes overnight secured to the cell door.

In return, I read the consul my letter and told them I had sent it weeks ago and further inquired had they received it yet? Knowing the answer already. I could see the consul look at her interpreter and she at once started to take notes. The air could have been cut with broken glass.

The chatter of the guards sounded to me like buck-passing time and who's going to be left responsible for this breach of jail security.

I had been painting every day since getting oils brushes and canvas with the assistance of the British consul. As the visit was now over, I collected the art materials I had requested, plus some gifts from the consul staff and mail from my family was handed in.

I loved painting it was the best discovery of my life, and it occupied all of my days. It was so interesting to see shapes appear with a resemblance to what I was copying. It made me laugh to myself when discovered the illusions that could be created by a few strokes of a brush.

.oOo.

It was a surprise welcoming for us all at the end of 1999 when a meeting known as the year-end assessment or known as the agitprop show gave us this information. As usual, we were told that we should write about the achievements we made throughout the year and what were our plans for the coming year. It was Captain Ma of the criminal affairs presiding over the meeting. He was in the presence of another guard who was smaller and older and he wore a white shirt. I immediately thought he was a Warden. It turned out he was to be a new addition to our unit and that he spoke English. Captain Shao was a slight built man around 168cm in height he was quietly spoken and well educated. The meeting had another purpose Captain Ma informed us that we would be moving over to the building opposite as they were going to renovate our unit. With a smile on his face portraying the look at how civilized we are then continued by saying and putting toilets in your cells. That caused a bit of fidgeting. Then Lativ immediately stated that we would prefer it the way it is with the toilets outside the cell. It was ignored the decision was already made. The other thing to be taken away was the veranda.

It was good while it lasted to be able to sit outside at times and paint and just chill out. That space was being used for the new inside toilet. We were asked to write down any suggestions to improve the unit and the meeting was called to an end.

I stopped Captain Shao on the stairs going down and asked him where he learned English. He replied he had travelled overseas as an engineer on a ship the conversation was interrupted when Captain Ma said something and Captain Shao went off to attend to whatever duty. I immediately took a liking to this guard he was very gentle in a humane sort of way

.oOo.

I was sitting outside on the veranda on the third floor it was a warm autumn day hearing voices coming from the cell below called who are you talking with Stanley?

A voice with a distinctive American accent replied, "Hi there, my name is Jude Shao an innocent American imprisoned in China."

I ran down the stairs immediately thinking he was a pilot who we had heard about on the news and that had been arrested for spying. As it turned out it was a young well-educated native Chinaman age around 36 who greeted me shaking his hand and asked if he had met Cranky or Bo, yet – or the other two Americans imprisoned there.

"Not yet," he replied and I took that as my cue to leave.

I was about to depart when Eddie said, "Another new person from Ghana is moving onto your floor."

I went upstairs and met Kofi he was a young, tall, broad-shouldered, and proud man. He had been arrested for traveller check fraud and sentenced to four years. Jude on the other had gotten sixteen years for tax evasion, which he claimed was all a setup.

.oOo.

As it turned out regardless of our written reports not to put toilets in the cells or remove the veranda, they shipped out the Chinese from across the way whilst we were all moved to the opposite building. We were kept six to a cell. The cherry on the cake for me was on our first day settling in we had a meeting that was the introduction of another new Captain his name was Chang. He would take charge of us. He was around 34 years in age and he looked enthusiastic and most importantly that meant Jiang was gone.

I had wondered why he wasn't at that meeting and was so happy to hear that evil Jiang was no longer here. I felt victorious. Then I realised he would be in some other cellblock disrupting some other people's lives – it was just a vicious circle.

2000

As the New Millennium approached with the year 2000, there were predictions from disaster to a new messiah coming. I was on my illusion bubble ride again thinking that 1999 would be the 50th anniversary of the founding of the People's Republic of China and they might grant me amnesty.

I had even submitted a report stating that the King of Thailand granted amnesty to drug offenders. As usual no response.

The millennium bug had died a death in the end all sorts of predictions made from every nationality in there but they came to nothing.

I was lying on top of my bed one day when someone walked into the cell and introduced himself as Mick. I looked at him and saw he was a Westerner.

"Hi," I said nonchalantly, "where did you just come from?"

Mick replied in an offhanded way, "Oh I came by special escort."

I looked at him again; he was dressed in top designer sportswear.

Just then Stanley came into the cell and started speaking Chinese to which Mick replied in Chinese and left saying, "See you later mate," in a not very distinguishable Australian accent.

I immediately thought that he was a Consul Staff member but then remembered there were no Australians here. It turned out that Mick was a new inmate sentenced to 15 years for a mobile phone deal deception between Hong Kong and Shanghai. When his gear arrived, it took six of us to carry it into the storeroom. Mick was from Greek parents and he had that look and body like a well-sculpted Greek statue. As it happened, he had some medical problem so was kept at a hospital before coming here and not the detention cells.

.oOo.

The arrival of five more new inmates caused quite a lot of gossip. It was three South Koreans Mr Kim the eldest in his seventies Mr Lee in his sixties and Mr Chun in his forties. They arrived along with two Nepalese guys, Bijay age 39, and Min aged 32 - they had been arrested for attempting to smuggle cannabis into Japan. The story was that Mr Kim and Mr Chun really did think they were smuggling herbal medicines and felt a bitter resentment towards Mr Lee and Bijay the ringleaders of the scam. Mr Kim and Mr Chun had gotten five years each whilst Bijay got nine; Min got eight and Mr Lee got six.

I sat and listened to Chun speak quite a bit and he was angry you could taste it. I knew he had approached Bijay immediately upon arriving at the jail and confronted him for an explanation. Whatever was said, there was nothing forthcoming to calm Chun so it brewed on.

The renovation work was to be finished before spring festival 2000 and there was a lot of friction in the unit due to the shortage of space. That was when, if you were aware you tried to remain silent. It was one of those things when history comes in, the Koreans, Chinese, and the Japanese do not always mix too well. They have their past conflicts and each is equally patriotic.

It was not easy living, especially under these conditions. On top of that, there was an ongoing political issue regarding the Japanese government's duty to apologize for past war crimes and their use of comfort women.

You can imagine how the local inmates felt towards them but they were safe in this unit. I also had a run-in with Cranky over the remains of the hot water container. After sports, we sometimes collected it to wash after a game. You may think a water bucket is a trivial issue but you become possessive to odd things in jail. Fights can start over something as simple as not saying good morning to someone who greeted you.

I was content to be a loner most times and was mostly left to my own devices. No longer having that curiosity anymore wanting to know what other people were in for, I had exhausted that avenue of illusions thinking that I could put them straight with how the system works. I was the worst example being the one with the littlest remission.

.oOo.

It was February 2000 that we moved back into our old building. The cells were all bigger with the veranda gone. As you went inside the cell on your right-hand side was a flushing toilet with a half door and on the left side a washbasin and running water. Each cell had four beds and by each bed a stool and a small table plus one small wooden cupboard for keeping a variety of things. Above the beds at the entrance wall were four large linen storage spaces. It was the normal procedure that the building was finished to have a meeting and have our new cell allocation. I had asked Stanley to try to secure my old cell on the third floor.

The meeting turned out to be more than the normal humdrum of Chinese prison reform. We were told that we were having a change of staff and that Captain Jin would be our new brigade unit leader and was introducing transparency in our reform. The two guards who had been with us since the beginning - Captain Hua and Wu - were going also.

It was time for the new guards to be introduced. There was Captain Chang who had already taken over from Jiang and was in charge of us. Captain Shao was the eldest with the white collar who spoke English and was doing translation when needed. Then there was Captain Chung and Captain Liu one a university graduate and the other a young man of around twenty-two.

I got my cell on the top floor, sharing it with Stanley again.

I did not have any complaints about the arrangements but some others did. It would take time to settle in and get used to the new setup. There was one more floor above, which was the dining room area. A large room had been set out with tables and chairs plus an area for serving and collecting food. On the back wall was a fourteen-foot by eight-foot blackboard with a completely new set of conditions and rules. It was the merit point system under the title transparency you could see how many points you got each month and why you were given them.

There was an open rooftop area where you could hang out bedding and was used to sit out on hot summer evenings to play chess or just relax. It was rather civilized one could say.

.oOo.

There was an outdoor meeting it was propagated through reform that if you inform on someone and the case leads to confession or conviction whether that is inside or outside of the jail you will be rewarded with remission. That was the scenario going on rewarding the informers publicly. Sitting along with about 600, Chinese guys on what I named the criticism stools, and did not have to pay any attention to the long speeches made by Wardens and other would-be reformers of men. I perked my ear up only when they started calling names out but how would it ever be possible to hear Campbell amongst this madness?

Then Stanley called me and said I was wanted in the office.

I had butterflies in my stomach thinking that it might be some sort of reduction in my sentence. As it happened, Captain Shao returned taking me from the crowd, and escorted me to the guard's office in brigade five passing en route the hotbox confinement block. Captain Shao told me to wait at the office door and so waiting stood there with my best face of the day.

Five minutes later I was standing in front of three Judges and Captain Shao. I was given another ten-month reduction from my sentence as a present for the May Day holidays. This was only the second reduction I had received since the first ten-month reduction at the old prison.

Returning to the unit with a fake smile not wanting the authorities or anyone else for that matter to see how gutted I was. It was usual procedure if you were having a second reduction that it be more than your first. Having gotten ten months first time everyone estimated would get a fourteen-month minimum the next time.

Cranky had gotten fourteen months on his second reduction although he had missed out at the old jail when we had gotten a ten-month cut. He already had two reductions amounting to 26-month remission and I had 20-month remission. Cranky must have been doing something right or me something wrong. My new liberation date was December 5, 2004, and I could see the gate in my mind's eye but did not feel any closer to it.

.oOo.

The exercise yard had been the forefront of many a debated argument and fight. The issue was basketball as opposed to football during the afternoon period. It was true that football was played most days unless Captain Jin organized a basketball game against the opposite unit. This he did quite often as he himself enjoyed the game when on duty, and he was still a very skilful player, being aged around fifty and fit.

It was decided three days each and one day rest for those who wanted to walk around without ducking from balls. The football team we had was unbeaten within the jail. Bijay was an ex-British army officer and the Gurkas are well known for their loyalty and fierceness - he was a good strong and skilful player. Min - the other Nepali - was small around 160cm but built like an ox, and he was also not a bad player. Wavi was very fast, nobody at the jail could catch him. Grand Joe as we named him was also good and then Happy who often played in goal had surprised us all with how well he read the game. Matsuda had all the best gear sent from Japan and he was someone who ran for every ball everywhere on the field, then there was Stanley the hardest defender in our unit. He let nobody pass him and he was good.

I was still very reliable at my ball distribution and scoring my share of goals. However, none of us was as good as Elah he was as good as George Weah - as far as our unit were concerned - and a fellow citizen to boot being Liberian.

The days they played basketball we sometimes sat and watched. It seemed to me every move constituted a foul. It did not have the flow of football. Then one day Jude explained to me the rules, and I saw the game in a new light, and began to enjoy watching that sport on television. *I believe I can fly* with air Jordan was big at the time also Kobe Bryant and my favourite was Iverson. I learned new words like a *Shaq attack* but wouldn't trade football for it though. I preferred the echo of old chants of football legends. The likes of Jinxy Johnston or Slim Jim Baxter both of whom were rivals from the same city but different clubs I had heard the Hamden roar on many occasions as a boy going to games in Glasgow.

It was a mixed house in Glasgow, our family shared my father's religion, a protestant, and my mother's, a catholic. I was a blue nose my brother Robert was a Tim and Tommy wisely supported Scotland. Football is a passion once possessed it never dies so in my eyes football should have been the sole exercise yard game but we were the foreign unit and a democracy ruled.

It remained that way until autumn, then another obstacle arrived. The complaint was the football was leaving dirty marks on the washing that the Chinese inmates had been hanging out behind the goalposts.

We objected to the guard that this was our exercise ground, not the drying area. The Chinese inmates did not like our setup as opposed to theirs and they had a right to complain regarding daily exercise. The foreigners could play sports twice a day and they were lucky if they could get a game once a week. I helped a lot with this problem and started to arrange mixed games or at times play against each other. The problem was easily solved by arranging for Stanley to collect all the washing at four o'clock and pass it into the building opposite.

It was those sorts of obstacles that you could not foresee we had been playing for years without any mention of dirtying the bedding.

.oOo.

The foreign unit was supplied with two English papers every day. It was arranged that the paper would go to cell one on Monday then to cell two first on Tuesday then on along the line to five. Cranky was always circling over articles or even cutting them out before some people had read them. By the time cell, five got the paper it was the following day and often later. Therefore, another rote system was set up. Cell, one got the newspaper first for one week then it started at cell two, and so on same but different. Bo had come up with the suggestion that we buy our papers, Jude supported that as he wanted papers from other parts of China. This was submitted in a written report and the outcome was that we could buy our own and that stopped any more squabble over the newspaper.

One day Bo was taken over to the hospital and he never returned. He was transferred to the old jail hospital with a heart problem. The story was he was being returned to the USA for surgery. Bo had good connections and he was not a criminal and I wished him the best of luck and a speedy recovery.

.oOo.

Mustafa and Syed returned home before the October 1st holiday and I wished them good fortune. As they departed three more new guys arrived.

There appeared to be a waiting game to get into this jail as stories were coming that a gang of Malaysians were on their way.

The new guys were one from Burma age 42 - doing life for heroin possession – a Chinese American called Matt, doing two years for deception, and the third was a Korean guy named Pang – who had got four years for smuggling fake alcohol into of China.

The only cell space left for two people was my own or the one Mustafa and Syed had vacated so Lativ didn't get the luxury of a single cell he got the two new guys and the third Pang was put into cell two with the Koreans.

.oOo.

It was a few days before Christmas 2000, when three more new people arrived, they came from Malaysia all on separate charges. Jimmy Huang was in his forties and had gotten eight years for company fraud- he said he was innocent. Then there was Mr Tsai age forty - life sentence for possession of a large amount of ecstasy. Then Mr Wong had gotten years for possession of a small amount of ecstasy.

Cell five - our storeroom - was cleared and moved to the ground floor again. The unit was getting quite a mix of nationalities all three were Malaysian Chinese so there was a mix of Cantonese Hokkim and other dialects spoken amongst them and this was throwing the local Shanghai boys into confusion.

One of the major problems for foreigners was you mostly needed an interpreter to inquire about certain matters from the guards. The overseas Chinese did not have this invasion of privacy as they could ask directly everything they needed. As to the non-Chinese speakers, they either had to put it in writing or with assistance. It was the same with outgoing mail. They wrote in Chinese so it did not need to lie around waiting in a pile to be translated. Their mail was out within the week.

This caused a bit of friction, as the foreign mail issue had been ongoing since my first week of arriving in jail back in 1991. It appeared the overseas Chinese were getting preferential treatment.

Lativ had been getting a hard time as his writing was in Persian and it was taking a minimum of one month before his letters went out. He even got permission to pay a government-approved translator to get his letters out quicker which they did for a few months then it slipped back to the snail mail system. Lativ also wrote in English to his children he was very loving in his words. Sometimes asking me to put a cartoon drawing on a card to which I gladly obliged.

Mail is a well-known power tool for the authorities and it would not be something our voice of discontent would overthrow.

It was Jude who came up with what we thought was an eventual solution Jude suggested during a meeting that the mail be photocopied and sent immediately then checked later.

The eventual outcome was nothing changed that you could notice.

2001

The weather is perfect in China during spring of 2001, I had been doing a lot of painting, and was working on an idea for an exhibition. It was to involve myself, Kofi from Ghana and Min from Nepal. I had put forward a report to the education department asking for materials and it was accepted – so I wrote a list of what was needed.

The exhibition was titled *An Inside insight - behind the great wall of prisons in China* and was a very interesting experience with the three of us sitting discussing what we should portray. All knowing that propaganda paintings highlighting the modern civilized prison would have to be present so we broke it into four parts.

Part one. Public security issues five paintings.
Part two. The Cultural Gap four paintings.
Part three communication breakdown four paintings.
Part four: Sport and food four paintings.

These four topics were the outcome of advice received in a letter from a lady called Sarah Travelon. I had asked her about getting counselling. Sarah had told me that giving counselling from Scotland to China was impossible but suggested sitting in front of a blank canvas and painting what's in my mind. I sat for days before breaking into my mind and the outcome was not too nice to look at but it was a step forward to accepting who am and that was all mixed up. I was finished with the paintings and the time came to exhibit our work. The three of us knew we would be rewarded in some way or another and it was remission we all desired. It was set out in the visiting area in the main building and would be exhibited there during inmates' family visits and my Consul visit so that the public could see that foreign criminals reformed actively as well as the Chinese. At the end of that month of July 2001 Kofi Min and I were told to write crime acknowledgment reports and that usually meant one thing remission of sentence. Asking the guard about my crime acknowledgement report having already gotten remission six months ago and according to the prison law could not have another reduction of sentence until a minimum of one year passed. The guard assured me that this new crime acknowledgment report would be better and that adding the exhibition reward would make it good for me. I walked away dejected knowing this report would lie in some desk drawer or file cabinet and when it came time for me to get a reduction, they would ask me to write a new one adding other supposed achievements.

It was easy to convince myself that it would be better to get a bigger reduction with this new report but felt deep down the longer they can delay my reduction I was bound to fuck up and lose it before getting it. They are masters at trips and traps lies and illusions leading you into a false security and then kicking your legs away. That is reform you are there to suffer so you do not forget so quickly in the future and to live an honest life.

.oOo.

I had been given the test results of a medical checkup we all had back in November 2000 and was shocked to read I was HIV+ and Hepatitis C+.

In a panic, I immediately wrote to the Consul knowing that I had been infected by the system. Talk about being fucked - I was so God dammed angry I wanted to kill someone. But who was to blame?

Seething, I immediately thought of Cranky. Could he have managed to put his infected blood into my food? The answer was yes, he could easily do that, but would he? I didn't doubt it - so he was my first suspect.

Then I recalled what he had to say when he discovered he was HEP C+ Cranky was enraged and swore to sue the Chinese prison authority for infecting him. It seemed to me this time he was on the right track. We had both been infected with two deadly viruses.

If Cranky was Hep C + away back before our previous medical checkup then I must have been clean as no mention nor was treatment given to me. I was in some sort of shock and could not shake myself from it. I was going to die. My mind screamed. I wanted another checkup, this time done by the consul doctor.

I spoke with the guard about the urgency of this and asked them to arrange a special visit just to give my blood. That night lying in bed I thought that those dirty, evil, communist, bastards had infected me and I knew why.

I had always voiced my opinion at meetings and had written numerous articles on the rights of prisoners, not with malice but with genuine inquiry. Qing Pu jail was civilized in many aspects that I respected and thought surely, they hadn't intentionally infected me because of my racial discrimination report against Captain Jiang in July 1999 or for telling them to stick their communist thinking up their ass back on June 2nd, 1998. I had also gotten shingles - Dragon skin disease, as it's known in Chinese - a ring of painful blisters running from my left nipple over my shoulder down to under my armpit onto my back - another virus. I was truly demented during that period and requested a special visit but instead received this letter sent on by the consul.

> Consul Letter.
> We have sent you the medical check result of British citizen Lauchlan Campbell in the letter dated 14 August. Unfortunately, we had made a mistake in that letter: in one of his check items, the check result HIV (-) has been put as HIV (+) by mistake. We apologize for the mistake we made.
> Foreign Affairs Department Shanghai Justice Bureau. 24/08/01

I did not let out any sigh of relief but instead reacted rather angrily not at the Consul during this visit but by the way, my life was being handled stating one test said positive and the other negative - which one was correct. By that stage, I did not honestly know. I wrote and asked the consul to arrange for their nurse to take my blood and give me an independent test result - this was granted and I left that consul meeting at least with a feeling that I would find out.

I needed to know how long I would have to live, and not how soon was going to die. One up for the wonders of positive thinking. I had to give credit here to the consul for their efficiency, knowing about the psychological damage such news carries and still being in the dark and not knowing if was infected or not. I had the consul test results in print within two weeks stating HIV- HEP C+.

It was good news in one respect to not have HIV. The consul also enclosed 30 pages of HEP C information on how to treat it and what dietary requirements are best for infected patients. After reading parts of every page, it all came down to the fact that you are slowly dying. No cures just do not drink alcohol or abuse your body.

It is a wonderful sight to see a letter heading British Consulate-General made it official for me that I wasn't HIV+. I could trust that.

Cranky and I seldom spoke we came to tolerate each other and live and let live. Having to ask him one day about his Hep C, wanting to know how he knew he had it. The doctor at the hospital had told me Cranky specially asked for that test. "Is that true?" I inquired.

"No way," was how Cranky responded. "It took my consul months to get that information," and only recently had he received it in writing.

The system liked to turn us around in circles putting out misinformation. It was well manipulated in these Chinese jails and it worked to keep us in the dark for years with the many games they experimented with.

During this period, my family had written to the foreign office asking for my return on medical grounds. I didn't see any chance of that happening as Cranky was still here and I had heard no talk of him going home for a transplant. Jail thrives on hope even if that hope is killing you, it still might get you home quicker.

.oOo.

Mick was proving to be a real thorn in the side of the authorities he was intelligent and spoke reasonably well in Mandarin. Having sat with him and looked through his photos one day, it is not something you do unless you feel at ease with someone. Mick and I got along ok. His Chinese girlfriend was a beauty but his ex-wife was gorgeous and his two son's fine young lads. Mick was a body builder but the sort with ribbed outlines in short; he liked the look of himself. The parcels of the highest quality proteins vitamins muscle enlarger, and so on arrived on a monthly basis. Mick also had an ongoing medical problem and had even managed to get out to a hospital for tests with the assistance of his consul.

I shared a cell with him on the third floor after Stanley and I had a punch-up and cell change. Mick would get up in the middle of the night and press the buzzer stumbling and moaning and often vomiting. This got the guards back up as they got out of bed to take him across to the prison doctor who also had to get out of bed. This went on for months and then the guards stopped opening our door. That was all Mick needed he was a man who took note of every detail and he logged the dates and times not only when getting treatment but also when he had not been attended to.

When his consul visited, he read out his notes and embarrassed the face out of the system. For whatever reason Mick did not give a fuck and rang that night bell until some of the cons were shouting, "Mick give us a sleep tonight mate." Then that extended to, "Shut the fuck up Mick!" from the cell next door.

Sympathy is harder to come by than remission in a Chinese jail.

The arrival of another Chinese inmate with Australian citizenship was a pleasant addition. Simon was in his early forties and doing life imprisonment for embezzlement. I got on with him and we started doing workouts together. One day he asked me about Mick and why he made so much trouble and I answered, "You had better ask him that yourself."

.oOo.

On Christmas day 2001 fed up with the pretentious merriments of the festive season. I was happy though, after receiving a book from my friend Ralph McLaren Paintings of Radiant light by the artist Thomas Kinkade. I looked at the paintings and marvelled at his distribution of light. I wrote into my diary *light in a Godless land* and immediately started to copy his work. I was so enwrapped in this that I was doing two paintings a week. The wall in my workplace looked like a gallery every time one finished an old one got taken down and rolled up and added to my mounting collection. The Kinkade paintings were in big demand in our unit and I painted one for half the people there charging a jar of coffee for each. The guards were in on it also, I got Stanley to pass them the book to select their choice and then copied them.

Being on artistic high learning landscapes I came to realize his paintings were just that bit heavenly and that combining art with spirituality was a wise, wonderful, and colourful way to work.

.oOo.

Jude had been fighting to clear his name non-stop from the first day of arrival and he was not having any of it regarding his Consul mail and his rights being violated. Jude secured a copy of a Vienna Convention Consular agreement. Article 36 states *any communication addressed to the consular by the person arrested, in prison custody the said authorities shall also forward mail immediately the said authorities shall inform the person concerned immediately of his rights under this sub-paragraph.*

This was a revelation and the bandwagon started, everyone wanted a consular agreement, me included.

It was as if you had this piece of paper your rights could not be denied you. It was written in the Vienna convention and that made it official.

Along with some of the newfound international law protectors we soon discovered things went along at the pace suiting the Chinese authorities.

I should have foreseen it would not matter what convention, Vienna, Geneva, or Miss World, we were all in jail in fucking China and no convention tells the Great Wall to stand or fall.

I will say Jude Shao did deserve another trial his case was shaky, to say the least, and he had gathered documents to prove his points but would it ever be heard? I doubted it and voiced this opinion to Jude one day telling him about my brother and his fight for justice.

I had written to my brother and said take a deal and get out of jail. His reply was he would die first, innocent and unbroken by the system.

I was trying to persuade Jude to do the same and make a deal, telling him to just get out of here, the sooner the better.

Jude, like my brother, was having none of it. He wanted his name cleared. I respected that strength, which I felt, I did not have.

2002

It was early February of the year 2002 and you had all sorts of dates, times, seasons, and reasons in your head for release dates. One day out of the blue Wavi Eli and Kofi were called down to the office. The subject was about buying their air tickets home.

Kofi was sorted out, and the Ghanaian consulate in Beijing secured his flight. As the other two were from Liberia, this proved to be a problem due to the political instability and their civil war. Wavi had family living in the USA and it was arranged he would fly to Paris and meet someone from the UN office regarding refugees. Eli was allowed to fly into the Ivory Coast where he had a wife and son.

I watched as they left the building, I thought Kofi was a really fine young man with principles and intelligence to go with it. I wished him well on his return to Ghana and gave him my son's email address. The other two were different smart streetwise guys like me but from another culture – with different principles and less experience.

The other two being released were Josikawa and Matsuda from Japan. During their stay at the prison, the Japanese and Koreans were quiet, never causing trouble, and always obedient. They did not have as much of a cultural gap to bridge as some of us had. The two Japanese inmates Matsuda and Josikawa had paid a small fine and gotten several months cut from their sentence. It was a very unusual situation in China regarding fines nobody ever paid them. The two Germans had paid theirs and Bull had paid his in the hope that the system would reduce their time. It had not worked for them but maybe the communist regime was seeing foreigners would pay their fine if they were assured a reduction in sentence. That assurance was never forthcoming so most never paid. I did not have any fine to pay but then all my money was confiscated.

I wished them well and laughed when Matsuda said to give his football gear to Stanley, as Stanley was a lot smaller. That is the Japanese for you, always polite.

.oOo.

The six new arrivals put a stir in the air looking out for football players as the two-star men at our unit had gone. There was an old man from Singapore aged 67 serving 6 years for business fraud, a Chinese Bolivian age 38 serving 4 years for fraud, a Chinese American age 50 got 6 years for firearm possession, one more Korean age 35 got 6 years for smuggling technology into China, and there was Abdul from Pakistan who got 2 years for fraud.

The sixth person was a new guard called Captain Li who we nicknamed the Professor because he had a PhD in physics and taught at the university for years. I got on well with him - he was the same age as me but he carried an air of calm. He was tall and thin with a straight back.

The Professor called me into the office one day while resting from painting a Chinese river scene. The Professor had me sit while he told me the wonders of drinking Chinese tea. Taking note of what he said I wrote to the Consul and requested they buy me a tea-making set, which they did. I grew to love the taste of Longjing tea. It is not all negative in jail and you learn a lot if you were willing to listen.

.oOo.

I was happy and somewhat apprehensive that my son Scott assured me he was coming and had booked his ticket for March 20. My mind was in turmoil thinking they might arrest him for the suitcase Lochy Junior had been arrested with - but he was determined.

I waited in fear and excitement that my son was coming to visit his old man. I had written to the Prison Administration Bureau requesting to have a meal with Scott and had written to the consul that they request on my behalf, as it is not often that foreigners get visits. This would only be my third visit in eleven years and I wanted the equal opportunity as Chinese inmates had.

Mick had also had a visit from his parents and had taken over a flask of hot water too, plus one coffee pack with coffee cups and biscuits. His request for a meal wasn't granted so he broke new ground by bringing his supply. Well, done Mick - liking his style at times.

Scott arrived and I was elated to see him - enquiring immediately to how young Lochy was. I had been worried that his stay at the Shanghai shackle house would have severely damaged him at the tender age of 17, spending 6 months in a 12-man cell is hard on the mind.

Scott assured me he was fine and all at home were well and still petitioning on my behalf to be returned on medical grounds.

I looked at my son and he seemed tired but put that down to the flight. Scott and I spoke in colloquial Glaswegian and he told me he had an apartment and my Chinese friend was showing him around town. I had secretly arranged for Scott to meet an old local inmate whom I had got along well with and was released. I was glad to hear that, as many promises made in jail are seldom fulfilled – but this one was.

I left the visiting room both arms full of gifts brought from the UK and gave Scott a list of what to bring on his next visit as I had arranged for two meetings. I returned to the unit and left my goodies at the office for inspection and went up and laid in my cell. It was great to see my son he looked well enough but a bit pale – but I put that down to the Scottish weather - and dozed into a contented sleep.

The next few days went by and doing a workout with Simon, he was very interesting but a bit above my head when it came to talking about the futures market and how he used it. I liked Simon he was very softly spoken and never got involved with jail politics. He said to me that he expected to serve fifteen years unless something changed in the remission system.

I explained to him all the hopes I had of an early release from the Hong Kong takeover to the 50th anniversary of the founding of the People's Republic of China - all illusions created by me.

Simon was under no illusion but did hope something would change. "Starting a life sentence at age 40 is not much of a bright future," he said.

.oOo.

March 25th, 2002, was cold wet and windy outside. Sitting in my cell just after lunch, I had on my feather-down jacket my brother had bought when he visited. I was called to the office going downstairs expecting to pick up the remains of the parcels my son had brought and ready to enter the office when the guard said I had a Consul visit. He directed me towards the exit.

I immediately had a panic attack, first I thought something had happened to Scott and could only think the worst. Had he had been arrested for the suitcase that I had said he left behind in my first letter?

Walking into the visit room I could see straight away something was wrong. A striking tall blonde woman who introduced herself as Emma met me. Lisa the translator was with her and we sat down.

"Lauchlan," she said, "I am sorry to inform you that Scott has taken ill."

I nearly shouted, "Thank fuck," but instead said, "What is wrong with him?"

Emma in a soft and comforting tone told me it was nothing to worry about it was stress-related and he had taken some sort of epileptic fit. Emma also told me he was returning home and that they had arranged for a flight and someone to return with him to make sure he was ok. I was shaken up but did feel some relief that he was not lying in jail waiting to visit me on a long-term basis.

That was such a bummer I could not face anyone who spoke with me, just hung my head, and said my son was on his way home.

It was more than a month later that Scott sent me a letter explaining it was stressful to come to visit me and he had been billed by the foreign office for £6000 for the escort and fare back to the UK. I was just glad to know he was all right. Scott had enclosed a few photos of Shanghai Don Fang tower and my granddaughter Ashton who was a little heartbreaker.

.oOo.

There was a meeting in July and the new rule was that we would not be staying in our unit all day but from the next week, we would go over to the classroom area and study computer skills.

"What if I don't want to study computers and want to paint all day," I asked.

The guards replied then bring your paints across with you.

When we did transfer over it was a godsend in more than one way for me. Ceiling fans are desperately needed and that room had two. Plus, the full-length room windows gave great light for painting and a good breeze. July in Shanghai is so hot and to sit for hours you become sweaty and wet from head to toe. It was the rash season and the hospital was next door so overall the move was better for the collective.

It did not take too long before curiosity as to how a computer worked got hold on me and ventured next door where it was all set up. Tip toeing into the room with a feeling that I might disturb something and was met by Jude.

"Hi Lockie," he greeted me.

The Chinese inmates had started using my first name also this had begun since Jude's arrival and I appreciated his respect for using the proper name-calling system of the West and educating the Chinese cons who stayed at our unit with us.

Jude lived in America and was a very intelligent young man. It got irritating for me at times when he would sit and talk about his case, he was correct in his views but I also knew he knew how the Chinese system worked. So why was he opposing it, I inquired, his reply was direct and to the point.

"The reason is I am innocent," he would say determinedly. Jude then showed me how to work a computer. He was in charge of the setup and linked six computers up. Jude then asked Wong the Malaysian person to let him have the computer while he showed me some things.

Wong got up and Jude started by showing me how to open a window then went on to some other computer talk. I stood looking over his shoulder in amazement and never remembered a word he had said. After a few minutes I told him to stop and excused myself saying, "Enough, I will return tomorrow." Leaving that room none the wiser but more afraid of computers having heard the google words spoken by Jude and typing at the same time this wasn't going to be as easy as learning to paint.

.oOo.

The arrival of a Chinese Australian inmate was quite a surprise as usually beforehand you heard news about the arrest or information got through one way or another. I never spoke with him when he first arrived but was hearing second hand what he had been sentenced to five years in jail for. It could only be possible in China, Jude told me. It seems that Gordon and his girlfriend had gone down to Australia and got another university degree – an MBA - and they were allowed to take residence partly due to these educational qualifications. He and his girlfriend married and settled in Australia building a life and a family with two sons. Being young, intelligent, and computer literate, he worked at creating programs for a cheaper communications network. Gordon had a contract from a Chinese company related to such network link-ups. It was all officially done and so the venture took off. In the first year, massive profits were going to Gordon's network system and bypassing the usual government setup. In the second year, they threw him in jail. It was an unprecedented case and there was no law as to why he was arrested.

The Australian consulate did all they could but nothing changed the verdict. It was down to money and Gordon was getting a better slice of the pie by using his intelligence. It was still a communist country although it was supposed to be free enterprise - money not going to the state and going on to another plate was soon stopped.

I do not have any explanation as to why innocents are imprisoned but it is dammed well shameful knowing they suffer like the guilty. I can say a couple of the guards there knew the truth and showed Jude and Gordon mutual respect and sometimes one on one they openly excused their systems error in their particular cases. It could never be shown that any guard sympathized with a criminal. Our status was firmly stamped into our psyches - remember you're a criminal. I became friendly with the young man who spoke good English with an Australian accent.

.oOo.

Abdul came from Pakistan and had been in jail in China several times all for fraud. It was a way of life he told me one day. In Pakistan he can do nothing, no job, no money, no wife, nothing. Going on to tell me his connection in Islamabad got him a new passport and he returned back again to China. He was happy to do that as he owned his own house and would return to Pakistan once he had changed between $5,000 and $8,000 to drop off to his supplier. He would get his share then return with more stolen cheques and continued to do so until his arrest. He seemed to be only around for weeks then he was gone, spending more than one year waiting in detention, so his sentence was nearly over when he arrived.

I got on all right with him, he was a devout Muslim and was proud to show me the hard skin mark on his forehead from praying to Allah. He said in his Pakistani accent, "See you soon Campbell," then he was on the van, and off to the airport. One more gone and that was always good to see.

.oOo.

I had been waiting on some reduction of sentence for about two years and my liberation date was 5th December 2004. I was hoping to get at least one more year of remission.

The unit was changing a lot, short-term people had gone and a new person from Mexico was due to arrive. We also heard about a man from Japan convicted of killing his father, and seemingly, he was soon on his way to the prison too.

The Mexican person had been arrested in Beijing and was telling us stories that the jail there was much easier. He told us about the guards letting them use their mobile phones in exchange for money or other items they desired. They could buy cigarettes and other foodstuffs. I assured him that would not be happening and his reply was if they don't get my smokes, I want my patches.

I said, "Listen to me, my friend, there is no smoking here. Trust me they even add time onto people's sentences if they get caught smoking cigarettes."

Then he explained to me what a nicotine patch is and that was fascinating to hear of such a wonder that if you put it onto your arm, it prevented the cravings for nicotine.

God the world had changed in the last decade. Mobiles phones, computers and nicotine patches - what next?

The October reduction of sentences had passed and I never got one and was not pleased in the least.

Cranky had gotten another reduction and had only four months left until his release date. I had been inside jail ten months longer and he was going out two years sooner than I was.

It was only a couple of weeks before Xmas when I was called downstairs to the office where Captain Jin and one Judge sat. The captain smiled at me as if to say, "Didn't, I tell you so," and was given a one-year remission of sentence.

That was it. I was happy as a pig in shit as the saying goes. It was December 22nd and getting the remission meant I would be going home on December 5th, 2003, less than one more year. Seeing the gate and smell of freedom, it was a feeling that cannot be explained by me. All I knew was I would be leaving that place - civilized jail or not. God, it felt good.

2003

I had decided as my New Year resolution to do the following starting January 1, 2003. Monday Wednesday Friday workout Tuesday and Thursday stair run. Finish one painting or more a week. Do no more labour voluntarily or other. Don't hand in monthly ideological remoulding reports. Start following Prisoners Abroad guidelines to resettle in the UK.

.oOo.

Having gathered all my things what, I deemed important and valuable to me was my writings and paintings. Having had so much paperwork collected over the years, it filled a large box. Then started to sift through it to see what could be discarded. I picked out price lists from the old jail back in 1992 and the prices had tripled and more. I found the prison law copy and other paperwork, wanted to keep so sat for hours one evening and separated it and tore up loads, and binned about half of it. I was not aware of it then but that was gate fever and did not want any surprises. My hopes were well battered I was not looking for any more 50th anniversary amnesty or other hopes for compassionate parole. I wanted to be ready and prepared.

This was it for me just counting down the celebrations still to come all taking me closer to that gate and freedom. I would eat my favourite moon cakes and still had May Day to come then founding of the People's Republic of China Day. That was when we got to eat eight-treasured rice a mixed fruit and dates dish that tasted like heaven to me. The games and karaoke had played their last tune for me and I became a full-time observer.

.oOo.

As part of the transparency policy, the prison had opened a shop and we were allowed to go once per month to buy rations. It was a revelation to us to walk into a small supermarket inside the jail. It was not big but enough for 10 people to shop at a time so we were taken in groups. It also had a bookshop with mostly old classics like Jane Ayres or Dickens books. Jean Marie Happy bought a collection of Mao's writings but all in Chinese. There were some magazines with Chinese art and got me a few for study and copying.

It was set up that we all got a swipe card and that would register what we had in our accounts. There was a limit on how much you could spend which was 200 Yuan around $25 each month but there was no limit on how much fruit you could buy of what was available in season. The changes to the unit were coming fast, we had a small multi gym installed. They renovated the second-floor guards office to make space. Moreover, there was talk of getting to use the phone

They had installed a telephone for us to use but of course, there were rules to follow. The first thing to work out was the time zones as we came from all over the world. We would be allowed to call home once per month and talk for 20 minutes. It could only be family members and we had to hand in a list of who we would likely phone.

On my list, I put my sons and my sisters. The next object was paying for the call. The prison shop had them in store for the following month costing 50 to 100 Yuan each and there was no limit on how many you could buy. Mick being the big spender got 1000 Yuan worth I got 100 as nobody knew the costs of a call. Gordon told me it would not cost more than 100 to call England for 20 minutes and trusted his judgment. Gordon had bought cards also for phoning Australia he got four 50-Yuan cards telling me he would not need more.

The day arrived when the phone was to be operational it was agreed that the Malaysian people phone first. The stairway was crowded with people leaning over the rail to listen to someone talk on a phone. When those people were finished, we excitedly asked how it was, "Can they hear you okay?" and they assured us all, it was clear.

I was going to phone my sister in Glasgow on Sunday and felt excited listening to Mick telling me about talking with his children, Happy had got in touch with his ex-wife - he hadn't had contact from anyone in years. Jude spoke with his sister, Bijay with his daughter whom he had not seen yet.

It was just a stir of excitement from everyone and a calmed atmosphere emerged immediately.

When I did call my sister Sarah, she asked me again and again, "Is that you Lockie, have you escaped?"

Shaking inside I shouted, "No I am here in Shanghai jail, we can use the phone."

It was surreal listening to my sister talking - then she put on my niece Karen on the phone, and to hear her clear Scottish voice was amazing to my ear. She was talking Glaswegian - my mother tongue it sounded unusual coming so rapidly. I had a good talk and assured my family that all was well and I was healthy - doing gym workouts and taking the vitamins that they had sent to me. It was something special not like a family visit but closer than that phantom mail carrier - and this was instant no more sending mail.

.oOo.

I had been getting my consul visit every month since Emma arrived and looked forward to everyone. She brought in such a refreshing feminine scent. She was married and her husband was a Rugby player called Big Baz. I could not put into words what Emma did for me. She was sisterly and seemed to really care about me in a humanitarian way. She was a tall striking blonde-haired woman with a smile that made their Mandarin smile a Mona Lisa in comparison.

Emma guided me through some of the obstacles that would be coming my way upon release. She let me know that things had changed in the UK since I was last there and she gave me the latest English newspapers and told me to try to catch up on some current affairs.

I asked her about not returning to the UK but going to Thailand instead she was informed that I would be deported directly to the UK. Emma had also brought me telephone cards and to my surprise, she handed me 600 Yuan worth and had asked for only three. Then Lisa explained to me that different companies offer different deals this one was buy 100 and get 100 free. I was delighted and thanked them both for their consideration. As the visit ended, I said, "See you next month," handing her an order for some special food goodies for my next visit.

The consul was great in that respect and I did not overdo it with my requests.

Mick would and did overdo it at times asking his consul to make deliveries of special foods. Mick was still undiagnosed from a mysterious illness that kept him at the doctor's door every other day since his arrival. A determined man for sure.

I told some of the people about the telephone card deal, and they asked me to buy some for them as their consuls did not visit.

Wong the Malaysian person approached me and asked if I wanted to do some trading and business. I asked what the deal was. He asked me to get 1000 worth of cards which would give me 2000 he would pay me 1500 in fruits and foodstuffs. I told him to let me think it over.

I did not take up his offer but instead ordered them for Bijay and Min whenever they asked. Nick was doing a bit of wheeling and dealing but it all soon came to a stop. All cards handed in by consuls were to be placed in the office.

The calls were now once every week so that cost a bit more for those with children but the guards allowed me to give out cards knowing I wasn't making any profit. Now that is civilized.

.oOo.

October 2003 came around and I could not believe what was going on – there was a new virus called SARS which was killing people all over China. I was two months from release and about to go home and they had stopped flights coming into China, AND the ones going out, to try and slow down the spread of the deadly disease.

All visits stopped and there was no incoming parcels or mail. The whole jail went on shutdown. The guards were not even allowed to go home they stayed on duty one full week. Then went home for one week with very restricted guidelines as to where they could travel.

The whole unit was sprayed every morning and evening with a disinfectant. The jail was in upheaval and paranoia spread fast.

The foreigners, ie Non-Chinese, felt that the Asian convicts were more likely to catch it than we international convicts were. It was an Asian virus just as mad cow disease was European. It was amazing to watch how we all changed our attitudes towards each other.

One Malaysian guy Michael was seriously sick and we were all sure it was SARS the poor person was shipped over to the hospital on isolation row. The SARS scare lasted a whole month before we started to get visits again but only through a glass pane separating us from any contact whatsoever.

It sadly reminded me of going to visit my father in the 1950s at Barlinnie jail in Glasgow when he was shipped down from Peterhead prison for visits.

It turned out that Michael the Malaysian had another undiagnosed disease and returned to our unit under much suspicion among us all. Everyone was scared to let him or others breathe on us.

It was frightening for me afraid I might be going to die just before my release. I had my suspicions as I was already surviving HIV+ HEP C + and Shingles now it was SARS - what else would these people do to kill me?

I started to cover my mouth and nose whenever anyone spoke with me so did a few others.

Then SARS had gone and life went back to normal.

.oOo.

There was a last open-air concert before heading home – it was something that was done several times a year and the foreigners always had put on a show. Vern, Bull, Cranky, and the Old Reformers had usually sung a song and I did too. This was the time to make a statement.

Mick was testing me out asking me, "What you are going to say? If I was you," he advised me, "just denounce the whole system."

Having thought of saying something regarding parole but that was all had in mind. When it came around to my turn sang a song by Loudon Wainwright the third song called *Smoky Joe's Cafe*. I did my usual funny Max Wall walk around the stage then said my few words on parole for foreigners and handed the microphone to the next person.

I sat down and Bijay said, "Well done Campbell," and raised his eyebrows towards Mick as if to say let him speak for himself.

These cooling parties had ice cream brought around and soft drinks with plenty of watermelon to eat. The guards would also go up and sing and that was when the cons got their laughs by shouting all sorts of compliments tongue in cheek of course but that was their style mandarin smiles all the way - never showing emotion.

Goodbye

The time had come I did not sleep well that last night knowing I was going home the next day. My brother Robert had brought me a new suit and other nice clothes during his visit to see me and they lay spread on the bed opposite me, pressed and ready to be worn.

I had said goodbye to most of the people who got along with me the night before. We had a small farewell party Jude, Gordon, and Bijay had given me email addresses – which was new to me but I had gotten one from my son Scott too. I gave that to Jude to pass around.

Jude was inquisitive when he found a new word and asked me what *scunner* meant – as it was part of the email address Scott had given me. I gave him an example and said, "In short it's making a fool of yourself."

The next question was why your son would choose such a distasteful name and did not want to try to go into the psychology of it with Jude so instead said this. "You know how Michael Jackson says *it's bad* but that means *it's good*?"

Jude replied, "Yeah."

"Well," I went on, "my son chose *scunner* because it may be true, he is a scunner at times but to be upfront admitting it then it becomes good. You got that Jude?" I asked.

"Sort of," he replied then asked what RFC was – which was also part of the email address.

That was easy to explain *Rangers Football Club*.

.oOo.

I stood in front of the cell mirror, shaved and dressed, like a very well-preserved man of 53. My weight was 78kg and I could still play an hour or more football a day. I walked downstairs and nodded my head at a few guys in the corridor. Every step, my last one inside this place.

My hands were free having my luggage put into the office downstairs the night before for inspection. Entering the office, I picked up the small suitcase that the consul had bought for me - which was full only of my diaries and writings over the years. Having also a roll of 108 oil canvasses plus 40 UN Anti-drug posters it was a heavy load.

I entered the police escort van, turned my head to look up at the unit for the last time, and could see many faces. Sticking out my hand from the window I waved.

I looked ahead as the gates opened and a moment later was on the road to freedom.

On the way to the airport a song in my head by John Lennon, "It's a long way to go, a hard road to hoe, but in the meantime…" In the meantime, Greenwich meantime here, I come.

The SARS check was still being done at the airport departures having my blood pressure taken. I was allowed into the check-in area having overweight baggage but did not give a dam as had no money other than a fifty-pound note Emma brought for me to get me across London if nobody was meeting me or I got lost.

I shook hands with Captain Chang and Captain Shao then headed for immigration with my piece of white stamped paper and no passport it was easy enough and walked into the departure lounge with my Virgin Airlines boarding pass. I smelled the human mix of international odours. I looked around me the feeling of being in an airport again something I once had enjoyed and did regularly in years gone by. This time it was all so strange.

Final boarding for the flight Virgin Airlines but sitting back until the last passengers were boarding before getting up and then getting on.

It was Emma the British consul attaché who had secured my flight. Emma had worked for Virgin Airlines and got me this ticket rather reasonably priced.

Once seated, I fastened my seatbelt and then looked at the magazines in front of me. A young Canadian man around 36 sat beside me leaving the centre seat free and not wanting to strike up any talk. I was happy to stay locked in my mind.

When the plane was up and the sign to unfasten seatbelts was announced the person next to me introduced himself as Don and told me he worked at selling computer programs all across Asia.

Then I told my story, that I had worked at the British consul cultural section studying art and Chinese, and teaching English part-time. Don set up my movie screen, and film programs list for me, and coming to one called *Anger Management* pressed play. I do not know what the Lord was doing but it was a clear message he was letting me know something how could it be possible that the new release, *Anger Management* with Jack Nicholson would be the movie of choice after twelve-plus years away in jail.

Watching I listened open-mouthed and wet-eyed. To compare your situation with others and feel the portrayed emotion from the film - some of the characters seemed worse off than me.

An article from a Prisoners Abroad newsletter popped back into my mind of the person complaining that he could not understand or speak the language, he was far away from home, did not like the food, and the final straw he was serving six months in France. I recall thinking *six months and far from home.* You wimp.

Then sometime later the penny dropped we all suffered equally six months was his suffering, and fifteen years was mine. Some of those scenes in that *Anger Management* movie related to my daily happenings in jail that I cried with pain and laughter through the whole film and kept turning my head to see if I was disturbing anyone, hearing no complaint, I cried more - this time with a dinner napkin to soak me up.

.oOo.

Walking along the tarmac and upon entering the immigration area I was caught in a throng of non-residents pushing to be stamped in and collect their luggage. The sign was large and clear UK passport holders this way. I had just passed through showing my travel paper and was immediately joined by two civilian-dressed men one of whom said, "Did you have a good flight, Mr Campbell?" Then went on to say that they were Foreign Office workers assigned to ask me a few questions and I followed them into a room.

They asked me how my health was and I replied fine.

"Do you harbour any revenge thoughts against the Chinese people or government?"

"No," I said.
"Good to be home, eh?" one said.
"You bet," was my reply.

.oOo.

Who was waiting for me in the arrival lounge but my son Scott. My son had been there all the way when it all began in Islamabad. He had stood by me through my jail journey, taking out the cannabis from the detention holding cells. When I reached him, we hugged and headed for the world outside. With him was a friend of mine Jeff and his wife Kath whom Scott had linked up with when knowing my liberation date.

.oOo.

I entered the house in Bethnal Green and my brother's wife Vonny embraced me and said, "Welcome back Lockie."

Standing there was her two sons Jason and Joshua and we also shook hands. Jason says, "Welcome back Lock," in 100% cockney.

Jason and I had met up in Thailand before my arrest and he was a man of real good character - a hard worker and never got into trouble with the law or been to jail. Joshua, I did not know. He had been a baby when I left, who still slept with the old Scottie dog that was loved so much. Here stood a still growing six-foot teenager handsome with strong McLaren features.

That evening we all went to the pub to have a drink and meet more in-laws and trust me the McLarens are a clan - eleven girls, three boys, some of them living in London forty years and more and many had grandchildren.

As soon as the bar door opened several old friends of mine waved me over it was Andy McCarthy and James Marr it was a warm exciting atmosphere, music playing, people talking over each other.

My brother-in-Law Jim McLaren approached me and we shook hands and hugged then Jim slipped an envelope into my pocket, "You're looking great Lockie," he said and commented on the nice, stripped suit my brother Robert had brought me when he had visited me in China.

"You always looked well yourself Jim," returning the compliment and it was true Jim was known for his style and enjoyed shopping in Bond Street in his younger days duty-free shopping I might add as they never paid, they were professional shoplifters along with our mutual friends from our youth.

We joined Andy and Marsy at a table and Andy offered me cocaine which I politely declined and wasn't drinking alcohol either.

"What about a wee joint son," Marsy offered.

"No thanks, I gave it up. I don't smoke."

Marsy went on, "You know Lockie, the last time I saw you was walking down the London Road with two empty beer bottles. Then the next time was from a photo you sent Rab ten years later standing on a mountain path in Tibet - with a donkey full of dope. You get yourself about a bit Lockie." That is typical Glasgow humour.

We reminisced and laughed at past encounters and shared experiences. The names that were brought up all asked me, do you remember him, or her, Lockie? I would then be told what had happened to them - good and bad.

Living in Glasgow in the 1960s was producing not only fighting men but also a new breed of entrepreneurs setting up across the UK. Jim told me Tommy McGuiness whom I had last seen in 1967 had since opened some of the most exclusive clubs and restaurants in the city and became a property developer and millionaire.

Andy mentioned Robert Caruthers from Maryhill who had taken me under his wing in Manchester, both of us wearing suits stolen from Frazer's of Perth in Scotland - along with Pringle crew neck sweaters – and dating two sisters, Barbara and Pauline. Another name came up who taught me skills in stealing was a guy called Cool – this was in my early days when living in London Cool was King to coin a phrase.

Those days were gone and my mind was on the present and was in no way impressed by the amount of alcohol and drug consumption by some of the bar crowd but it was going on openly. The McLaren family was united against any type of drug even cannabis.

My brother Robert was talked about nearly as much as old Ray McLaren the mother of them all. A lovely lady who wisely foresaw that living in the East End of Glasgow with eleven good-looking daughters would spell trouble, so where Mum goes the family follows - having a very loving family bond.

That night I slept in my brother's old bed and I lay looking at the ceiling. Rab had slept there for years and little flashes of his face would sometime skip into my inner vision. I smiled at him, then cried for my loss, and wept away my mourning knowing Rab wouldn't want any of us to suffer. He was a cracking wee guy and left a wife and family that loved him.

Before leaving for the train to Scotland, Vonny took me into Red Rab's wardrobes and told me to take all I wanted - it was the finest range of clothing from cashmere coats, suits and sweaters, casuals for all seasons, top designer labels. I crammed two suitcases with Knightsbridge quality clothing and would have him by me most days - see you in heaven Red Rab.

.oOo.

The train journey back to Scotland was pleasant - Scott looked through some paintings we had unwrapped. My stomach was rattling with nerves. TC Campbell and my son Lochy were going to be at the station to meet us.

I was still worried about how Lochy's six months in detention might have affected him – at the young age of 17. Then there was TC Campbell - my youngest brother had always been somebody and had earned that respect length and breadth of Scotland. He was a straight talker, a fair leader, and a hard hitter if you crossed him.

My mind danced with the imaginary reunion dialogues that we would have.

The train pulled into the station, and we were bundled off with the excess luggage. My brother called out and waved then I saw him walk past the ticked gate to assist with the bags.

We embraced and shook hands looking each other up and down.

My brother looked well enough to me especially after what he had endured during his campaign for justice. "Lockie," he said, "I was thinking you would be skinnier, but you look as if you just came from a health resort rather than a Chinese jail!"

That broke the ice and we laughed.

Just then, Lochy arrived, saying he had been at the wrong arrival gate. He came over, and said, "Good to see you again Dad."

I was choked and we embraced.

It was arranged for me to stay with Scott until getting my place and we all drove there to Hag Hill where his flat was located. Scott offered me the bedroom, but I preferred to sleep on the floor in the lounge room.

We did not talk for long. My brother Tommy had arranged for a gathering at my sister Sarah's house for that evening where other family members would join us. Tommy and Lochy departed leaving Scott and me to relax. It was just past midday in my city in Scotland, my homeland.

.oOo.

In the order of age, there was Helen, Sarah, Agnes, and Patricia my brother George wasn't there - and they had all aged. It wasn't just the twelve-plus years in jail that we hadn't seen each other. I hadn't seen Helen in thirty years, nor Sarah and Patricia in over twenty. I had made a short visit to see Agnes in 1990, not long before my trip through China. My siblings had greyed hair and the lines on Sarah's face reminded me of hill tribe women from some minority group in Burma - with graceful and intelligent eyes.

The house was full of nephews and nieces many of them with their children. Good food was served and plenty of it and the Malt whiskey flowed into the glasses of those who wanted them - me again declining, to which all my sisters commented, "That's a wise move son, you're dry, stay that way."

It was a wonderful reunion, both my sons with me again and the party carried on till into the morning - before Scott and I took a taxi to his place.

Lying on the floor that night I thought about what I would do next. What could I do? A reformed criminal and anti-drug campaigner. I could paint in oils and acrylics, and I could get by with basic Chinese conversation.

I slept that night with big ideas of working with drug addicts and counselling them - all I wanted was to be useful. The following morning, I got off the floor and folded the quilt then put the kettle on to make myself coffee. I sat looking out from Scott's window where I could see Celtic Park – football stadium also known as Paradise, being a lover of that sport – and I thought what an amazing view to see the park of the first British team ever to win the European Champions Cup. It made me feel proud when comparing the football scene from where I had just come from. This view was paradise and I smiled inwardly after sleeping my first night, back on Scottish soil.

Home at last.

Printed in Great Britain
by Amazon